D0200165

Santa Fe

Taos and Northern Pueblos

Lawrence W. Cheek
Updated by Andrew Collins
Photography by Eduardo Fuss

HILLSBORO PUBLIC LIBRARIES
Hillsboro, OR
Member of Washington County
COOPERATIVE LIBRARY SERVICES
WITHDRAWN

COMPASS AMERICAN GUIDES
An imprint of Fodor's Travel Publications

Compass American Guides: Santa Fe

Editors: Nancy Zimmerman, Jennifer Paull
Designer: Siobhan O'Hare
Compass Editorial Director: Paul Eisenberg
Photo Editor: Jolie Novak
Archival Research: Melanie Marin
Map Design: Mark Stroud, Moon Street Cartography
Editorial Production: Linda K. Schmidt

Cover Photo: Eduardo Fuss, Inn at Loretto, Santa Fe
Copyright © 2008 Fodor's Travel, a division of Random House, Inc.
Maps copyright © 2008 Fodor's Travel, a division of Random House, Inc.

Compass American Guides and colophon are registered trademarks of Random House, Inc.
Fodor's is a registered trademark of Random House, Inc.

All rights reserved. Published in the United States by Fodor's Travel Publications, a unit
of Fodor's Travel, a division of Random House, Inc., and simultaneously in Canada by
Random House of Canada Limited, Toronto. Distributed by Random House, Inc., New York.

*No maps, illustrations, or other portions of this book may be reproduced in any form without written
permission from the publisher.*

Fifth Edition
ISBN 978–1–4000–1866–6 *3688 9722 12/07*
ISSN 1543–1657

Compass American Guides, 1745 Broadway, New York, NY 10019

PRINTED IN SINGAPORE

10 9 8 7 6 5 4 3 2 1

To Ann Aceves, whose grace, generosity, and intelligence illuminate Santa Fe.

C O N T E N T S

SANTA FE ❖ FANTA SE 12

FIRST NEW MEXICANS 21
Hunters, Gatherers,
Farmers, Spirits 21
Chaco Culture National
Historical Park 29
Bandelier National
Monument 29
Petroglyph National
Monument 30
Pueblo Culture 31

HISPANIC SANTA FE 36
Early Santa Fe 41
Resettlement 44
The "Mournful" Capital 45
Mexican Santa Fe 47
Taking New Mexico 53

CONTEMPORARY SANTA FE . .58

ART AND MUSEUMS 70
Shopping for Art 77
Indian Arts 78
Buying Pottery 80
Hispanic Art 85
Art Museums 87
Santa Fe Opera 90
Adobe and Modern Architecture 93

SEEING SANTA FE 98
Downtown Walking Tour 98
Walking Acequia Madre/Canyon
Road .112
Acequia Madre/Canyon Road
Highlights 112

TOWN OF TAOS 118
Early Taos 122
American Artists Discover Taos .124

Growth and the Art Market . . .128
Visiting Taos 131
Taos Highlights 132
Greater Taos Sights 135
Taos Pueblo 137

EIGHT NORTHERN
PUEBLOS 138
Durable Community 140
Visiting the Pueblos 144
Tesuque 144
Pojoaque 144
Nambé 146
San Ildefonso 147
Santa Clara 148
Ohkay Owingeh 151
Picurís 151
Taos .154

SIDE TRIPS FROM SANTA FE 156
Roads to Taos and Back 159
Tesuque 159
Velarde 162
Dixon 162
Taos and the
Rio Grande Gorge 162
Las Trampas 165
Truchas 167
Chimayó 170
East to Pecos and Las Vegas 174
Pecos National
Historical Park 174
Las Vegas 175
Los Alamos and the
Jémez Mountains 176
Los Alamos 177
Bandelier National
Monument 179
Jémez Mountains 182

Historic Western Loop 185
Kasha-Katuwe Tent Rocks
National Monument 185
Petroglyph National
Monument 185
Old Town Albuquerque 187
Ácoma Pueblo 190
Northwest to Chaco Canyon . .193

CUISINE ❖ RESTAURANTS . .196
Santa Fe Farmers Market 198
New Trends in New Mexican
Cuisine 202
Chiles 202
Tortillas 205
Santa Fe Area Restaurants 207
Santa Fe 207
Near Santa Fe 211
Chimayó 212
Taos 212

LODGING 216
Lodging Listings 219
Central Santa Fe 220
Greater Santa Fe 224
Beyond Santa Fe 226
Taos 227

PRACTICAL INFORMATION . .228
Area Code 228
Metric Conversions 228
Climate/When to Go 228
Getting There 229
Getting Around 232
Outdoors 233
Tours 236
Official Tourist Information . . .238
Useful Web Sites 238
Festivals and Events 240

RECOMMENDED READING . .244

GLOSSARY 248

INDEX 252

Topical Essays and Sidebars

Santa Fe Facts 8
An Ancient Tradition in Pottery 24–25
History Time Line 38–40
The Population of Santa Fe in 1790 45
La Patrona de Santa Fe 51–52
Jean Baptiste Lamy 54–57
Otherworldly St. John's College 68
Classic Southwest Jewelry 76
Pueblo Pottery of New Mexico 81–84
Photographing Santa Fe 117
Pueblo Etiquette 145
Feast Days and Dances 153
Euralia Vigil: The Teacher and Her Apples 168–169
Santa Fe School of Cooking 200–201
Chile Scorch Scale 203
Climate Averages 229
Northern New Mexico Ski Resorts 235

Literary Extracts

Josiah Gregg *on arriving in Santa Fe* 9
Lewis Thompson *on the old days in Santa Fe* 18
Fray Alonso de Benavides *on the kingdom's capital* 42
Josiah Gregg *on Mexican manners* 48
The Santa Fe New Mexican *reports on a fandango* 50
Susan Hazen-Hammond *on Santa Fe's future* 63
Charles Lummis *on mud houses* 96–97
Georgia O'Keeffe's *letters from Taos* 127
Mabel Dodge Luhan *on D. H. Lawrence* 136
Paul Horgan *on hacienda life* 197
Susan Shelby Magoffin *on a U.S. Army ball* 241

Maps

Greater Santa Fe 7
Native Americans 20
Central Santa Fe 99
Acequia Madre/Canyon Road 116
Greater Taos 119
Downtown Taos 133
North-Central New Mexico 139
Side Trips 157
Santa Fe Restaurants 206
Santa Fe Lodging 218
Taos Lodging and Restaurants 225

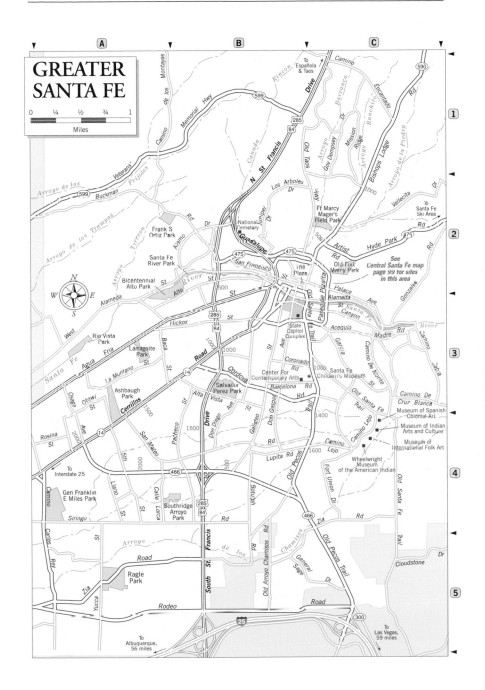

GREATER SANTA FE

0   ¼   ½   ¾   1

Miles

SANTA FE FACTS

■ **SANTA FE BASICS**

Name Derivation: Spanish for "Holy Faith"
Founded: 1607–1610
Designated Capital of New Mexico: 1610
Elevation: 7,000 feet
Population: 66,500

■ **CLIMATE**

Hottest Day: 99 degrees Fahrenheit, on June 2, 1994
Coldest Day: minus 18 degrees Fahrenheit, on January 13, 1963
Heaviest Rainfall: 3.61 inches, July 26, 1968
Heaviest Snowfall: 27 inches, December 30, 2006

■ **INTERESTING FACTS**

- Santa Fe is the oldest capital city in what is now the United States. The official founding date is 1610, but evidence records 1607 as the true founding.

- Santa Fe annually receives an average of 10 more inches of snow than Barrow, Alaska, but also averages 300 days of sunshine.

- The oldest road in the United States runs from Santa Fe to Chihuahua, Mexico. It first served travelers in 1581. It is now I-25.

- Chaco Canyon is the site of the world's largest excavated pre-Columbian Indian ruins.

- For more than 200 years, Santa Fe was the administrative center for Spain's northern territories, which stretched west to the Pacific Ocean.

- The *Places Rated Almanac* ranks Santa Fe as the 36th most expensive American metropolitan area (out of 354) to live in.

ARRIVING IN SANTA FE

A few miles before reaching the [capital] city, the road again emerges into an open plain. Ascending a table ridge, we spied in an extended valley to the northwest, occasional groups of trees, skirted with verdant corn and wheat fields, with here and there a square block-like protuberance reared in the midst. A little further, and just ahead of us to the north, irregular clusters of the same opened to our view. "Oh, we are approaching the suburbs!" thought I, on perceiving the cornfields, and what I supposed to be brick-kilns scattered in every direction. These and other observations of the same nature becoming audible, a friend at my elbow said, "It is true those are heaps of unburnt bricks, nevertheless they are *houses*—this is the city of Santa Fé."

—*Josiah Gregg*, Commerce of the Prairies, *1844*

A view of Santa Fe, ca. 1846–47. (Museum of New Mexico)

(following pages) A winter sunset highlights the Sangre de Cristo (Blood of Christ) Mountains, forming a golden backdrop in this photograph of Santa Fe.

SANTA FE ✦ FANTA SE

I am waiting in the checkout line at Kaune's, a cluttered but tony gourmet grocery across Paseo de Peralta from the New Mexico state capitol. I think I've seen the clerk before at a competing store. I ask.

"I actually work three jobs," she admits. "Two days here, three at another grocery, and another day at an architect's office filing and keeping books."

"Sounds like a typical Santa Fe story," I say. "Work three jobs so you can afford to live here."

"No," she sighs. "I work three jobs and I *can't* afford to live here."

Richard Mahler, a Santa Fean since 1988, tells me another quintessentially Santa Fe story.

For improved privacy, he wanted to add a couple of feet to the height of his fence. He decided to gamble on the city bureaucracy not noticing and, following an ancient and honorable New Mexico tradition, bypassed the inconvenience of applying for a building permit. But just before the job was finished, a city official noticed the attentions and red-tagged the renovation.

The issue slogged through the city bureaucracy for months. Finally, Mahler got a call. An official told him that his fence modification would be on the city council's agenda the next evening.

"I can't be there," Mahler pleaded. "I'm on a flight to Singapore in the morning."

The bureaucrat paused for a moment, pondering. Finally he said, "Well, just go ahead and finish your fence. In Santa Fe it's easier to get forgiveness than permission."

■ ■ ■

This is not a conventional guidebook to Santa Fe. This is the work of a visiting journalist whose decades-long relationship with the city has flitted among love, fascination, amazement, aggravation, and exasperation. This is a guidebook in which no subject is out of bounds, one in which Santa Feans tell their amazing and preposterous stories about work and art and love and trying to build fences. It explains how one of North America's oldest cities manages to survive and thrive—and charm practically everyone who visits it—in a high-tech world that would seem to have little use for such an anachronistic place.

Santa Fe inspires spirituality, homespun or imported—as at this Tibetan Buddhist center.

La Villa Real de la Santa Fé de San Francisco de Asís (the city's original Spanish name), founded in 1607, claims more history, more fascinating characters, more art, and more multicultural energy than any other city in America with the possible exception of New York, which is more than 100 times Santa Fe's size. Santa Fe possesses an unusual climate: two basic seasons, summer and winter, neither too extreme, with an interlude of autumn color that almost rivals New England's. It has three colleges, including a thoroughly unconventional one whose recent president unashamedly told me, "We don't know much about the 20th century."

Santa Fe may well be the most concentrated arts center in the world: the city's convention & visitors bureau claims that one in every six residents is employed, in some way or another, in the art business. In the 1980s, Santa Fe style, for better or worse, captured the nation's imagination, inspiring crafts, furniture, and architecture designed in an "antiqued" 18th-century Spanish colonial dress. Santa Fe style's popularity has since waned slightly, but the city has become one of America's culinary capitals, perhaps the only one, save New Orleans, that has evolved a broad and distinctive regional menu. Anyone for crab and mango on tortilla "spaghetti" with *habanero* chile sour cream? (I did not—could not—make this up.)

The above entrée, courtesy of a prestigious Santa Fe hotel kitchen, brings up the exasperating side of Santa Fe today. The city can be pretentious and outrageously expensive, and it ain't what it used to be.

Downtown, which appears on the surface to be lively, is really naught but tourists until dusk—locals just don't go there because they can't afford anything in the stores and they wouldn't be able to find parking anyway. The spiritual heart of Santa Fe's unique aesthetic, its adobe architecture, has been seriously corrupted— about 95 percent of the modern houses in town are thrown up with 2x6 studs and chicken wire and stuccoed with soft corners to masquerade as adobe. We might call it the *Santa Faux* style. In 2006 the median sale price of a home in the city was $398,000. New (real) adobe houses start at around half a million.

Historic adobe houses can wear price tags even farther removed from planet Earth. Actual example: *Antique adobe on quiet lane . . . glowing wood floors, fun eat-in kitchen, and lush garden courtyards under a canopy of old trees. Walk to Plaza and Canyon Road. Priced to sell! $695,000.* Nobody earns such money in Santa Fe; prospective buyers for such houses invariably have created their fortunes elsewhere.

The San Francisco de Asís Church of Ranchos de Taos was the subject of one of Georgia O'Keeffe's most important paintings.

Yet the old, uneven brown town is ineffably alluring. Sweep into Santa Fe on I-25 from Albuquerque—stay on the freeway until the Old Pecos Trail exit; avoid Cerrillos Road—and you'll see the last city in North America that truly embraces its natural environment. Almost nothing man-made save the cathedral and neighboring Loretto Chapel rises more than three stories to scrape the sapphire New Mexico sky. Houses and even commercial buildings snore under a quieting blanket of foliage. Even where the adobe is fake, the muted brown colors help connect the architecture to Mother Earth.

Or is it the other way around? As Susan Hazen-Hammond observed in her delightfully wry book, *Only in Santa Fe,* this is the only city in America where the more money you have, the more likely you are to live on a dirt road. Santa Feans love to indulge in simulated rusticity. (A common gibe, even among locals, is to call the city "Fanta Se.") Some critics deride its pretensions, but there is also a deep and honest desire to perpetuate the city's unique qualities.

This is an irrepressibly friendly place. Strangers out for morning walks routinely offer greetings to each other. On one of my strolls, a light drizzle had started, and a stranger in a car—a woman—offered me a ride. (I later learned that she might have been going beyond simple neighborliness; single women in Santa Fe claim the ratio of eligible, heterosexual, nonpsychotic males is skewed against them one to five.) The young family that owned my apartment, correctly suspecting that I might be lonely 500 miles away from my family at Thanksgiving, invited me to spend the holiday with them. This is the cultural landscape of Santa Fe.

That landscape comprises many different cultures including Indian, Hispanic, and Anglo. This is even more important to the textural richness of the city than its architecture and art. The cultures all depend on each other, and interact where they need to, but remain to a large extent distinct. There are race and class tensions in Santa Fe, as in every diverse community, and they grow as the chasm widens between rich and poor.

Whatever their cultural heritage, Santa Feans are fiercely in love with their city and the stunning land around it. They will endure any economic hardship in order to live with it. So will visitors. There are, however, many ideas in this book for saving money, something important to most of us.

The other side of the coin of friendliness is contentiousness. Santa Feans fight furiously over their city's present and past, and the battle frequently unfolds like

(following pages) El Rancho de las Golondrinas, south of Santa Fe, has buildings dating from the early 1700s, when it was a stop along the Camino Real from Mexico City.

OLD DAYS WERE BETTER FOR SANTA FE

When I first moved to Santa Fe [1957] it was so quiet on the plaza you could hear a rooster crow at the Delgado house on Palace Avenue, now headquarters for Banquest, which isn't a catering outfit as you might suspect but a quarter-of-a-billion-dollar bank holding company.

When I first moved to Santa Fe there was a San Ildefonso Indian named Joe who got paid five dollars a day for just sitting in the lobby of the Desert Inn, providing atmosphere for tourists. Joe would condescend to have coffee with me if I bought him some apple pie à la mode. We talked about growing Indian corn and how you could make Sears linoleum tile look like turquoise in jewelry.

When I first moved to Santa Fe cutting down billboards on Saturday night was a big social event, the only haciendas of consequence were built over three or four or more generations without the help of architects or regulated by city planners and building codes, and Fiesta was a family event with Dr. Deforrest Lord and his wife doing their handmade puppet show in La Fonda's lobby.

If you had a party you didn't have to think about what to serve; you just naturally cooked up some beans and posole and served that with both green and red chile stew, or you asked Mrs. Delgado to put you on her list for three or four dozen tamales.

When I first moved to Santa Fe, us Anglos knew our place.

But Santa Fe has changed. Now we have instant haciendas costing a million or more and we have a Fiesta that is still a spectacle, but it isn't OUR spectacle, so it doesn't amount to much, and I suppose that those imported caterers will run Mrs. Delgado out of business.

The people I feel sorriest for are not the old-timers who remember how it was but the newcomers who missed it all, and I particularly feel sorry for those people at *People* magazine who can't find anything genuine to write about so they make up a bunch of lies, calling Santa Fe a Shangri-la. Privately, we always thought it was Shangri-la, but no one would ever dream of calling it that for fear of Santa Fe becoming something other than what it was meant to be, like another Disneyland with tour buses, wall-to-wall tourists, fast-food chains and a plaza that exudes all the charm of a carnival midway.

Viva la Sagebrush Shangri-la.

—Lewis Thompson,
letter to the editor in the *Santa Fe New Mexican*, August 27, 1982

the theater of the absurd. City Hall operates like a third-world government, rife with nepotism and creaky bureaucracy. One homeowner was denied a permit to demolish a chicken coop on his property; the city deemed it a "historic structure." A telling local joke: How many Santa Feans does it take to change a light bulb? Six: One to screw it in and five to mill around and bitch about how much better they liked the old one. As several Santa Fe residents told me, this sort of thing makes great copy (and even the *New Yorker* has gleefully reported on Santa Fe's local controversies), but it's a little tiring to endure year after year.

The *Santa Fe New Mexican,* the city's paper, bursts with letters daily decrying Santa Fe's allegedly fading uniqueness. Debbie Jaramillo, the city's controversial mayor in the mid-1990s, told me with her trademark frankness that the place has changed since she was a girl, and not for the better. "Growing up here it was almost like a third-world country: passive, a great mix of people, a tomorrow-is-just-another-day attitude. Today, it seems so hurried, fast-paced, people just figuring how they can make another dollar." Every Santa Fean who doesn't wring a living from the tourist industry is aching to crank back the clock.

The cranky conservatives have a point. Santa Fe was more charming and more accessible 30 years ago. But in compensation, now it is vastly more sophisticated, and has much more to offer the visitor. Whatever you do, don't plan on spending just two or three days here. The city and the surrounding Indian pueblos, Spanish colonial towns, Taos, Anasazi ruins, mountains, canyons, gorges, skiing, fishing, hiking, river rafting—not to mention grazing those *habanero* sour cream sauces—Santa Fe asks for as much of a month as you can spare.

A *month* at Santa Fe's prices? Well, my one-room apartment sounded pricey indeed at $800, but that works out to $26.66 a night, it was a 15-minute walk from the Plaza, and it had a TV that sometimes worked and foot-thick honest adobe walls. I was living near the heart of the most intriguing small city in America, working hours so long it seemed I had three jobs, and having a pretty damned good time.

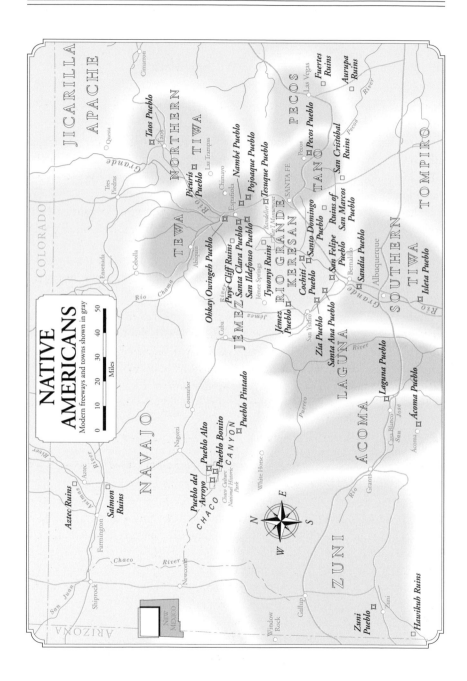

FIRST NEW MEXICANS

New Mexico is redolent with history; we all know that. But New Mexico's prehistoric past swirls also in mystery.

A few years back, a visitor from Arizona was stretched out in a sleeping bag at Chaco Canyon, the strange nexus of the northwestern New Mexico Anasazi in the 11th century. Shortly before dawn, he awoke with a bizarre and terrifying image exploding in his head.

"I had this very strong feeling that there had been sacrifices at some ancient time *right here*," he said. "And then I started hyperventilating. I couldn't breathe normally. I thought I was having a heart attack."

He woke his wife, and she rushed him to the nearest emergency room, 90 miles distant. The doctors ran an EKG and found nothing wrong. Finally, after blowing into a paper bag he calmed down.

Years after he described that frightening morning, I told him something I had uncovered in my years of research on the Anasazi: that some archaeologists, most notably Christy Turner in the astounding book *Man Corn*, published in 1999, had concluded that the Anasazi of Chaco Canyon had practiced ritual sacrifice, including cannibalism, as a form of organized terror to maintain their power.

He stared at me, blood draining from his face. "I didn't know any of that," he said.

■ HUNTERS, GATHERERS, FARMERS, SPIRITS

At least 575 generations of people have lived in northern New Mexico—11,500 years of continuous occupation.

Archaeologists call the earliest people Paleo-Indians and know almost nothing about them except that they were nomads who hunted bison with lances equipped with spearheads of finely fluted and sharpened stone. By around 5000 B.C., the climate had become drier, the surviving bison plodded north in search of greener pastures, and a new culture of plant-gatherers now called the Archaic moved in. Or perhaps the Paleo-Indians just shrugged, changed their diet, and became the Archaic. Archaeologists don't know much about them either.

Southwestern prehistory starts becoming interesting around 300 B.C., when corn, probably brought by itinerant traders from southern Mexico, began to be cultivated. This was the most profound event in New Mexico's entire history, at

(above) La Fajada Butte in Chaco Canyon. (opposite) A potter of Santa Clara Pueblo, taken by Edward S. Curtis, ca. 1905. (Library of Congress)

least until the arrival of the Spaniards. Agriculture led to permanent settlements, and that to pottery, architecture, town planning, government, and—who knows?—prehistoric bureaucrats and lawyers to make rules and settle disputes. The very pervasive and elaborate Pueblo Indian religion of today probably began to germinate along with these first seeds of corn, because people depending on the weather for successful crops would need allies in the spirit world.

The prehistoric builders who left the stunning ruins in northwestern New Mexico at Chaco Canyon are called the Anasazi. The word is of Navajo origin, and often is blandly translated as "the ancient ones." The more accurate translation is also the more ominous one: "enemy ancestors." To this day, Navajos steeped in tribal tradition avoid the ruins, believing that irritable spirits still lurk about. Some modern Pueblo Indians find the term offensive, preferring "ancestral Puebloans." The National Park Service has adopted this usage.

The early Anasazi, also known as "Basketmakers," lived in dismal pit houses with floors excavated about 20 inches below ground and a framework of poles, sticks, and mud mortar heaped overhead. Around A.D. 750, the first small pueblos of stone masonry began to appear. The Chacoan "great houses" followed in the 10th and 11th centuries, and cliff dwellings in the 13th.

AN ANCIENT TRADITION IN POTTERY

Pottery makers of the Southwest have been experimenting with clays, slips, and forms, both useful and decorative, for about 1,500 years. Designs common in the pots shown below are still part of the pottery tradition today.

Hohokam pot
This Sacaton red-on-buff–style pot was found at Casa Grande National Monument in Arizona. Its sloping shoulders make it typical of this period of pottery-making among the Hohokam people. A.D. 1100.

Anasazi pot and bowl
Found at Canyon de Chelly in Arizona, the cooking pot to the left was made for everyday use by the Kayenta Anasazi. The corrugations are made by pinching coils of clay. The black-on-white bowl to the right was found at Mesa Verde in southwestern Colorado. It measures more than 13 inches in diameter. The Mesa Verde region was a major center of pottery manufacture. A.D. 500–1300.

Sinagua bowl

The redware bowl to the right was made by the paddle-and-anvil technique and was found near Flagstaff, Arizona. The Sinagua culture, whose name means "without water," flourished between A.D. 500–1450.

Salado jar with handle

An unusual pottery type, found in the vicinity of Roosevelt Dam in central Arizona. Its linear design was applied after the piece was polished. A.D. 1150–1450.

Eastern Pueblo pot

This glazed pot was made in an Anasazi pueblo in the Rio Grande Valley in New Mexico between A.D. 1425 and 1475. It was probably used for storing food or water.

Early archaeologists assumed, as do casual visitors today, that cliff dwellings were built for defense. The issue is still a matter of debate. True, a cliff dwelling would be almost impossible to assault, but it would also make defending distant fields and hauling up water supplies much more difficult. Some archaeologists believe the Anasazi were mainly defending themselves from wind, snow, and rain. But I have climbed to sites so imposing (and frightening) that I side with archaeologist Christian Downum, who told me about some of the sites: "There was no reason on earth people would have built them unless they were afraid for their lives every night when they went to sleep."

The ascent of Anasazi art closely paralleled the rise in architectural sophistication. Until around A.D. 700, all Anasazi pottery was undecorated plainware. Gradually, painted designs began to appear, and by the 1100s the Anasazi were crafting pots, bowls, and mugs in astonishing variety and with dazzling skill. Elaborate turquoise, bone, and shell jewelry appeared, as did decorated clothing. There are

(above and opposite) The exceptional skills of Anasazi masons are readily evident at Pueblo Bonito in Chaco Culture National Historical Park, one of the most important archaeological sites in the United States. Built in the 11th century, Pueblo Bonito had between 600 and 800 rooms, making it the largest of the "great houses" at Chaco Canyon.

beautifully preserved Anasazi sashes woven from dog hair with repeating diamond patterns that are as sophisticated as anything sold in Santa Fe boutiques today.

Anasazi culture was not at all monolithic. There were striking variations in architecture, pottery, and clothing from place to place, and the people probably spoke several different languages. They occupied the adjoining corners of four of today's states: New Mexico, Colorado, Utah, and Arizona. Then, in the short span of time from A.D. 1250 to 1300, the Anasazi world dispersed—a phenomenon that popular writers like to call a "mystery," and one that archaeologists term the "abandonment."

There is no mystery about it. Overpopulation in what is mostly a high, semiarid plateau had consumed the scarce natural resources. And tree-ring studies tell of a devastating drought that persisted from 1276 to 1299. By 1300, most of the Anasazi cliff dwellings were left to the spirits, and the survivors, apparently, were surging into New Mexico's Rio Grande Valley, where the region's most reliable river ran.

What happened then was "a great mix of people," in the words of Curtis Schaafsma, curator of anthropology for the Museum of New Mexico. There were Anasazi from the west, Mogollon from the south, possibly Sinagua, Salado, and Hohokam from Arizona—as well as native Puebloans who had occupied the valley since A.D. 600. All this would account for the babel of languages spoken in the pueblos today—Keresan in Ácoma and Laguna; various dialects of Tanoan in Taos, Santa Clara, and Jémez; and Zuni in Zuni Pueblo. All these Puebloans are the direct descendants of the great migration to the Rio Grande Valley.

Beginning around 1250 to 1300, immense stone and adobe pueblos—some with 2,000 to 4,000 rooms for living and storage—arose in the valley. Santa Fe's City Hall rests atop one; it probably was abandoned just a few decades before the Spaniards arrived. "When you go into the adobe brick of the Palace of the Governors," says Schaafsma, "you find potsherds. I think they [the Spaniards] just went to this big pile of dirt for their adobe."

Given the modern examples of India, Yugoslavia, and Russia—to name just a few—how is it that people from so many ethnic stocks could come and live together in an increasingly crowded valley? Well, nothing in Southwestern archaeology today is as likely to start a fight among authorities as the question of prehistoric warfare. Joe S. Sando, a Jémez Pueblo Indian, wrote in *Pueblo Nations: Eight Centuries of Pueblo Indian History:* "There were guidelines for well-ordered living. What the Pueblos have now as an unwritten 'tribal code' was essentially in operation in ancient times, remembered and obeyed as though carved in stone. The code was respected, understood, and taught from generation to generation." The code, Sando explained simply, came from the Great Spirit.

"They *didn't* merge peacefully," Schaafsma contends. "Rock art in the Rio Grande Valley is jam-packed full of all kinds of warrior imagery. The idea of the 'peaceful pueblos' is something people made up because it sounded good. However, 'warfare' is too broad a term. 'Squabbling' probably describes it better. The fighting was more opportunistic than ritualized."

Archaeologists are sure to squabble about the internal conflict for generations to come. Meanwhile, there are several fascinating Pueblo ruins within a comfortable drive of Santa Fe for the rest of us to explore. Listed below are three important prehistoric sites in the vicinity of Santa Fe. They are also listed and more fully described in the chapter "SIDE TRIPS FROM SANTA FE."

■ CHACO CULTURE NATIONAL HISTORICAL PARK

Within Chaco Canyon are an astounding 2,000-plus prehistoric ruins, including 11 major pueblos. Startling in its scale, the canyon's Pueblo Bonito, built mainly between 1030 and 1079, once contained between 600 and 800 rooms. The Anasazis' sophisticated construction techniques are apparent at Chaco, one of the most significant archaeological sites in the United States.

From Santa Fe take I-25 south 41 miles to U.S. 550. Follow U.S. 550 north about 120 miles to the turnoff for County Road 7900 (3 miles east of Nageezi Trading Post) and then drive south along County Road 7950 for 27 miles to Chaco Canyon; 505-786-7014.

■ BANDELIER NATIONAL MONUMENT

This astonishing spectacle of prehistoric dwellings and volcanic rock formations covers nearly 50 square miles. The Anasazi migrated here in about A.D. 1150 and the tribe thrived for 400 years. Most of the inhabitants had deserted the area by the 1600s. Seventy-five miles of trails lead to the cliff dwellings, ceremonial caves, and ancient pueblos. The largest pueblo is Tyuonyi, an oval-shaped structure encircling a large plaza. The construction took about a century, supposedly reaching 400 rooms on three levels at its peak.

The first New Mexicans left petroglyphs in several areas of the state, including these of a bird and a club in Petroglyph National Monument. (National Park Service)

About a one-hour drive from Santa Fe. Take U.S. 84/285 north about 12 miles, then turn west on N.M. 502. At the junction with N.M. 4, continue 6 miles to the parking area. Follow one of the hiking trails to reach the ruins; 505-672-0343.

■ **PETROGLYPH NATIONAL MONUMENT**
The monument preserves more than 15,000 Anasazi petroglyphs and other prehistoric images dating back 2,000 to 3,000 years. Most of the petroglyphs—depictions of birds, other animals, and humans—were left by Puebloans between A.D. 1300 and 1650. Three easy, self-guided trails take you past many of the petroglyphs.

From Santa Fe take I-25 south to Albuquerque about 56 miles, then take I-40 west to Coors Road exit north. Turn left on Atrisco Drive, which becomes Unser Boulevard. The visitors center is at Unser Boulevard and Western Trail Road; 505-899-0205.

■ PUEBLO CULTURE

What occurred in the lives of the people living along the Rio Grande between the time the Anasazi abandoned their cliff dwellings and the Spanish arrived 250 years later is a matter of speculation. Presumably, Anasazi people came down from the drier canyon lands to live along the Rio Grande, integrating their lives with those of others already there. The landscape the Anasazi had come from was one of deep, fertile canyons where rocks suitable for use in masonry buildings were numerous. Between Santa Fe and Taos, the landscape was wide open to the sky. The tributaries to the Rio Grande along which people came to live—the Taos, Santa Cruz, Pojoaque, Santa Fe, and Galisteo—dried up for months at a time, and in the spring, when they flooded with snowmelt, the waters ran red. The villages that grew up beside them were made not of rock, as were the Anasazi villages, or shrubs, as were those of earlier inhabitants in this area, but of packed mud in connected rooms, sometimes on several levels.

These were short, lean people with dark eyes and hair and brown skin well adapted to blazing sunlight at high elevations. In warm months, children went naked, women walked barefoot, and men wore breechcloths. In colder weather people wore moccasins; men, kilts about their waists and cloaks of turkey feathers or rabbit fur. Some wore on their ankles little copper bells and beads made far to the south in what is now Mexico. Women wrapped themselves in pieces of cloth, 4 to 5 feet long and 3 feet wide, worn under the left arm and over the right shoulder and held together with decorated belts.

A girl of Taos Pueblo, photographed by Edward S. Curtis in 1905. (Museum of New Mexico)

Ceremonial kiva at Bandelier National Monument, near Los Alamos.

Within Pueblo villages, all aspects of life were carefully prescribed by tradition. Rituals governed the tasks of planting, hunting, and building, as well as the emotional dramas of birth and death. If one fear was pervasive, it was the fear of witches, who were believed to be responsible for the mystifying events that intervened even in the most carefully ordered lives. People wanted to avoid being the subject of a witch's spell, and, most likely, they wanted to avoid being identified as witches themselves. Alleged witches were purged, sometimes in groups.

All members of a pueblo owned the village and land in common, but families were granted plots of land on which to grow crops for their own use, as well as a room to live in. They were small rooms, reached by a ladder from the ceiling and made comfortable by mats of native cotton and yucca fiber woven on looms and by stools made from cottonwood trunks. A new husband joined his wife in her family's room or rooms; if he left his wife, an ex-husband returned to his mother or sister.

Life outside the family was organized around the duties of cults and secret societies, to which men belonged by heredity and women joined through marriage. Each society was obligated to undertake particular civic duties, and its ceremonies took place in a large, usually round chamber, or kiva.

For the most part, this was a harmonious world. The cultural memories of the 1200s, a time of terrible conflict, were fresh, and the Puebloans devised a new way of cooperative living based on the katsina religion, still practiced in the Hopi tribe today. Networking with other cultures came in the form of goods that moved along ancient trade routes all over the Southwest and Mexico. Traders brought seashells from oceans, copper bells and macaw feathers from Mexico, and news from pueblos to the west—those of the Zuni, Hopi, or Ácoma.

Yet with the exception of trouble from nomadic warrior people who trekked down from the north and the west, occasionally attacking their villages, the citizens of these pueblos remained in place. Seasons came and went, the rivers ran full or sank into the sand, the villagers prayed for rain and crops. When dawn brightened the horizon, the familiar routine unfolded and the stillness was broken only by familiar sounds: the whispering of younger members of the tribe in childish versions of their dialect, the rippling creek water, the wind in the cottonwoods, a dog barking, an owl hooting one last time.

Sometime in the year 1540, the Puebloans along the rivers between what is now Santa Fe and Taos heard rumors that a group of strange men had arrived near the pueblos to the west, in the desert. These men rode enormous animals and some dressed in shining clothes that arrows couldn't pierce. When native people went to do battle with these men, they raised sticks that killed with noises and fire.

What the Puebloans had encountered was a scouting party sent by Gen. Francisco Vásquez de Coronado under the command of Capt. Hernando de Alvarado and accompanied by a chaplain, 16 cavalrymen, and four foot soldiers. The group was moving toward what is now north-central New Mexico with the encouragement of the viceroy of Mexico,

The interior of a kiva, scene of religious rites.

(above) Edward S. Curtis shot this image while visiting Ácoma Pueblo in 1904. (Museum of New Mexico) (opposite) This classic Puebloan ladder was shot at Picurís Pueblo.

whose ultimate allegiance, like theirs, was to His Most Catholic Majesty, King Carlos I of Spain. The next chapter will explain the devastating effect this incursion had on the Puebloans along the river; the remarkable fact is that they still exist and maintain a traditional, viable culture. Between Santa Fe and Taos is a cluster of eight pueblos consisting of both ruins and modern villages. These pueblos, listed below, are described more fully in the chapter "EIGHT NORTHERN PUEBLOS."

Nambé	Ohkay Owingeh (formerly San Juan)
Picurís	Santa Clara
Pojoaque	Taos
San Ildefonso	Tesuque

Ácoma Pueblo, which is described in "SIDE TRIPS FROM SANTA FE," is one of several pueblos southwest of Santa Fe. Visitors to all pueblos should remember that these are quiet villages, where people prefer to go about their daily lives in peace, without intense scrutiny.

HISPANIC SANTA FE

The Spanish provincial capital of Santa Fe was conceived of imperialist ambition and born of conflict between church and state. Its adolescence consisted of more than two centuries of skirmishes, revolts, sieges, wars, executions, persecutions, ethnic divisions, and, for good measure, random violence.

No American city has a richer history; few have been surrounded by more tragedy and turmoil. The streets of 21st-century Santa Fe, generally peaceful and lined with glittering galleries and boutiques, deceive. The full story is worth knowing.

The recorded history of New Mexico began in the summer of 1540, when part of an expeditionary army led by Francisco Vásquez de Coronado mustered across the present-day Arizona border along the Zuni River. Coronado, the governor of New Galicia, then the northernmost province of New Spain, was a mere 30 years old. His monumental foray—the curtain-raiser of the Spanish *Entrada* into the history of southwestern North America—was spurred by rumors of the fabled Seven Cities of Cíbola, the cities of gold, a legend whose roots extended deep into medieval Spain and originally had nothing to do with the New World. His recruits were mostly teenagers and men younger than himself who had grown up in privileged families but had found themselves instantly impoverished by the draconian inheritance laws of Spain: everything went to the firstborn son. These later-born sons were easily seduced by visions of wealth for the taking.

Coronado's expedition set the stage for the next 100 years. He had firm orders from the viceroy of New Spain to treat the Indians he encountered "as if they were Spaniards"—in other words, with decency and dignity. But how could his party follow this mandate when they were essentially searching for plunder—and, incidentally, were determined to harness the barbarians to the yoke of Roman Catholicism?

Each time they entered a pueblo, the Spaniards would fire their guns and read the *requerimiento,* a proclamation claiming the village *en nombre del rey*—"in the name of the king of Spain." Furthermore, those who lived in the towns were ordered to consent to the teachings of the church. If they refused, the proclamation continued, "We shall forcefully enter your country and make war against you in all ways and manners that we can . . . and the deaths and losses which shall accrue from this are your fault. . . ." Since these men were the first Spaniards the Indians had ever seen, the proclamation might as well have been read to them in classical Greek as in Spanish. But they quickly came to understand the Spaniards' intentions.

On July 7, 1540, Coronado's advance guard approached the Zuni pueblo of Hawikuh. Rumors had it that this was one of the fabled Cities of Cíbola. What the Spaniards saw was an unprepossessing huddle of houses made of rocks and mud. Still, they demanded that the village surrender in the name of their king and God. The Zunis answered with a hail of arrows. The Spaniards responded with crossbows and muskets and took by force what was, to them, a worthless pueblo. Many of the defenders were killed.

Coronado's band passed within a few miles of present-day Santa Fe, wandered as far as Kansas in a futile search for gold, and finally slunk back to Mexico in disgrace. Coronado himself was charged with abuse of the Pueblo Indians—at Tiguex, near present-day Albuquerque, the Spaniards had burned 30 rebellious Indians alive at the stake—but eventually he was acquitted.

A French map drawn by G. Samson in 1669 depicts the territory of Spanish North America and shows the Rio Grande flowing into the Pacific Ocean just east of the island of California, rather than into the Gulf of Mexico. (Museum of New Mexico)

History Time Line

ca. A.D. 1250–1400 Pueblo Indian villages thrive along the Rio Grande.

ca. 1415–1425 Santa Fe region suffers worst drought in 1,000 years; many pueblos are abandoned.

1540 Francisco Vásquez de Coronado comes upon Zuni Pueblo in search of the Seven Cities of Cíbola.

1598 Under the leadership of Spanish explorer Juan de Oñate the first permanent European colony in New Mexico (the second in the United States) is established at San Juan Pueblo.

1607–1610 Don Pedro de Peralta names La Villa de Santa Fé (the City of the Holy Faith) as capital of the new colony. Construction begins on the Palace of the Governors.

1617 A Spanish priest, the first European settler in Taos, builds the Mission Church near the centuries-old Taos Pueblo.

1680 Pueblo Indians revolt against Spanish rule and colonists are exiled to what is now Ciudad Juárez, Mexico, across the river from El Paso.

1692 Don Diego de Vargas recaptures Santa Fe for Spain.

1792 Spain acquires the Louisiana Territory and commissions Pedro de Vial to blaze a trail between St. Louis and Santa Fe. New Mexicans are forbidden to trade with anyone other than Mexico or its colonies.

1806 American explorer Capt. Zebulon Pike, celebrated for his daring expeditions up the Arkansas River and along the Rio del Norte, is captured and taken to Spanish Santa Fe.

1821 Mexico secedes from Spain. The following year American William Becknell opens the Santa Fe Trail and brings wagonloads of northeastern goods to the residents of Santa Fe.

1846 Gen. Stephen Watts Kearny leads the Army of the West into the Santa Fe Plaza and proclaims New Mexico a U.S. territory.

1848 Treaty of Guadalupe Hidalgo cedes New Mexico to the United States.

1851 Jean Baptiste Lamy arrives in Santa Fe.

1862 The Confederate Army of New Mexico captures Santa Fe on March 10; Union forces retake the capital on April 8.

1869 Work begins on St. Francis Cathedral and is completed 17 years later.

1878 Lew Wallace is appointed governor; two years later, while still in office, he completes an epic romance novel set in ancient Rome, *Ben-Hur.*

1880 The railroad reaches Santa Fe. Streetlights are put up in the Plaza and the main streets. Billy the Kid spends the night in Santa Fe's jail.

1881 The first telephone rings in Santa Fe.

1912 New Mexico becomes the 47th state.

1915 Ernest Blumenschein, Robert Henri, Joseph Henry Sharp, and Bert Geer Phillips, among others, form the Taos Society of Artists.

1922 Author D. H. Lawrence and his wife, Frieda, arrive in Taos.

1929 Arts patron Mabel Dodge Luhan invites Georgia O'Keeffe to New Mexico.

Santa Fe Plaza in the 1880s, painted by Francis X. Grosshenney.
(New Mexico Museum of Fine Arts)

1942–1945 The first atomic bomb is developed in top-secret laboratories in Los Alamos.

1956 Swiss émigré Ernie Blake builds Taos Ski Valley.

1957 John Crosby, 30, founds Santa Fe Opera; first production is Puccini's *Madama Butterfly.*

1967 The New Buffalo Commune, one of the first hippie communities in the nation, is founded in Taos.

1987 King Juan Carlos I is the first Spanish king ever to visit the former colonial capital of Spain.

1997 Santa Fe honors (finally!) New Mexico's most celebrated artist, Georgia O'Keeffe, opening a museum of her work.

2001 The Lensic, a glorious vaudeville and movie theater, reopens as Santa Fe's premier performing arts center after major renovation.

2002 Water becomes the fighting word in the desert city, as residents face severe restrictions while private golf courses gulp a million gallons a day.

The Koshare clowns at San Juan Pueblo in 1935. (Museum of New Mexico)

■ EARLY SANTA FE

The first group of Spanish settlers to arrive in northern New Mexico came in 1598 under the leadership of Gov. Juan de Oñate. Among them were 130 families, 270 single men, and 11 Franciscan friars, along with 7,000 head of cattle and 83 wagons and carts. After enduring incredible hardships in the Chihuahuan Desert as they traveled north from Mexico, they settled along the Rio Grande near San Juan Pueblo. Soon the settlement was embroiled in disputes, and by 1610, Gov. Oñate had been replaced by a new governor. The original settlers regrouped and joined with newly arrived colonists led by Gov. Pedro de Peralta to build a villa on the Rio Santa Fe. Six districts and a block for government buildings were marked out. Residents elected four councilmen, two of whom were to act as judges.

Within a few years, the villa of Santa Fe was a fortresslike compound, with arsenals, a jail, a chapel, and governor's offices. Two interior plazas were joined by outer walls, and entry was gained through a single gate with a trench in front of it. Settlers lived outside the gate and were given two lots, for a house and garden; fields in which to plant vegetables, vineyards, and olive groves; and another 133 acres of land. In return they agreed to live in the area for 10 consecutive years.

In 1612, a Franciscan friar named Isidro Ordóñez rumbled into Santa Fe with a contingent of missionaries and a letter from the viceroy authorizing him to take charge of the New Mexican missions. The secular governor, Peralta, correctly felt that his authority was being challenged.

In less than a year, the friction ignited. Just before a Sunday mass in 1613, Ordóñez ordered Peralta's honorific governor's chair placed outside the church. When Peralta arrived he was furious and brought it back in. Ordóñez excommunicated him. Later that week Peralta ordered the priest out of town. When Ordóñez refused to go, the governor whipped out his pistolet and fired. Ordóñez was only grazed by the bullet, but he vowed revenge. Ordóñez organized a posse and arrested Peralta, imprisoning him first at Sandía Pueblo, then at Zía. Eventually the Inquisition in Mexico City reprimanded Ordóñez and vindicated Peralta, but neither man returned to his post. For decades to follow, governors and priests in the little capital village would swap threats, excommunications, and arrests.

There was also trouble between church and state over the treatment of the Indians. The colonists saw a human resource to be exploited, extracting tribute in the form of bushels of corn and animal skins from the Puebloans and sometimes forcing them to "donate" labor. Even more injurious, the Europeans passed along

Kingdom's Capital

Seven leagues west of the aforesaid pueblo is the town of Santa Fé, capital of this kingdom. There reside the governors and the Spaniards, who number about two hundred and fifty, although for lack of weapons only fifty can be armed. Though they are few and poorly equipped, God has always enabled them to come forth victorious and has instilled into the Indians such a fear of them and of their harquebuses that at the mere mention of a Spaniard's coming to their pueblos they run away. In order to keep them in constant fear, they deal very severely with them whenever occasion arises for punishing a rebellious pueblo. . . . When I arrived there as custos, I started the construction of the church and friary, which—to the honor and glory of God—would merit admiration anywhere. There the friars are already teaching the Spaniards and Indians to read, write, play musical instruments, sing, and to practice all the arts of the civilized society.

—Fray Alonso de Benavides, Memorial of 1630

diseases that devastated the Pueblo population. In the first 80 years of Spanish contact, the Pueblo population became substantially reduced, an occurrence that greatly vexed the church, which was losing potential converts—and tithes. It cannot be said, though, that the church was always kinder or gentler than the colonists. In 1675, four Tewa Indians were charged with "bewitching" local priests and hanged as "sorcerers."

Yet most of the priests were men of dedication and energy. By 1625, 26 friars had built 50 churches in New Mexico, and in their own era they were considered idealists with a highly respectable vocation. Franciscans left for the New World convinced they represented the only salvation available to man, in a form sanctified by God. In this they were backed by the religious training of their childhood and their years of seminary education. The severe discipline and punishment they meted out to the Indians paralleled what the Spanish Inquisition was visiting upon Spanish citizens at home.

As early as 1650 the Puebloans began mumbling of revolt against the unwelcome Europeans. (Potential revolutionaries were also hanged, whenever the Spaniards could find them.) In 1680, the war finally commenced, and with a

Don Diego de Vargas, governor of New Mexico from 1691 to 1697, came from an aristocratic Spanish family. (Museum of New Mexico)

vengeance. A Tewa warrior named Popé sent messengers to all the pueblos, each carrying a cord of yucca fiber tied with knots to remind them how many days were left until the revolt. On August 11 the last knots disappeared and the storm began. The Puebloans killed most of the settlers outside Santa Fe and then laid siege to the Palace of the Governors, where a thousand defenders were holed up. After days without water, the Spaniards decided they had to fight, even though they were badly outnumbered. At sunrise on August 20 they poured out of the Palace and successfully took back the town, killing 300 Indians in the process.

Still, the future looked bleak, and Gov. Antonio Otermín decided to abandon the capital, at least temporarily. The settlers retreated 300 miles south to El Paso del Norte (present-day Ciudad Juárez, Mexico). Of the 2,500 colonists and servants who joined in the retreat, 1,946 were recorded by the Spanish authorities as having arrived in El Paso, where they were to remain for a dozen years. In 1692 the governor-in-exile, Don Diego de Vargas, led an expedition to Santa Fe, found the Indians surprised and disorganized, and retook the capital without firing a shot. At Galisteo, de Vargas's captain of artillery, Francisco Lucero de Godoy, found his young nephew, who had been held captive by the Puebloans since they had killed his family at their hacienda 13 years before.

Unfortunately, de Vargas had to return to El Paso to collect the rest of his flock of settlers. When they set out again in October, almost 100 years after Oñate first brought treasure seekers and settlers to the region, most of those who followed were returning to the landscape of their childhood, where a parent, child, husband, or wife was buried. In all, there were 70 families, a contingent of soldiers, Indians from Mexico, convicts, lawyers, and chaplains. The group was supported by 18 wagons and three cannons, 1,000 mules, 2,000 horses, and 900 head of cattle. Their sacred object was *La Conquistadora,* a statue of the Virgin (now on display at Santa Fe's St. Francis Cathedral). They made their arduous journey behind the imposing figure of de Vargas, the son of a distinguished Spanish family, a tall man with dark eyes who wore his beard narrow and his hair long and carried in his saddlebag a full court dress.

When the colonists again arrived in Santa Fe in 1693, a battle ensued. Twenty-one Spaniards and 81 Puebloans died. De Vargas reclaimed the village, but the cost had been high.

■ RESETTLEMENT

As the next century proceeded, the colonists whose farming and ranching supported the capital at Santa Fe scattered across the landscape of northern New Mexico. They had arrived with different motives than those of the conquistadors. They were looking for cultivatable land rather than gold, and they brought new varieties of beans, chiles, onions, oats, barley, wheat, peas, and melons, as well as chocolate and tomatoes. Their grazing animals spread out across the countryside, and their sheep provided wool to be spun and woven into cloth.

Family and community life were tightly structured, and deeply religious in their focus. Comanches occasionally swept down from the north on raiding parties. Near Taos in 1760, 50 Spanish women and children were carried off and not seen again.

Feast days, Christmas celebrations, and weddings were the center of social life, as was shared work like the yearly cleaning of irrigation ditches. *Santeros* traveled from Santa Fe to the villages and haciendas, selling thin, large-eyed wood carvings of the saints to sanctify homes and fields. Men joined *Penitente* societies—lay religious fraternities that exist to this day—flagellating themselves to atone for Christ's suffering on the cross. The church officially disapproved of these practices, causing the *Penitentes* to go underground. Another outcast group were descendants of Spanish Jews who had fled the Inquisition, ostensibly converted to Catholicism and resettled in the kingdom's most far-flung outposts.

The Population of Santa Fe in 1790

CATEGORY	MALE	PERCENT	FEMALE	PERCENT
Pure Spanish	820	67.38	875	66.04
Mixed Race				
Color Quebrado	185	15.20	195	14.72
Mestizo	101	8.30	121	9.13
Mulato	42	3.45	43	3.25
Indian Servants	31	2.55	5	0.38
Indio	36	2.96	85	6.42
Coyote	2	0.16	1	0.08
TOTAL POPULATION	1,217		1,325	

■ The "Mournful" Capital

Eighteenth-century Santa Fe had very little of the charm and élan it began to acquire toward the end of the next one. A famous description by visiting Friar Francisco Atanacio Domínguez, written in 1776, betrays the priest's disappointment at not finding much in the way of civilization:

> This villa . . . in the final analysis . . . lacks everything. Its appearance is mournful because not only are the houses of earth, but they are not adorned by any artifice of brush or construction. . . .

Although the population was small (the first census, in 1790, counted just 2,542 residents), urban sprawl was already a problem. As Domínguez went on to observe, most people lived on "small ranches at various distances from one another, with no plan as to their location." The real problem was not aesthetics, but Apaches: without a garrison wall, the town could not be defended. In 1777 the new governor, Don Juan Bautista de Anza, devised a plan to rebuild the town compactly on the south side of the Santa Fe River, but was rebuffed by the ranchers, who wanted to stay close to their fields so they could guard them. According to New Mexican historian Marc Simmons, the ranchers actually worried more about bears prowling down from the Sangre de Cristo Mountains to poach than they did about Indian raids. (On rare occasions, bears still wander into Santa Fe today. One morning in 1994, a 250-pound black bear showed up just a few blocks from the government complex on Cerrillos Road. A state Game and Fish officer shot and killed it, prompting a furor that lasted for weeks.)

Other menaces of daily life included rattlesnakes, smallpox epidemics, floods, droughts, and shootings. There was little organized commerce; the 1790 census listed exactly one merchant. The reason was Santa Fe's isolation and the Crown's prohibition against trade with any nation except Spain and her colonies. Potential trade with Mexico City was an arduous 1,400 miles away. Most goods were either handmade or bartered with Indians at trade fairs at distant Taos and Pecos.

The church, as always, managed to import at least some of the trappings of culture. Although adobe was the only building material available, the military chapel of 1760 called *La Castrense* showed off a stunningly intricate baroque altar screen carved by stonemasons from more settled parts of Mexico. (The chapel is gone, but today the screen is the focal point of Cristo Rey Church.)

Cristo Rey Church.

The echoes of Santa Fe history still resonate in the city's character to this day, although with the waves of newcomers that character is rapidly being submerged. The hardship and isolation fostered a sense of fatalism, independence, and especially a stubborn pride in being a unique people. If a modern Santa Fean should shout a cranky epithet at the occupant of a luxury car with out-of-state plates, well, it's not very different from Santa Feans in 1777 telling carpetbagging Gov. de Anza to go to hell with his plans for their town.

By 1800, foreigners—trappers, traders, and haphazard voyagers from abroad—began to arrive with increasing frequency on the borders of the Spanish frontier. They brought news of a changing outside world: the city of New Orleans, Spanish in 1800, reverted to France in 1803, only to be sold to the United States. In 1805, nothing was more unnerving to the people of Santa Fe than an incomprehensible medical innovation: the Spanish government decided to vaccinate its people for smallpox. When the government doctor went through the city and out to pueblos and haciendas with his vials of fluid, Indian and Spanish parents were equally suspicious of his intentions.

Although periodic hostilities between the Puebloans and the Spaniards continued into the 19th century, the two gradually became allies in the face of Apache and Comanche raids. After generations of enmity and retributions following the Pueblo revolt, they began intermarrying, the Indians learned Spanish, and many even returned to the Catholic Church. The Puebloan diet surely diversified with new foods introduced by the Europeans. And the Puebloans didn't lose their traditional lands, as did so many other Native American tribes. But Spanish rule still had been a tragedy of epic proportions. Historian Marc Simmons estimates that in 1540 the Puebloans had numbered from 40,000 to 50,000 people; by 1700 they had dwindled to no more than 14,000. Today, however the population has climbed back up to nearly 40,000.

■ MEXICAN SANTA FE

In 1810, an event pivotal to the development of Santa Fe took place hundreds of miles away in Dolores, a poor Indian town 120 miles northwest of Mexico City. With the famous *grito de dolores,* still celebrated throughout Mexico and the American Southwest on September 16, the priest exhorted his people to break the bondage of Spain. "My children!" shouted Padre Miguel Hidalgo y Costilla. "A new dispensation comes to us this day. Are you ready to receive it? Will you be

MEXICAN MANNERS

The Mexicans, like the French, are remarkable for their politeness and suavity of manners. You cannot visit a friend but he assures you that, *"Está Vd. en su casa, y puede mandar,"* etc. (You are in your own house, and can command, etc.), or, *"Estoy enteramente a su disposición"* (I am wholly at your disposal), without, however, meaning more than an expression of ordinary courtesy. Nor can you speak in commendation of any article, let its value be what it may, but the polite owner immediately replies, *"Tómelo Vd., Señor; es suyo"* (Take it, sir; it is yours), without the slightest intention or expectation that you should take him at his word.—Mr. Poinsett observes, "Remember, when you take leave of a Spanish grandee, to bow as you leave the room, at the head of the stairs, where the host accompanies you; and after descending the first flight, turn round and you will see him expecting a third salutation, which he returns with great courtesy, and remains until you are out of sight; so that as you wind down the stairs, if you catch a glimpse of him, kiss your hand, and he will think you a most accomplished cavalier." Graphic as this short sketch is, it hardly describes the full measure of Mexican politeness; for in that country, when the visitor reaches the street, another tip of the hat, and another inclination of the head, will be expected by the attentive host, who gently waves, with his hand, a final *'adiós'* from a window.

—Josiah Gregg, Commerce of the Prairies, *1844*

free?" Eleven years and 600,000 deaths later, Mexico was an independent nation—and an immense one, because its territories included California, Arizona, New Mexico, and Texas, an area larger than today's Spain, France, Germany, Italy, Great Britain, Sweden, Norway, and Finland combined. From the southern tip of Mexico the empire stretched a mind-boggling 3,000 miles to the northern stub of California.

Becoming part of this empire was the best thing that had yet happened to Santa Fe. The Mexican government welcomed trade with the United States, and within a year a trapper and Indian fighter named William Becknell had begun to blaze a wagon trail from Independence, Missouri, 780 miles to Santa Fe. The Santa Fe Trail was the first major trade route punching into what would soon become the American West.

There is an ironic footnote to Mexican independence in Santa Fe. A celebration was clearly in order, but the town's big cigars seemed not to know exactly what to do.

So the *alcalde* (mayor) summoned one of the first American merchants to reach Santa Fe, one Thomas James, to ask what Americans might have done to welcome their own relatively recent independence. James suggested cutting the tallest pine they could find, stripping the branches, erecting it in the Plaza, and running up the flag. On February 5, 1822, as all Santa Fe gathered for the ceremony, James logically suggested the honor belonged to the governor, Facundo Melgares.

"Oh, do it yourself, Señor James," said Melgares. "You understand such things." So an American citizen raised the first Mexican flag over the New Mexican capital, launching five days of bacchanalia. The party might have been more subdued had a wise man been able to foretell the future: that in just 24 years New Mexico would have another new flag—as a territory of the United States.

Carts pulled by lumbering mules and oxen brought tons of American and even European fabrics, clothing, building materials, tools, hardware, kitchenware, and booze along the Santa Fe Trail. But the wagons were in constant danger of attack by Indians, and the encounters were vicious. In 1828, Indians shot a Capt. John Means off his horse, and, according to one account, "scalped him before he had drawn his last breath." That same year a party of trappers invited the enemy to a parley, then fired on them, killing half a dozen Indians. Today, as we drive from

Arrival of a caravan at Santa Fe in 1844. The opening of the Santa Fe Trail in 1822 signaled the beginning of the Anglo period in the region. (Museum of New Mexico)

SHAMEFUL

January 23, 1864:

We have heard of what we hope never will again occur in Santa Fe. It is that, at a fandango, a few evenings since, two of the females became insulted and enraged at each other, and that American men present endeavored to inflame the ill will and violence of the two women, the one against the other, and that a ring was formed and knives placed in the hands of each, for a desperate fight.

We hope no American will so far forget the dignity of human nature—his name and race, as to be found encouraging, again, such an exhibition of passion and violence between two females who, but for being animated and excited by spectators, would restrain within decent bounds their personal animosities.

—*News clipping from the* Santa Fe New Mexican *as reprinted in*
Oliver La Farge's Santa Fe: The Autobiography of a Southwestern Town

---

Missouri to Santa Fe in a couple of days, risking no more than speeding tickets, it is hard to imagine the mixture of adventurousness, trepidation, and opportunism that animated these early dreamers.

The Americans who lumbered into Santa Fe encountered a culture that astounded them. For example, the Spanish women of Santa Fe routinely smoked, danced, and gambled in public; they owned their own businesses and even made small fortunes. Priests routinely and openly took mistresses.

The town was wide open to carousing, partying (for any imaginable excuse), drinking, and especially gambling. Yet, according to historian Janet Lecompte, "courtesy was the first rule of conduct." Against that backdrop, many of the Americans proved to be boors. "They jeered at New Mexican folkways, broke up fandangos with drunken violence, and seduced and then abandoned both wives and children." Disparaging comments permeated the Anglos' impressions. Traveler Albert Pike in 1833 labeled the New Mexicans as "a lazy gossiping people, always lounging on their blankets and smoking cigarillos." Later in the century, Gen. William T. Sherman quipped that "The United States ought to declare war on Mexico and make it take back New Mexico."

La Patrona de Santa Fe

Santa Fe once had a *patrona*, a godmother. Her name was Gertrudis Barceló, but she became famous as la Tules—the Tules. That name lingers today at the corner of Burro Alley and Palace and Grant Avenues. And for a brief time, historic Burro Alley was called Calle Barcelona, for it was here that the gambling *sala* and residence of the notorious *monte* player dominated the social and gambling scene during the 1830s and 1840s.

La doña Tules.
(Museum of New Mexico)

Never in the history of this fandango-loving town has a woman entertained citizens and visitors with such intelligent wit and style. The legend of the expert *monte* dealer (*monte,* a card game of pure chance) has been depicted in park murals, told in novels, newspapers, and magazines, and portrayed in musicals and dramatic monologues. Her legend (somewhat embellished) grew even larger in 1844 with the publication of Josiah Gregg's famous epic of the Santa Fe Trail, *Commerce of the Prairies.*

La doña Tules, born around 1800 in Sonora, Mexico, of Catalán heritage, traveled with her family up the Rio Grande Valley along the centuries-old *El Camino Real de Tierra Adentro,* the Royal Road to the Interior. The Apache-infested road from central Mexico had been the route of New Mexico's first colonists led by don Juan de Oñate in 1598.

The Barceló family settled in the *Río Abajo* (down river) in the wine-growing village of Valencia, south of today's Albuquerque. Here la Tules married Manuel Antonio Sisneros and gave birth to two sons, both of whom died as infants. Motherhood was the biological wealth coveted by the woman gambler whose name appears time and again in church records as a godmother to the children of her friends and family.

Despite the sexual license of early New Mexico, adultery was frowned upon and considered illegal. More than once la Tules defended her reputation against local rumors. Her neighbor had complained to the *alcalde* (mayor) of la Tules illegally cohabiting with an Anglo. Taking the offensive, la Tules demanded that the neighbor back down. The two women later signed an act of conciliation. Soon, however, la Tules was again back in the *alcalde* court demanding an apology from another woman for unnamed slander.

La Tules traveled long distances to gamble at trade fairs in Mexico and throughout New Mexico. But it was the political excitement and international flavor of Santa Fe that finally captured her. She attended *bailes* (balls) and dealt *monte* to fur trappers, soldiers, merchants, governors, generals, women, and even the local clergy. A $10,000 stake was not uncommon, and gamblers were known to have covered as much as $40,000 in a single bet. Hard specie for use by the U.S. Army was in short supply

Dancing the fandango. (Museum of New Mexico)

at the beginning of the Mexican War in 1846. The erudite Lt. Col. David Dawson Mitchell, who was said to have made the ladies swoon as he walked the streets of St. Louis, needed money for supplies for his men to travel to Chihuahua. In public appreciation for a loan of $1,000 from la doña Tules, Mitchell escorted her on his arm to a play entitled *Pizarro,* given in the old Palace of the Governors.

In January 1852, New Mexico's newly appointed Bishop Jean Baptiste Lamy officiated at the funeral of the gambling doña. La Tules paid the church and Lamy almost $2,000 to be buried in the Capilla de San José (a south chapel) of the *parroquia* (parish church), on the site of today's St. Francis Cathedral.

The *gente fina* of Santa Fe—Hispanic, Anglo, clergy, and military—attended the grand finale to the life of la doña Tules. In life she had achieved wealth and fame, and in death the unprecedented fortune to be the first woman in New Mexico history to be buried by a bishop who desperately needed money to restore his crumbling mud churches.

The subject of Bishop Lamy's homily was the importance of leading a good life. Had la Tules led that good life, her name might well have missed the pages of history.

—*Mary Jean Cook*

Taking New Mexico

> Oh, what a joy to fight the dons
> and wallop fat Armijo!
> So clear the way to Santa Fe!
> With that we all agree, O!

The cheerily militant ditty above was sung by 300 U.S. Army regulars and volunteers as they marched over the Santa Fe Trail from Missouri to New Mexico in 1846. The Americans were commanded by Brig. Gen. Stephen Watts Kearny, a renowned fighter and ardent patriot. Manuel Armijo, the New Mexican governor, had a reputation as a good governor, badgering Mexico City to serve the needs of distant New Mexico and constantly advocating something relatively rare in the province: literacy. But he must have felt himself between the proverbial rock and hard place when he heard that the United States had declared war on Mexico. Armijo was obligated to defend Santa Fe, which meant defending it against the Americans who were forming its prospering economy.

The priests, curiously, tried to whip up flames of resistance. They warned the New Mexicans that the Americans would destroy the churches, rape the women, and brand the men on the cheek, like cattle. At this news, many Santa Feans fled. Eventually, so did Armijo. Convinced he couldn't win, he loaded what he could into seven wagons and left town. On August 18, 1846, Kearny and his ad hoc army captured the capital of New Mexico without spilling a drop of blood. As Janet Lecompte described it:

> They met no opposition, only sullen faces and downcast eyes. The wail
> of women rose above the din of the horses' hooves. As cannons
> boomed, soldiers raised the American flag on a newly constructed pole
> in the plaza. One soldier wrote later that he saw black eyes peering
> from behind latticed windows, many filled with tears, but a few gleam-
> ing with joy. The moment held both despair and hope—sorrow that
> Santa Fe was no longer a loving child of Spain and Mexico, and antici-
> pation that the United States would prove a more attentive parent.

JEAN BAPTISTE LAMY

On an August Sunday in 1851, a French-born priest named Jean Baptiste Lamy rode into Santa Fe to become the territorial capital's first bishop. His Spanish was abysmal, his health questionable, and he had no idea of the scorpions' nest of trouble he was about to confront—or to create.

Born to a prosperous peasant family in a small French town, he had grown up on narrow, dusty streets and attended mass in an unexceptional provincial church. Of 11 brothers and sisters, he was one of four to survive to adulthood.

During his years in the seminary, Lamy heard heroic stories of priests carrying the word of God into the New World. Inspired to join their ranks, he took orders, and at the age of

The controversial and energetic Bishop Jean Baptiste Lamy. (Museum of New Mexico)

25 stepped aboard a sailing ship bound across the Atlantic from the port of Le Havre. During an uncomfortable voyage, he studied English and ate sparingly—the ship did not provide food to its passengers; they had to bring their own. Lamy arrived in New York after 44 days at sea, and he set out to meet with the bishop of Cincinnati, Ohio.

The year was 1839, and the United States was in the midst of a depression. Lamy's bishop sent him into the Ohio forest to build a congregation and a church. His contemporaries were Abraham Lincoln, recently elected to the Illinois state legislature, and Robert E. Lee, who was working as an army engineer rechanneling the Mississippi River near St. Louis. Lamy spent the next 11 years in parish work, first in Ohio and then in Kentucky, ministering to congregations, buying land, and designing churches and raising the money to build them. He must have identified with his new country because in 1847 he became a citizen of the United States. He did, however, return to France the following year and on other occasions, visiting family and trying to find priests willing to come to the New World.

In 1848, the United States signed treaties concluding its war with Mexico and annexing the American Southwest. Reports from U.S. soldiers about the questionable state of the church in the New Mexico Territory weren't long in coming to the attention of the American Catholic Church, and letters on the subject of its improvement were soon being sent back and forth between Baltimore and Rome. Various people were suggested for a bishopric in the newly acquired territory, and in the summer of 1850, Father Lamy—at work building a church school in Covington, Kentucky— was surprised to hear that Pope Pius IX had named him bishop of Santa Fe.

Lamy returned to Cincinnati, then traveled by steamer down the Ohio and on to the Mississippi River, bound for New Orleans on a boat that carried passengers, animals, cotton, and slaves for sale. Reaching the Gulf, he boarded a ship to travel west, and barely survived its wreck. But survive he did, and he continued west on land toward Santa Fe—an arduous trip through arid country whose few cultivatable areas were suffering from a severe drought. In this territory of 70,000 people, he'd been told, there were 15 priests, of whom six were infirm with age.

Several thousand citizens of Santa Fe turned out to welcome him on a Sunday in the summer of 1851. Directly upon arriving, he went to say mass in the old church of St. Francis, where the parishioners knelt on floors that were for the most part of mud-packed earth. Seemingly in honor of his arrival, clouds massed, and the rains came. Certainly an auspicious beginning; but the next day the vicar of Santa Fe told Lamy he refused to recognize him as a bishop, despite the papal bulls Lamy had in hand, because there'd been no word of such a thing from the bishop in Durango, Mexico.

■ ■ ■

Willa Cather immortalized Lamy in her famous historical novel, *Death Comes for the Archbishop,* published in 1927. But the real Lamy was more intriguing than the "brave, sensitive, courteous" and one-dimensional creature of Cather's creation.

Bishop Lamy disapproved of santos carvings such as this one when he arrived in Santa Fe.

You can begin to sense Lamy's character at the east end of San Francisco Street in downtown Santa Fe, where the great, gray Romanesque cathedral towers over the low, brown adobe town. This is Lamy's legacy. He conceived it, imported the architects and stonemasons for it, and had it built literally around the adobe parish church that had stood there before.

The Catholic Church that Bishop Lamy encountered in New Mexico was little better than pagan, he felt. One Santa Fe priest, Lamy discovered, was "keeping a very young and beautiful married woman in his house." When Lamy ordered her out, the padre essentially told his bishop to go to hell. In little more than a year, Lamy and the Spanish-speaking priests in his see were at war, and Lamy was still struggling to learn Spanish.

Lamy felt a moral obligation to rehabilitate the New Mexican church, but he never understood New Mexicans. He couldn't tolerate the primitive, sometimes macabre folk-art carvings of santos (saints) that inhabited the churches, and at one point ordered them thrown out.

Santa Fe's Catholic cathedral dominates East San Francisco Street in this 1865 photo. (Museum of New Mexico)

Lamy's most controversial act was his excommunication of an elderly New Mexican priest, Padre Antonio José Martínez of Taos. Martínez was an intelligent and respected activist who had battled the practice of compulsory tithing to the church. Bishop Lamy, while he decried priestly greed and corruption, reinstated the tithe, cut the percentage paid to the priests, and increased the amount under his own control. He wasn't out for personal gain; nobody has ever accused him of that. He did dream of a French cathedral towering over Santa Fe.

Lamy appointed a Spanish friend, Don Damaso Taladrid, to replace Martínez. Martínez didn't budge, and sent laundry lists of grievances to his bishop. Lamy didn't answer. In 1857 Lamy dispatched his vicar apostolate, Priest Joseph Machebeuf, to Taos to kick Martínez out of the church. But even after

A statue of Bishop Lamy stands in front of the Santa Fe cathedral.

excommunication, Martínez maintained an independent, crypto-Catholic Church with his own followers.

"Bishop Lamy's removal of the native clergy was tragic," writes historian Ray John de Aragón, voicing a common viewpoint among Hispanics. "It deprived the Hispanic New Mexicans of their leaders, leaving a 'wound that was long to heal and a scar that can still be felt.'" On the other hand, Lamy gave a great deal to Santa Fe at a pivotal moment in its development: he set up a school for boys in his own house and summoned the Sisters of Loretto to establish an academy for girls. Writes author Paul Horgan, "Affirmation was the theme of his life. Who knew how much spiritual energy was thoughtlessly inherited, absorbed, and reactivated in later inheritors?"

Arrogant, determined, and hardworking, kind in his own manner and unquestionably honest—this is the complex mosaic cobbled together from different points of view. Maybe the best tribute to Jean Baptiste Lamy, as you watch the evening light paint his statue and cathedral, is to think of him as a complex and contradictory figure.

CONTEMPORARY SANTA FE

Santa Fe has been casting its mysterious spell over visitors for more than a century. In 1880, the first locomotive huffed into town, bringing building materials and patients with tuberculosis or emphysema who prayed that the thin, dry air would cure them. Artists and tourists followed in growing waves. Between 1880 and 1900, the Anglo population of New Mexico quadrupled. Most fell in love with the place. Martha Summerhayes, a young army bride, rhapsodized in 1889:

> As we drove into the town, its appearance of placid content, its ancient buildings, its great trees, its clear air, its friendly, indolent-looking inhabitants, gave me a delightful feeling of home. A mysterious charm seemed to possess me. It was the spell which that old town loves to throw over the strangers who venture off the beaten track to come within her walls.

By 1900, Santa Fe was beginning to acquire a reputation as a colony of painters and writers. Statehood was still a dozen years away and the entire population of the territorial capital was about 5,000. "Santa Fe style," far from being a fabrication of the 1980s, was being talked about as early as 1912. Within the next few years, prescient architects, artists, and Museum of New Mexico director Edgar Lee Hewett published articles that advocated stripping the town of Victorian frou-frou, restoring the Plaza to its original dimensions (twice as large as we see it today), creating a linear river park, and fabricating all new building in the Spanish–Pueblo Revival style. They correctly realized that Santa Fe's future lay in tourism; they failed only to predict the monster that it would become.

Santa Feans date the birth of the "monster" to the early 1980s, when a tsunami of national publicity rolled over the little city. In 1981, *U.S. News & World Report* called it "a new Palm Springs." *Newsweek* hailed it as "America's Salzburg." In prose shamelessly empurpled, *People* termed it a "Sagebrush Shangri-la . . . a mecca of mesas and margaritas." A little higher on the literary scale, *National Geographic* called it "an enchantress among cities without the Circean evil that turns men into swine." In 2006, readers of *Condé Nast Traveler* voted Santa Fe the *number two* city in the United States, favoring it over New York City, Chicago, and Seattle.

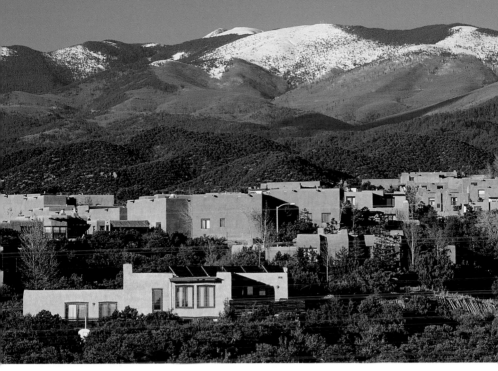

Blue skies, white capped mountains, and evergreens—nature's contribution to Santa Fe style.

But the article that created the biggest local howl was a 10-page piece in the May 1981 *Esquire* that said, in effect, pack your BMW and move to Santa Fe:

> There is, quite simply, a *here* here, a surfeit of it. Art and music. Bookstores. Thousands of acres to hike, climb, fish and ride. Good bars and worthy restaurants, warm and friendly nearly every one. Lots of single people. Nifty things to buy and wear: cowboy boots, Stetsons with peacock feathers, down-filled vests.
>
> And there is an attitude in the air that some townspeople call tolerant, others laid-back, still others *mañana* [tomorrow]. Finally, there is a prevailing live-and-let-live heritage, Santa Feans tell you, that promises privacy to the most hermitic, acceptance to the most eccentric. Imagine: all this set in a place as lovely as God could design. . . .

Not all the commentary was quite so breathless. In a funny and revealing 1982 *New Yorker* report about a raucous spat over a Santa Fe homeowner's roof design, author Calvin Trillin advanced the Theory of the Dumbest Sons:

CAROLE LAROCHE

According to this theory, there was a time when a number of wealthy Eastern families assigned their dumbest son—the son who was of no use in the bank or the factory—to a life of coupon-clipping in Santa Fe, and everything that has happened since can be traced to either the customs or the genes brought from the East by those founding offspring.

Turning slightly more serious, Trillin went on:

Although the Theory of the Dumbest Sons has a simplicity that has always appealed to me, I suspect that a theory closer to the truth would be the Theory of the Sons or Daughters Who Didn't Fit In— didn't fit in because of being uninterested in business or being artistic or sickly or eccentric or dumb or not dumb enough to devote their lives to a family bank. In northern New Mexico, they found a romantic setting inhabited by romantic people. . . .

Other commentators found no romance in Santa Fe. English writer John M. Taylor invented a whole new word to vilify the city's modern character: *boutiquery*.

Wherever it appears, boutiquery is a sure sign of sterility; only the cause varies. In Santa Fe effete pretension supplants genuine creative impulse because the rugged scenery of northern New Mexico is over powering. Paradoxically, the vast and pitiless landscape that is all too real provokes a fussiness of response that is all too phony. Without scenery Santa Fe would scarcely exist, yet scenery on the grandest scale vitiates the town's existence. . . . The locals are willing enough that life among the mesas be mindless. . . .

Mindless? Contemporary Santa Fe can legitimately be indicted for vanity, excessive self-promotion, cutesypoo-ing itself—but not mindlessness. There are more than 30 bookstores in town. There are three colleges. A typical week's lectures and meetings listed in the *Santa Fe New Mexican's* "¿Qué Pasa?" (What's Happening?) section includes options such as: Tibetan Buddhist meditation; meetings of a baroque recorder society, literacy volunteers, French, Spanish, and Portuguese con-

A door to a gallery on Canyon Road is typical of the "new" Santa Fe style.

versation groups, and the Santa Fe Green Party; lessons in "Zen and the Art of Making a Living"; and a "Full Moon Ceremony: Meditations and Teachings with Wild Horse Woman in the Tradition of Grandfather Thundercloud." Something, surely, for every mind.

The small amount of bad publicity flung at Santa Fe in the 1980s hardly hurt— the plaudits did the damage, turning the city into a place too expensive for most people to live. In the 1990s, the city's Office of Community Development estimated that Santa Fe's middle class was evaporating at the rate of 2 percent every year. Nearly everyone thinks the city has grown too fast, and water is becoming a serious worry. In the early 2000s the city declared its worst-ever water shortages, restricting outdoor garden watering severely. Somehow, Las Campanas, a private golf course, continued slurping as much as a million gallons a day to stay lush and green, infuriating longtime Santa Feans.

Resenting newcomers and their wealth is a time-honored Santa Fe sport. In the 1980s, a wave of wealthy Texans swamped Santa Fe; in the 1990s came a flood of second-homers from California. A columnist for the *Santa Fe Reporter* who drove a borrowed car with California plates for a week wrote that she was hailed on the streets with invective and reproving sign language. Debbie Jaramillo, a former mayor, said the new gated communities on the city's periphery have created tension: "Many old Santa Feans asked me when they look at these gates, 'Why do I feel like I'm the stranger in this town?' "

Other longtime residents say the water issue separates the people who belong to Santa Fe from the interlopers. "If you grew up here, you understand this as a desert," one told me. "We would shower once a week, just before we went to confession." She said it wistfully, as if it were a memory of halcyon days.

But halcyon days for Santa Fe developers ebb and flow. Over the past few years, Santa Fe has taken a welcome step back from the madding crowds. Some merchants are grumbling, but visitors and locals are happy they can actually score a table in a good restaurant without reservations—sometimes.

It's just another cycle, and Santa Fe's allure has persisted through four centuries of stressful changes. Not even the most obdurate pessimist imagines that it will ever become an ordinary place. It is too resilient, too rich in history, in culture, in scenery for that.

Start with that scenery. Santa Fe stretches out on a valley between the majestic Sangre de Cristo ("Blood of Christ") and Jémez mountain ranges, the twin south-

LOSING HISTORY

In varying degrees, and for varying reasons, probably most of the . . . residents of Santa Fe today have some sense of the city's long past and rich traditions. But that very awareness of the city's priceless history makes many contemporary Santa Feans worry that the city is highly vulnerable to the risk of being cut loose from its moorings, in serious danger of losing its identity and its sense of the past.

To many Santa Feans, the major force at work in the city today appears to be a generalized drive towards standardizing Santa Fe and turning it into a typical resort community of upscale condominiums, golf courses, and wealthy part-time residents. As the Santa Fe mystique receives continuing attention from the national press, drawing more and more people from other parts of the country to experience for themselves the special light, the unpolluted blue sky, the cultural diversity, and that certain lifestyle embodied in the term "Santa Fe Style," the question remains whether the ancient city can retain its sense of identity and heritage in the face of rapid change.

—Susan Hazen-Hammond, *A Short History of Santa Fe*, 1988

ern tails of the Rockies. The surrounding hills are decorated in sweet-scented piñon, juniper, and sage, which give way to towering ponderosa and aspen in the higher elevations. The sunlight is sharp yet somehow sensuous at the same time, giving an unusual definition to every leaf, limb, and rock. In Santa Fe, one's senses seem sharpened.

That goes for within the city, too. Cerrillos Road is as much a strip mall–lined eyesore as any major artery in Albuquerque or Tucson, but the compensation is a walk along the Santa Fe River Park (William Johnson's idea come true), or even along the Acequia Madre, shaded by cottonwoods and American elm—surely the most romantic ditch in the country.

Santa Fe's man-made scenery is protected by one of the oldest historic-district zoning ordinances in the country, first adopted in 1957. There are 7,000 buildings in five historic districts, and any remodeling or new building must be approved by the Historic Design Review Board. Originally, the ordinance decreed that everything in these districts had to conform to the Spanish-Pueblo or Territorial style.

The Sangre de Cristo Mountains stretch north of Santa Fe.

This led to some laughable architectural mongrels, such as when the owner of a Victorian house was forced to graft a Pueblo Revival addition onto it. A 1992 revision made the ordinance more realistic while still guaranteeing that Santa Fe's unique historic style would be preserved.

Ah, Santa Fe style. *Ristras* (strings) of red chiles hung by the front door. A cozy beehive fireplace in a corner of the living room. A Chimayó rug on the wall. Hand-painted pine cabinets, chairs, and table in the dining room. Kokopelli coffee mugs on the table. Always more of a marketing scheme than an actual catalog of design or state of mind, Santa Fe style eventually became a caricature of itself. Carmella Padilla analyzed it beautifully in a *Dallas Morning News* piece about products from Old Spice Santa Fe Men's Cologne to Pepperidge Farm's oatmeal-raisin Santa Fe Cookies. According to the marketing gurus Padilla quoted, Santa Fe represented the quintessential relaxed Southwestern lifestyle, while still suggesting urban sophistication.

Or what they *imagine* that life to be. Santa Fe author Susan Hazen-Hammond notes that "Santa Fe Style can mean Ph.D.'s working as waitresses and former executives driving cabs, even when the rest of the U.S. economy is booming."

Making ristras, *the strands of chile peppers that have become a visual symbol of the Santa Fe area.*

Surveying the streets of Santa Fe, the visitor would swear that current Santa Fe style includes a $70,000 SUV. But this is just common-sense prestige transportation. Few wealthy locals own Lexuses or BMWs because on snowy winter days the cars' only use would be as ice sculptures.

There is a real Santa Fe style, but it's not something that can be packaged and exported, hung on a wall or stuffed in a burrito. Santa Fe style was illustrated in a 1974 controversy over the commemorative obelisk in the Plaza that honored "the heroes who have fallen in the various battles with *savage* Indians in the territory of New Mexico." After nearly a year of furious debate, one August day a stranger calmly climbed over the low wrought-iron fence around the memorial, chiseled out the offending adjective, and disappeared. End of problem.

Santa Fe style *was* Municipal Court Judge Tom Fiorina's annual tradition of dismissing parking tickets during Thanksgiving week in exchange for turkeys donated to the needy (a tradition ended, alas, by higher judicial fiat in 1995).

Santa Fe style is also an old Hispanic gentleman slowly wandering about St. Francis Cathedral, playing tunes on a scratchy violin day after day. He bothers no one, and no one bothers him. It is the ceremonial autumn torching of Zozobra, a 40-foot-high effigy of Old Man Gloom. When the muslin, paper, and wood monster goes up in flames, the troubles and sorrows of Santa Feans symbolically burn with him. It is a cold Christmas Eve on Canyon Road, with flickering *farolitos* outlining uneven parapets and dirt driveways, and 30,000 people strolling the street, sipping hot cider and singing carols. It is street names that evoke 400 years of real history—Paseo de Peralta, Calle de Anza—rather than a developer's Spanish rhapsodizing.

It is a soft Hispanic edge to the quality of life, like the unevenly rounded corners of an adobe house, that perseveres even after 400 years of tumultuous change. It is a tolerance of eccentricity left over from the days when Spanish women shocked gringo traders by their gambling, smoking, and entrepreneurship. Santa Fe never tolerated a Puritan, and it mostly dodged the Victorian era, and the positive effects are still evident today. "There are enough good qualities left here," says Jaramillo, "that if we can protect them, we have something worth hanging onto."

When the towering image of Zozobra is burned every year, the troubles and sorrows of Santa Feans symbolically burn with him.

OTHERWORLDLY ST. JOHN'S COLLEGE

It's called St. John's College, but "cloister" might be a better description. It is a fully accredited four-year liberal arts college, and 80 percent of its graduates go on to law school, medical school, or graduate school, but otherwise it is not of this world.

I told John Agresto, the former president, that if I were a Martian anthropologist who had crashed onto St. John's Santa Fe campus and stumbled over his curriculum, I'd assume that the 20th century didn't much matter. "Well, I'll be honest about it," he replied. "We as a faculty don't know much about the 20th century."

St. John's was founded in Annapolis, Maryland, in 1696, as King William School. The name was changed during the American Revolution. In 1937, the conventional liberal-arts curriculum was replaced by a program centered on the study of 200 "great books" of Western civilization, from Plato's *Republic* to Werner Heisenberg's *The Physical Principles of the Quantum Theory*. In 1964, St. John's opened a second campus in Santa Fe.

A more idyllic setting would be hard to imagine. Santa Fe–style buildings step down the piñon-forested slope of Sun Mountain at the city's southeastern edge. A man-made pond with a miniature waterfall gurgles fetchingly in the plaza. But this isn't a place to kick off shoes, doze through the afternoon, party through the night. Though grades are not emphasized, St. John's is tough.

Agresto described how the students have to publicly defend their senior essays: "You wear a robe, the faculty members are in their academic gowns, you proceed into the room, the doors are barred, and for one full hour—and it stops exactly when the hour is over, in mid-sentence if necessary—you are taken apart. There have been oral exams postponed three, four, or five times because of intense vomiting."

But St. John's offers a gentle, nurturing, remarkably civilized environment for serious students. In class discussions they must address each other as "Mr." or "Ms." Grades are determined more by how thoughtfully students teach each other than how well they act like students.

St. John's is tough for the 60 faculty members too. Each one has to be able to teach every course, from Mozart's operas through nuclear physics. Every student takes four years of geometry, calculus, astronomy, biology, and physics (in which modern texts are allowed).

That aside, the 20th century remains the future. T. S. Eliot, Wallace Stevens, and Virginia Woolf have made guest appearances among the "great books," but haven't yet been incorporated into the curriculum. "The faculty fights about this all the time," Agresto said. "Some of this will find its way in, probably too late."

At Christmastime the town's residents place farolitos *along the city streets.*

Santa Fe style is an enduring informality best illustrated in the title anecdote of John Pen La Farge's *Turn Left at the Sleeping Dog,* a book of Santa Feans' oral histories published in 2001. La Farge related the story of a resident who lived just off Acequia Madre in the 1950s and gave directions to friends to turn left "where you should see a large shaggy black dog sleeping. . . . It never occurred to me that to give directions using living animals as guideposts was a strange thing to do." No, in Santa Fe, at that time, it would have been perfectly normal—and reliable.

Santa Fe, in the end, is much more than "mesas and margaritas." The place has an ineffable spiritual quality, something that changes people who come here even as they change the city. What D. H. Lawrence wrote three-quarters of a century ago remains true today:

> I think New Mexico was the greatest experience from the outside world that I have ever had. It certainly changed me forever. . . . The moment I saw the brilliant, proud morning shine high over the deserts of Santa Fe, something stood still in my soul, and I started to attend. . . . In the magnificent fierce morning of New Mexico one sprang awake, a new part of the soul woke up suddenly, and the old world gave way to the new.

ART AND MUSEUMS

In a 1-mile, several-hour walk along Canyon Road, Santa Fe's gallery ghetto, you could see and buy:

- Twelfth-century Anasazi pottery
- Nineteenth-century Sioux ceremonial moccasins
- Twentieth-century American bowling pins
- Native-American prayer feather fetishes
- Contemporary American impressionist painting
- Contemporary American abstract expressionist painting
- Contemporary Russian painting
- Contemporary Czech furniture
- Handmade turquoise, silver, or gold jewelry
- Kinetic sculpture with neon lighting
- Tibetan Buddha sculptures
- Moose and mule-deer antler chandeliers
- Cowboy art
- Gay erotic cowboy art

And vastly more. The list could run on for pages. There are about 85 galleries on Canyon Road, said to be the most concentrated art market on earth—and another 125 galleries scattered about Santa Fe. You can choose among a dozen openings every Friday night. You can discover fine art, kitsch, and schlock, cheek by jowl. You can spend 10 bucks or $100,000. This is the most democratic art market on earth, eager to accommodate the whole spectrum of taste and budget.

There is more music and theater in Santa Fe than in other American cities many times its size. You can listen to a professional men's chorus perform in the acoustically brilliant Loretto Chapel and then walk three blocks to the famous La Casa Sena Cantina for an enchilada and a concert of Broadway tunes by professional singing waiters. There are several theater companies, including the Santa Fe Community Theater, the oldest such group in New Mexico. "Pasatiempo," the weekly arts and entertainment section published by the *Santa Fe New Mexican*, usually runs from 64 to 80 pages, bursting with previews, reviews, and features.

Landscape No. 3 (Cash Entry Mines, New Mexico), *painted by Marsden Hartley while he was living in Berlin in 1920, was based upon his recollections of a visit to New Mexico in 1918 and 1919. (Art Institute of Chicago)*

Northern New Mexico has been fertile ground for the arts for centuries. In the 1830s one commentator sniffed, "There is no part of the civilized globe, perhaps, where the arts have been so much neglected." True, nobody was buying symphony tickets in Santa Fe in the 1830s, but neither were they anywhere else west of the Mississippi in that era. Although their 19th-century wares were clearly inferior, Pueblo Indians had been making distinguished painted pottery since the A.D. 700s. The Ortega family of Chimayó began weaving lovely woolen rugs in the late 1700s; its eighth generation continues today.

The modern blossoming of the arts in Santa Fe (and Taos) began more than a century ago. It started as a tentative trickle, a handful of painters and writers from the East coming out to visit the strange and exotic territory of New Mexico, and finding themselves utterly captivated. By the 1890s, there were art exhibits in the

Palace of the Governors. By 1920, dozens of distinguished artists had made Santa Fe their home, and the isolated little town was becoming a major center in the abstract expressionist movement. When Georgia O'Keeffe began spending summers in New Mexico in 1929, the course of her artistic life was forever changed. She wrote to a friend of her experiences:

> I have frozen in the mountains in rain and hail—and slept out under the stars—and cooked and burned on the desert. . . . It has been like the wind and the sun. . . there doesn't seem to have been a crack of the waking day or night that wasnt full. . . .

What lured artists of days gone by are the elements that still attract creators of all varieties: the land, the light, the people. One contemporary abstract painter in Santa Fe told me he is inspired by "the ferocity of the landscape." A jewelry artist, in contrast, said she derives inner peace from Santa Fe's natural environment. "If a piece hasn't gone well, or if someone's criticized my work, all I have to do is drive 10 minutes out of town, and the grandeur of this place really puts everything in perspective. Human beings, in the grand scheme of things, aren't very damned important."

(preceding pages) The Rio Chama near Abiquiú. (above) Black Mesa Landscape, New Mexico/Out Back of Marie's II *(ca. 1930), by Georgia O'Keeffe. (Georgia O'Keeffe Museum)*

The light in northern New Mexico is unlike anyplace else in the country: intense and powerful but not harsh or punishing. The expressionist landscape painter Marsden Hartley, who worked around Taos in 1918 and 1919, said that New Mexico "is not a country of light on things, but a country of things in light"—a wonderfully enlightening description.

And then there were the indigenous and Hispanic cultures that obviously provided many artists with fascinating subject matter, but also influenced others, even landscape painters and sculptors, in more subtle ways. Says James Rutherford, a Santa Fe gallery owner, "New Mexico became more of a mecca for the arts than other places in the Southwest: there's a blend of cultures here that doesn't quite exist anywhere else."

Shidoni, 5 miles north of Santa Fe, is a foundry and art gallery displaying work by emerging and established sculptors.

For a long time, Santa Fe was also an inexpensive place to live and work—an eternal concern of struggling artists. Gallery owner William Vincent, who moved to Santa Fe in 1956, reminisced in the *Santa Fe New Mexican* that "Back then, Canyon Road was loaded with artists. They lived there and painted there, and it wasn't high-priced at all."

It is now, for sure. Although Santa Fe is still loaded with artists, many have grown discouraged by the stratospheric cost of living. The result is that the artists' colony has dispersed, to some extent, and resettled in small towns nearby, such as Chimayó, Madrid, Abiquiu, and Galisteo. "However, Santa Fe's economy is a blessing to artists as well as a curse," says Rutherford, "because while wealthy people are moving here and driving up the cost of housing, they're also buying art."

Perhaps because of this, the art scene in Santa Fe is more eclectic, adventurous, and vital than it was even 30 years ago. Back then, art collectors could find themselves wearying of the commercialized sameness of much of the stuff in the

CLASSIC SOUTHWEST JEWELRY

COCHITÍ PUEBLO SILVER SQUASH BLOSSOM NECKLACE

Traditional squash blossom necklaces feature side pendants in the shape of a squash or pumpkin flower. In this necklace from Cochití Pueblo, 25 miles southwest of Santa Fe, the squash blossoms have been replaced with crosses; this particular design has a double-barred cross with a heartlike bottom, resembling the Catholic sacred heart and the Indian dragonfly that in many Pueblo cultures was the symbol for water.

ZUNI BRACELET

The Zuni Pueblo, the largest pueblo in New Mexico, is located south of Gallup near the Arizona border. For centuries, Zunis traded turquoise to Plains Indians for buffalo hides and to Mexican tribes for parrot plumes. Over the years the Zuni have become famous for their extraordinary work in turquoise and silver as exemplified in the huge sunburst-design cluster bracelet to the left. Circa 1930.

NAVAJO CONCHA BELTS

The idea for concha belts derived from disk-shaped hair ornaments sold to Plains Indians by white traders as early as 1750. Navajos linked hair ornaments to form decorative belts, impressing Mexican designs into the silver. Circa 1885.

galleries—paintings of aerodynamic Indians, pueblos in the sunset, weathered corrals capped with snow. "It was a tough place to show if you didn't do coyotes," says one artist. Kitsch still abounds in Santa Fe, particularly in the downtown boutique galleries (where Kokopelli, the prehistoric rock-art figure of a hunchbacked flute player, has replaced the howling coyote as the ubiquitous decoration on everything from earrings to, incredibly, toilet-paper holders). But the profusion of serious art in every medium from jewelry to monumental sculpture is amazing. One gallery, for example, once hung a show of photographic portraits of Soviet female pilots who flew combat in World War II. Such an exhibit would have seemed very strange in the Santa Fe of a decade or so earlier.

"I would rank us among the top four art markets in the country, along with New York, Los Angeles, and Chicago," says downtown gallery owner Ray Dewey. "And I think we're more diverse than the others. We're very strong in realism, contemporary Indian art, Hispanic art, and regional art. And I think we have an undeserved reputation as an expensive art market. Sure, you can spend $1 million here. But you can also get something of real quality for $100 or $1,000. I think that's our greatest strength."

As for museums, Santa Fe has several that display extraordinary work, from the superb Museum of Indian Arts and Culture to the Museum of Fine Arts, near the Plaza. See "Art Museums," on page 87.

■ SHOPPING FOR ART

Shopping for art in Santa Fe can be both exhausting and exhilarating for the same reason—the sheer number of things to look at. Some suggestions:

Begin by picking up a few publications. Wingspread's *Collector's Guide to Santa Fe–Taos* is a free glossy book and helpful Web site packed with illustrated gallery ads and short features. A monthly magazine with the quirky name of *The* runs arts features and profiles. "Pasatiempo," published every Friday in the *Santa Fe New Mexican,* is an entertaining and indispensable guide to all the arts in town.

Watch for notices of studio tours. Several times a year, groups of artists in towns throughout the region open their studios to visitors for a whole afternoon. It's an excellent way to get to know the artists and their work. Show openings, usually on Friday or Saturday nights and always announced in "Pasatiempo," are convivial, informal, and not at all snobbish. Some galleries pour complimentary wine.

Look beyond the Santa Fe and Taos city limits. Small galleries of remarkable variety and depth thrive in the small outlying towns, and their prices can be delectably low—they show "emerging" artists at prices that don't reflect downtown overhead. And don't neglect Albuquerque, a short 60-mile drive away: Many of its galleries are as lively as Santa Fe's.

■ INDIAN ARTS

The modern era of Native American arts was foreshadowed when the first locomotive hissed into Albuquerque in 1880. Until then, tourism in Santa Fe and everywhere in the Southwest had been limited to itinerants and adventurers, few of whom had much interest in arts and crafts. But the railroads opened the territories to waves of families and settlers, many of whom were intrigued by the indigenous folk art.

By this time, though, New Mexican Indians had hardly any art at all. Puebloan pottery in the late 1800s was a pale remnant of the rich traditions of 600 years earlier. Most of it was utilitarian and indifferently made, and few people could have imagined selling or buying it. A San Ildefonso potter named María Martínez became the pivotal figure in not only the revival but the blossoming anew of an ancient art. A modest woman who said she "never cared about being well-known or anything," María and her husband Julian began making pots for the tourist trade in the early 1900s. María would build the pots, not on a wheel, but in the classic manner of coiling snakes of moist clay into the pot's rough shape, then scraping it smooth and finally polishing it with a "slip" or skin of fine clay. Julian, a self-taught but gifted designer, would then apply the paint. In 1918 an

María Martínez on the patio of the Palace of the Governors, ca. 1920. (Museum of New Mexico)

experiment produced a whole new kind of pottery—matte black designs on a glossy black background—and it made both artistic and commercial history. In a few years, several potters in San Ildefonso were making a living creating black-on-black ceramics, and the other Rio Grande pueblos, sensing at last an opportunity to lift themselves from the mire of poverty, began to develop distinctive styles of their own.

Pueblo pottery today is a highly developed art form, intricate and expressive, constantly evolving beyond its utilitarian roots. Any good Pueblo pot is still formed in the laborious, time-honored coil-and-scrape fashion. This is important not merely for tradition's sake. Hand-forming a bowl or pot gives it a human, slightly imperfect architecture (like an adobe building) that provides a welcome retreat from the anonymity of machine production: the artist's character lives in the work.

Buyers new to the art of Pueblo pottery sometimes don't catch on. "It's the hardest thing for them to deal with, if they don't know how the pots are made," says Albuquerque dealer Richard Myers. "They can't rationalize paying $1,000 for something that's got a flaw in it."

A thousand dollars? Yes, or many times that. Fine Pueblo pottery is expensive. The price depends partly on size, partly on the quality of its sculpted or painted decoration, mostly on the artist's reputation. And it may not help to bypass the city galleries and buy directly from the potters in the pueblos: they know what the retail price should be, and that's usually what they sell it for. Many other Indian arts are thriving these days, particularly painting, sculpture, and jewelry.

The annual Indian Market, staged in the Santa Fe Plaza every summer since 1921, draws 1,200 exhibiting artists and fills every motel room from Albuquerque to Taos with eager buyers. The late Taos painter R. C. Gorman's *The Navajo Woman* is one of the most familiar icons of 20th-century American art, a notoriety that does not bother Gorman. *"The Navajo Woman,"* he told an interviewer in 1994, "has bought me my cars, my home, and my dinners in Venice. Venice, Italy, by the way." The late Santa Fe sculptor Allan Houser, a Chiricahua Apache, revived the art of monumental stone statuary in America with his spare, fluid, powerful human figures. What he once said about his work is an affirmation that a good many Indian artists would share: "I work not just for myself, but to honor the American Indian. I hope to draw attention to centuries-old Indian values, especially concepts of living in harmony with nature that can benefit all people, if only given the chance."

■ Buying Pottery

Psst!—want a bargain on some ancient Southwestern pottery?

No, you don't. If the price sounds too good to be true, it is. Chances are that it either was obtained illegally or is a fake.

The U.S. Archaeological Resources Protection Act of 1979 outlawed the removal of Indian artifacts from all federal lands, and most states, including New Mexico, have similar laws regarding their lands. Federal and New Mexican officials are coming down hard on violators, and consequently most—though not all—Indian arts galleries in Santa Fe have quit dealing in ancient artifacts.

As for counterfeits, "There is a terrific number of them out there, and they've become so good that it's difficult to tell the difference," says one former dealer of Indian artifacts. "There are some potters that can make them with the exact techniques and materials used 600 years ago."

There are potfuls of money to be made in bogus or illegal ceramics. Legitimate Mimbres or Puebloan vessels start at about $3,000 and can run as high as $40,000.

So beware of "bargain" prices. Buy from a reputable gallery or collector, and make certain the seller will take back the item you purchase if it proves to be fake. Insist on documentation certifying where and when the pot was recovered, the best proof being that it was in a private or museum collection before 1979.

Or maybe best of all, just go ahead and buy a fake—a signed one, sold legitimately as a reproduction. The price will be palatable, and you'll never lose any sleep over it.

The most important guideline for buying contemporary pottery is simple: buy what you like. Ignore its potential investment value; buying pottery as an investment is a crapshoot.

Run your finger along the inside of the pot. If it's made by the classic coil-and-scrape method it will be slightly rough and irregular, though it shouldn't be lumpy. Cast ceramics will be smoother (and much less valuable). The decorative painting or carving should be even and precise and geometrically pleasing. The architecture of the vessel is important, too; no poorly proportioned pot can be rendered elegant by the designs applied to it.

Indian pottery is a rapidly evolving art form; what you buy today may become an anthropological treasure in only a generation or two. The best pieces are worth their considerable prices.

PUEBLO POTTERY OF NEW MEXICO

Pueblo Indians have been making pottery for utilitarian use and for sale or barter for 1,300 years. The practice of making them for barter declined toward the middle of the 19th century, when the opening of the Santa Fe Trail flooded the region with imported goods. But with the coming of the railroad in the 1880s, and the arrival of appreciative visitors, pueblo potters realized the commercial potential of their pottery and entered a new period of improvement and exploration. These pots from the Zuni and Laguna pueblos were made during this period.

Zuni polychrome, 1890.

Zuni Pueblo, south of Gallup, New Mexico, near the Arizona border, was visited by conquistador Francisco de Coronado in 1540.

Laguna Pueblo, in central New Mexico between Albuquerque and Grants, has a long pottery tradition.

Zuni polychrome fetish, 1920.

Laguna polychrome, 1910.

Ácoma pots in black and white.

Ácoma pottery has long been valued by collectors. Hand-drawn geometric designs, such as the one above by S. Chino, are typical. Clays used by the different pueblos come from nearby sources, and Ácoma clay is noted for being especially white.

Ácoma Pueblo perches high on a mesa west of Albuquerque.

Santa Clara Pueblo has produced many famous pottery families, among them the Gutiérrez, Tafoya, and Naranjo. This pot by Anita Suazo is typical of Santa Clara carved pottery.

Santa Clara Pueblo is on the road from Santa Fe to Abiquiú.

Santa Clara pot with bear claw design.

San Ildefonso jar.

San Ildefonso pot, María Martínez.

The polychrome jar, above left, was typical of San Ildefonso Pueblo pottery until María and Julian Martínez began to make their famous black on-black pottery designs. Their work, now world-famous, often commands more than $5,000 per piece. Many members of the extended Martínez family have also become famous, and their work is invariably bought by collectors.

The Jémez Pueblo pot to the left is typical of the modern, sophisticated works found in Santa Fe galleries. Jémez Pueblo is in the Jémez Mountains northwest of Santa Fe.

Jémez polychrome pot.

Jémez pot.

The beautifully crafted 3-inch black-on-red pot to the left was made by C.G. Loretto of Jémez Pueblo.

Figurines have long been a part of Cochití Pueblo ceramics. Storyteller dolls, first made famous by Helen Cordero, are favorites, and cheap imitations abound. The male storyteller doll to the right was fashioned by Ada Suina, who puts coat after coat of slip on her figurines to achieve subtlety and gloss.

The figurine below in the shape of a turtle was made by Helen Cordero. Cochití Pueblo is by Cochití Lake, southwest of Santa Fe.

Cochití storyteller doll.

Cochití turtle figurine.

■ HISPANIC ART

The Spanish settlers of New Mexico lived hard lives on a hard land, but they were not barren of artistry. New Mexico's rigors never stifled the Spanish soul.

Among the earliest artistic expressions was furniture, adzed and built by hand out of soft ponderosa pine, and decorated with chiseled designs of religious icons, fruit, vines, prancing lions, and abstract geometric figures such as rosettes. As Pueblo craftsmen were employed to build some of the furniture, Indian motifs such as chevrons, cornstalks, and ziggurats cross-pollinated with the Spanish themes to create a unique New Mexican style. The hand-painted modern imitations that have formed the cornerstone of Santa Fe style reflect a yearning for simpler times—and a romanticization of the Spanish colonial era in the Southwest.

More important to the perpetuation of Spanish culture were the santos—small wooden statues of Roman Catholic saints that held places of honor in both home and church. The carving of santos in northern New Mexico is an art form that has continued in an unbroken line through four centuries, passed along from generation to generation.

Santa Fe merchant Rey Móntez, whose father was a *santero* (sculptor of saints), says that the art of making primitive santos began in New Mexico after Spain realized the new land was not the lode of gold that had been expected. The mother country made little effort to export its sophisticated religious art here, and because of the colony's isolation, New Mexican santos quickly acquired an artistic character of their own. The figures are usually elongated and almost always melancholy in expression—even today.

"We Spaniards are very fatalistic," says Móntez. "And we are not to forget the sorrow and suffering that was endured on our behalf, particularly in the images of Christ. The santos remind us."

A santo from the Spanish Market.

Furniture was one of the earliest artistic expressions of Hispanic art in New Mexico.

Móntez, who has a downtown Santa Fe gallery specializing in modern santos, says that all kinds of people buy them: Christians, Jews, Hispanics, Anglos. Some buy them for devotional purposes; others are collectors.

"I have an atheist who buys a santo every year," Móntez told me. "Finally I asked him why. He said, 'It's pretty and it makes me feel peaceful.' "

Contemporary Hispanic art is flourishing in the striking multimedia work and ceramics of artists like Pedro Romero and the paintings of artists like Anita Rodríguez and Federico Vigil. Vigil's work can be seen in several of the city's museums and in the county courthouse, where he was commissioned to paint a spectacular mural.

For one weekend each July, the Plaza is converted into an exhibition of traditional Spanish arts and crafts known as the Spanish Market. Among the items sold here, look for santos, carved and painted furniture, weavings, and embroidery. The Contemporary Hispanic Market is held on the same weekend, off the Plaza on Lincoln Avenue.

■ ART MUSEUMS

Santa Fe blooms with museums devoted to historic and modern crafts and fine arts. Unless otherwise noted, the museums below charge admission. You'll save substantially if you buy a four-day admission pass that covers all four branches of the Museum of New Mexico—the Museum of Fine Arts, the Museum of Indian Arts and Culture, the Museum of International Folk Art, and the Palace of the Governors—plus the Museum of Spanish Colonial Art. See the following descriptions.

Georgia O'Keeffe Museum

At the museum honoring New Mexico's most celebrated artist are more than 140 oils, watercolors, drawings, charcoals, sculptures, and photos that demonstrate her astonishing range. *217 Johnson Street; 505-995-1000.*

Institute of American Indian Arts Museum

The work at this division of Santa Fe's IAIA, a nationally recognized college for American Indian artists, is an alternative to the more commercially oriented Indian art in for-profit galleries. Paintings and sculpture here may be beautiful, enigmatic, ironic, or bitter—or all of these at once. *108 Cathedral Place (one block east of the Plaza); 505-983-1777.*

The Georgia O'Keeffe Museum has more than 140 works by its namesake artist, who lived more than half of her life in New Mexico. (Georgia O'Keeffe Museum)

Museum of Fine Arts

The emphasis at one of the Southwest's oldest and best art museums, founded in 1917, is on 20th-century New Mexican art. The museum's permanent collection includes several works by Georgia O'Keeffe, although only a few are on view at any given time. *107 West Palace Avenue (one block west of the Plaza); 505-476-5072.*

Museum of Indian Arts and Culture

This superb museum has an enormous display of pottery from 11th-century Pueblo to contemporary Navajo artists. Native artisans give demonstrations in pottery, jewelry, and other arts, and docents give worthwhile tours (call for times). *710 Camino Lejo (2.5 miles southeast of the Plaza off Old Santa Fe Trail); 505-476-1250.*

(opposite) Mexican dance masks on display in the Museum of International Folk Art.
(above) The Museum of Fine Arts.

Museum of International Folk Art

The permanent exhibit here is the immense Girard Collection of more than 106,000 dolls, dollhouses, masks, weavings, religious icons, angels, monsters, toy trains, and many other items. In the museum's own words, "the collection defies categorization." Some pieces border on fine art, some are pure kitsch. Occasionally visitors find it overwhelming. The Hispanic Heritage wing displays folk and religious art. *706 Camino Lejo (2.5 miles southeast of the Plaza off Old Santa Fe Trail); 505-476-1200.*

Museum of Spanish Colonial Art

This museum, opened in 2002, displays arts, crafts, and artifacts (even a 1780 Mexican house, shipped from Michoacán and reassembled on the site) from the worldwide Spanish Empire of the 16th through 19th centuries. Contemporary art influenced by Hispanic traditions is also included. The museum, in a warm and sprawling 1930 adobe house designed by John Gaw Meem, is conveniently located in the cluster of museums on Camino Lejo, known as Museum Hill. *750 Camino Lejo (2.5 miles southeast of the Plaza off Old Santa Fe Trail); 505-982-2226.*

SITE Santa Fe

This contemporary nonprofit museum that opened in 1995 inside a former beer warehouse is not reluctant to use the word "provocative" in its promotions. Shows have included Gary Simmons's modulated erasures of symbols and stereotypes of racism, and John F. Simons's software art displayed on everything from LCD screens to laser-cut linoleum tiles. The SITE Santa Fe Biennial, assembled in odd-numbered years by guest curators from around the world, has emerged as an important and often controversial event. *1606 Paseo de Peralta; 505-989-1199.*

Wheelwright Museum of the American Indian

This private museum was founded in 1937 by Mary Cabot Wheelwright, who became friends with Hastiin Klah, a Navajo medicine man. The exhibits here are generally by contemporary Native-American artists. *704 Camino Lejo (2.5 miles southeast of the Plaza off Old Santa Fe Trail); 505-982-4636.*

■ SANTA FE OPERA

No major American opera company has ever made a life in a city as small as Santa Fe, and surely none has ever had such an ambitious opening season. In July 1957, the late founder John Crosby staged Igor Stravinsky's *The Rake's Progress* and, audaciously, invited the composer to the rehearsals. (He came.)

When Crosby came to Santa Fe in 1956, he was a walking musical department store. He had learned half a dozen instruments, had formed a dance orchestra, had studied composition with Paul Hindemith and conducting with Rudolf Thomas. In his plan for the Santa Fe Opera, he observed, "We chase our talent off to Europe to perform, when we in this country have so many beautiful places, and Santa Fe is one of the most beautiful of all." He had also observed the summer rainfall at his parents' Santa Fe home in 1955 and 1956 and had concluded, incorrectly, that the climate was so dry that out of 18 performances over a two-week period, only two were likely to be rained out. These two summers, though, were abnormally dry.

Mark Doss and Madeline Bender in a Santa Fe Opera production of Rossini's Italian Girl in Algiers.

The acclaimed Santa Fe Opera, which performs in an open amphitheater near Tesuque, produces one contemporary opera every season.

After four decades of soggy *Zauberflötes* and *Traviatas,* the famous open-air amphitheater finally was roofed in 1998, although the sides of the building are still open to the nocturnal desert air.

Crosby retired in 2000, having built the Santa Fe Opera into one of the most famous companies in North America. His successor, Richard Gaddes, has continued the tradition of producing one new American opera among the five productions every season. He has made the opera more accessible, especially to Santa Feans. A seatback libretto system gives people a choice of translations in English or Spanish, and a family-friendly program provides amazingly cheap seats for dress rehearsals.

The 2,126-seat theater is 7 miles north of Santa Fe on U.S. 84/285. Tickets and hotel reservations, especially on weekends, can be snatched up many months in advance. *505-986-5900 or 800-280-4654.*

■ Adobe and Modern Architecture

"If you do it with your family, with your children, with someone you love, the act of laying adobes, of building shelter from earth, is one of the most profound experiences you can ever have. With every course of mud mortar you lay, and every adobe brick, as the walls rise, it's like watching your children grow up."

Orlando Romero is talking about the endeavor that forms the architectural soul of Santa Fe, but one that only a few modern Santa Feans have experienced—building one's own house with handmade adobe bricks. The tradition is almost extinct. Romero is a dinosaur with mud on his feet.

The paradox is that adobe—dirt, water, and straw, among the least expensive of building materials ever devised—is nearly unaffordable today. Adobe is dirt cheap, but the labor to create it isn't. Fifty years ago, a Santa Fe family could invest a year's labor, evenings and weekends, in building a house, but today most people work full-time jobs and time to build a house just doesn't exist. Even wealthy folks who import their money to Santa Fe are reluctant to invest in real adobe. Robert Vigil, a Santa Fe builder, says the shell of an adobe house today costs from 30 to 50 percent more than the same in wood frame and faux adobe stucco.

But adobe's romance abides.

You can begin to understand it in early-morning or evening light. The old houses on Acequia Madre and Old Santa Fe Trail, made of mud bricks and bathed in mud plaster infused with wisps of straw, actually appear to glow. The low sun transmutes the mud into gold. It's tempting to believe the popular story that the 16th-century Spanish explorers saw an adobe pueblo basking in the evening light from a distance and assumed it was gold—the fabled Seven Cities of Cíbola—but the legend of Cíbola dates from Spanish medieval times and has nothing to do with adobe. *Qué lástima,* what a pity.

There are other legends about adobe that ring untrue. One is that it is an excellent insulator, hostile to modern utility companies. No, says Vigil. When he builds an adobe house, he adds a layer of insulation between the bricks and the outside plaster. Another is that it lasts forever. Also not true: Adobe devises numerous strategies to try to melt back into the earth. It will lick up water from the ground by capillary action and erode from inside, or wash away on the outside in a rainstorm. Earthquakes are bad news; adobe has no tolerance for lateral movement.

On the other hand, the oldest building in use in New Mexico, Santa Fe's Palace of the Governors, built in 1610, is made of adobe. Carefully maintained, an adobe building will weather the centuries.

New Mexico's Indians had long built with mud before the *Entrada,* puddling it up into free-form walls, but the Spanish introduced the use of adobe bricks. They had learned it centuries earlier from their own occupiers, the Moors: the word "adobe" is derived from the Arabic *al-tub,* "the brick." The technique for making and laying the brick has changed little. Mix dirt, water, and straw, pour the mixture into wooden forms to make bricks of a standard 10 x 14 x 4 inches and let them dry in the sun. Pry them out of the forms and let them bake, or "cure," for a few more days. Then layer them into walls with mud mortar. Contemporary infi-

Making adobe bricks is a craft; making them into a building, an art.

dels sometimes mix asphalt into the adobe to improve its stability, but this compromises its earthen color and texture. Traditionally, mud plaster was applied to protect the exterior walls. It used to be the women's job to replaster them once a year. Today stucco clads most of Santa Fe's modern adobe homes, reducing the maintenance burden.

Vigil grew up in an adobe house in Santa Fe, which had more than a little to do with his current occupation as a homebuilder. In 1977, he was teaching school, needed a house, and didn't have much money—so he did exactly what his family had done for generations. He made 10,000 adobe bricks by himself. He chopped 35 trees in the Jémez Mountains for vigas, or ceiling beams. Then he built the house. Eleven hundred square feet in area, it cost $15,000. Romero, a historian who has written a beautiful book on adobe, did much the same thing. His 1,000-square-foot house cost him less than $10,000. "The contractors wanted $150,000," he says in amazement.

The emotional appeal of adobe architecture is easy to sense but hard to explain. Adobe enthusiasts often talk about feeling a sense of connection to the earth, that there is no sharp line where nature ends and architecture begins. Adobe has a reassuring sense of solidity; no other kind of building offers such comforting refuge in a howling storm. And it ages gracefully, acquiring character instead of shabbiness.

But Romero says the most fundamental reward of adobe is the act of creation, fashioning shelter out of the earth itself. "Maybe I'm speaking like a poet here, but you should do it with someone you love," he says. "It's like a monumental childbirth."

Santa Fe's earth-tone architecture forms the most distinctive part of the city's physical character, but in the past several years a handful of dramatically modern buildings has appeared—to general acclaim, which may be a measure of Santa Fe's increasing sophistication. Because they lie outside the historic districts, they have not disrupted the harmony of the classic adobe (or set off World War III at hearings in City Hall).

The best of these buildings are the Mexican architect Ricardo Legorreta's Visual Arts Center and Santa Fe Art Institute at the College of Santa Fe. Legorreta's trademarks are bold geometric forms—fins, pyramids, thrusting boxes—and a sizzling palette of colors. "Ah, we Mexicans, we're absolutely irresponsible in our use of color," he likes to joke, but he took the fearsome reds, cerulean blues, and electric violets used in these buildings straight from the New Mexico sky.

MUD HOUSES

In the winter of 1884–85, an enterprising journalist named Charles Lummis walked from Cincinnati to Los Angeles, sending dispatches to the Los Angeles Times *along the way. Unlike many other Anglos of his century, he was enchanted by Santa Fe's architecture and lifestyle.*

Around the four sides of the plaza are most of the leading business houses—some in rather handsome blocks—and outside these lies the residence portion of the city. These New Mexican dwellings look odd enough to Eastern eyes. Nearly all are adobe, and a majority only one story high, though there are some three-storied adobes. But don't let yourself be fooled by nincompoop correspondents who write back home about "mud houses." These adobes are made of baked dirt, it is true, but so is your Ross County [Ohio] Bank Block. The sole difference is that you roast your clay with a fire, and these people let the sun do their brick-burning. An adobe out here knocks the socks—pardon my territorial elegance of diction—off of any brick or frame building, so far as anything but looks is concerned. The thickness of the

Ácoma Pueblo, circa 1880. (Museum of New Mexico)

walls—from two to three feet—insures comfort all the year round, and an adobe is cool in summer and warm in winter.

These houses are not generally very gorgeous outside, but within they are as capable of decoration as any other kind of buildings. You get into one of those large, handsome rooms, 18 feet high, finely papered and furnished, carpeted with Brussels, and you will laugh at your prior conception of "mud houses." Even the ruder dwellings of the lower class are very comfortable and pleasant. It would be a good scheme if the board shacks of Eastern shantytowns could be replaced by these neat little adobes. The more pretentious houses here are built in a square, with a *placita* (little plaza) in the middle, and many have remarkable fine gardens besides. One thing strikes you as you look down upon the city—the universal flatness. Probably there are not 20 pitch roofs in the whole place, and but few mansards. A Mexican, you know, always has two stories to his house—the roof serving as floor to a sky-thatched attic as big as all outdoors.

The countless burros, driven through the streets by Mexicans or Pueblos at a reckless gait of half a mile an hour, and generally loaded with wood, will look queer to you. It must be a semi-science, loading these little fellows. The wood—in crooked sticks of cedar, about two feet long—is laid in a kidney-shaped pile as big as the burro, across the pack-saddle, and held in shape by an adroitly-wound rope. I'd like to see a tenderfoot pack one of these loads—bet he couldn't make three sticks stick. So what with the people, the burros, and the queer little houses that pay no more attention to alignment than a dog does to catnip, one finds here street scenes as unlike as possible to all American ideas.

—Charles Lummis, *Letters from the Southwest,* 1885

Two other contemporary buildings well worth visiting are the Genoveva Chavez Community Center, designed by Santa Fe architect Ed Mazria, and Fire Station No. 7, by Santa Fe's Michael Freeman. Ellen Berkovitch, a former critic for the *Santa Fe New Mexican,* wrote that they make "a confident statement about the compatibility of the past and the future." Indeed they do, repudiating the notion, prevalent for the last century, that Santa Fe could only be true to itself by replicating its own past.

SEEING SANTA FE

Santa Fe is a walker's city, and not only because it is compact and fairly flat. Those are the pedestrian reasons (forgive me). Much more importantly, Santa Fe has a visual and tactile romance that can't be fully appreciated through a car window.

An arched niche cut in an adobe wall, a vine or flower spilling color through it. An early-19th-century house wrapped around an all-but-hidden courtyard. A whimsical sculpture planted in a patio or vacant lot. A private shrine dedicated to St. Francis or the Virgin Mary. The ethereal auburn-to-gold glow of adobe walls in the early evening sun.

Also, the streets are narrow, the traffic befuddling, and there's hardly ever a place to park. So walking Santa Fe makes practical sense.

You can stroll at random, take a guided walking tour, buy an illustrated guidebook (the Historic Santa Fe Foundation's *Old Santa Fe Today* is thorough but arranged alphabetically instead of by routes), or guide yourself along the two walks described in this chapter. The first route snakes through four centuries of downtown sights; the second takes in two centuries along Acequia Madre and Canyon Road. Neither is strenuous, but if you visit the downtown museums and a few galleries, either walk might consume most of a day.

■ DOWNTOWN WALKING TOUR

Begin at ① **the Plaza,** which dates from the founding of Santa Fe and which has been the focus of a host of momentous events in Santa Fe history. In the 1680 Pueblo Revolt an army of furious Indians camped in the Plaza and besieged more than a thousand Spanish refugees huddled in the Palace of the Governors. In 1846, Gen. Stephen Watts Kearny led his army into the Plaza, proclaimed New Mexico a United States territory, and raised the Stars and Stripes over the Palace. In 1962 the Plaza became a National Historic Landmark.

Notice the obelisk honoring heroes of the Civil War and Indian wars at the center of the Plaza. The inscription on the obelisk's north side once commemorated the bravery of those who had "fallen in the various battles with savage Indians in the territory of New Mexico." The word *savage* has been chiseled out by an anonymous editor.

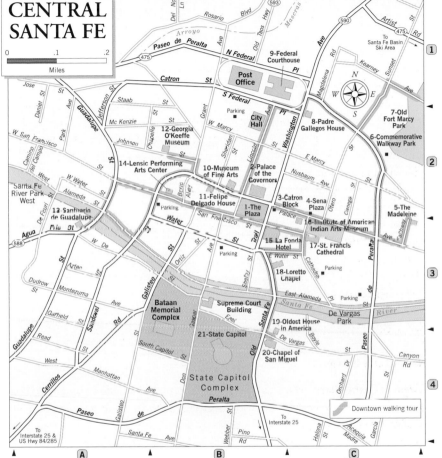

CENTRAL SANTA FE

0 .1 .2

Miles

Catron Block 3

Chapel of San Miguel 20

Commemorative Walkway Park 6

Federal Courthouse 9

Felipe Delgado House 11

Georgia O'Keeffe Museum 12

Institute of American Indian Arts Museum 16

La Fonda Hotel 15

Lensic Performing Arts Center 14

Loretto Chapel 18

Museum of Fine Arts 10

Old Fort Marcy Park 7

Oldest House in America 19

Padre Gallegos House 8

Palace of the Governors 2

The Plaza 1

The Madeleine 5

St. Francis Cathedral 17

Santuario de Guadalupe 13

Sena Plaza 4

State Capitol 21

*Museum of Indian Arts & Culture, Museum of International Folk Art,
Wheelwright Museum, and the Center for Contemporary Arts see Greater Santa Fe map page 7.*

(opposite) Farolitos *line the Plaza's walkways at Christmastime. (right)* The Ninth Cavalry Band *in the Plaza, July 1880.* *(Museum of New Mexico)*

The grassy Plaza, shaded with blue pine, American elm, spruce, cottonwood, and ornamental plum trees, remains Santa Fe's spiritual heart. Old people pass the time reading newspapers on benches, tourists stroll through in wonderment—wondering why every American city doesn't have such a gracious centerpiece—and in the evenings, when the tourist traffic begins to evaporate, teens congregate in clumps, flirting, smoking, and alternately looking cool and bored.

The ② **Palace of the Governors** (100 Palace Avenue) flanks the Plaza's north side. Built in 1610, it is the oldest government building, aside from prehistoric *kivas*, in the United States. As with the Plaza, remarkable events in New World history took place here. When Spanish governor Don Diego de Vargas recaptured Santa Fe from the Pueblo revolutionaries in 1693, he and his men were astounded to find that the Indians had, in essence, remodeled it into a pueblo, even converting a defensive tower on the east end into a kiva. Except for the 13 years of Pueblo occupation, the palace served as apartments for Spanish and then Mexican governors, and in 1862, Confederate soldiers borrowed it for their temporary headquarters. In the 1870s, Territorial Gov. Lew Wallace wrote part of *Ben-Hur* while living in it.

Today you can see the interior of the Palace, now part of the Museum of New Mexico, and get a sense of the world the early Spanish officials occupied. Thick adobe walls, painted white, surround a collection of artifacts—wooden wagons or *carretas,* antique gowns, vestments, spurs, and pottery—that evoke the mood of Spanish colonial life. Some museum docents are descendants of colonial families, and they relish retelling the story of the *Entrada* from the Spanish point of view.

Over the centuries the Palace has undergone much remodeling. The towers are gone, and the *portal,* a wide, covered porch that extends around the building, is a 1913 addition. Indians have been selling their jewelry and pottery in front of the Palace for hundreds of years. In recent times, vendors have been required to register with a museum program that ensures crafts are handmade by those who sell them or by their immediate families.

Now head east to the corner of Washington Avenue and East Palace Avenue and see the ③ **Catron Block,** a sophisticated Italianate Victorian building of 1891 and an example of what preservationists, in no great cheer, call "remuddling." The building's upper floor is original and beautifully preserved, but the awful (and fake) Territorial portal was tacked on in the 1960s as Santa Fe was dressing down to make itself appear more rustic and "Southwestern."

The main hall of the Palace of the Governors during Gov. L. B. Prince's tenure in 1893. (Museum of New Mexico)

Walk east along East Palace Avenue to a block-long row of contiguous adobe buildings beginning with 107 East Palace; this includes the Arias de Quiros site and ④ **Sena Plaza.** Governor de Vargas granted Quiros, a Spanish conquistador, a building site here for his help in the 1693 reconquest; he planted wheat and built a two-room house, now gone. Sena, scion of a prominent 19th-century Santa Fe family, later constructed the adjacent 33-room adobe mansion around a courtyard. Parts of these buildings date from the late 18th to the early 20th century, but sorting them out would be impossible. Many old Santa Fe houses grew like this, by accretion over generations and centuries. The walker's treat here is Sena's shady courtyard, dominated by a mammoth cottonwood tree and surrounded by shops. There are benches for relaxing here, along with a fountain, a biodegrading old wagon, and devil-barely-cares landscaping with vines and shrubs creeping over rough stone borders. It's the polar opposite of the primly manicured formal Victorian garden, and one of the loveliest public spaces in Santa Fe.

Continue walking east. Cross Paseo de Peralta, walk one more block east along Palace Avenue and then turn one block north to 106 Faithway Street. Here you will see a wild and crazy 1886 Queen Anne–style house, now ⑤ **The Madeleine,** a B&B. The original owner, George Cuyler Preston, was a lawyer, and his house, like the Catron Block, would have been comfortable in New England. As elsewhere in the Southwest, 19th-century Anglo newcomers replicated the architecture they had known back home.

Head back to Paseo de Peralta, then walk the three blocks that curl northwest to the ⑥ **Commemorative Walkway Park,** a paved path and staircase with 20 plaques outlining Santa Fe history along the way. Near the top is a tall, white steel cross commemorating the deaths of the 21 Franciscan missionaries killed in the Pueblo Revolt of 1680. There is no memorial to the 36,000 Pueblo Indians, who, according to historian Marc Simmons, died from the disease, famine, and war caused by the Spaniards.

At the hilltop is ⑦ **Old Fort Marcy Park,** the site of the first United States military post in the Southwest, begun immediately after General Kearny seized New Mexico in 1846. Though nothing of the adobe fort remains but mounds of dirt, the park is the prime place to watch sunsets over Santa Fe.

Descend from the hill, curve west (to your right) on Paseo de Peralta for two long blocks, and then walk south (left) on Washington Avenue to the ⑧ **Padre Gallegos House** (227 Washington), built around 1857. Padre José Manuel

Gallegos was one of the many Spanish priests French Bishop Jean Baptiste Lamy fired after his arrival in 1851. Gallegos later married and pursued a successful career in politics. His house is remarkable for its dignity, graceful proportions, and sheer size—Padre Gallegos didn't do badly after being punted out of the priesthood.

Directly across Washington Avenue looms the 1889 ⑨ **Federal Courthouse** (Federal Place and Lincoln Avenue), wrapped in native New Mexican granite, one of those heavyweight buildings from the time in which American courthouses were designed to convey Moral Authority through Architectural Power. Walk up the stairs to the entrance and you're being prepped to tell the truth, so help you God. The design is a mixture of Greek Revival and Romanesque style, with grand pediments and horseshoe curlicues over the third-story windows. Inside are six landscape murals painted by Santa Fe architect and artist William Penhallow Henderson from 1935 to 1937 as part of the Federal Arts Project.

Continue south on Lincoln Avenue to the ⑩ **Museum of Fine Arts** (107 West Palace Avenue). Designed by Rapp & Rapp of Trinidad, Colorado, and completed in 1917, this building shifted the Pueblo Revival style into high gear. The massive facade at the south end tries mightily to emulate the mission of San Esteban Rey at Ácoma, but its two-tone paint job and fussy decoration on the balcony spoil the effect. In New Mexico's old adobe churches, simplicity equaled nobility.

The museum's emphasis is on New Mexican art since about 1900. On permanent display are works by the Taos Society of Artists founders Ernest Blumenschein and Bert Geer Phillips, as well as works by Georgia O'Keeffe.

Head west (right) on Palace Avenue to the ⑪ **Felipe Delgado House** (124 West Palace). Delgado, a prominent merchant, built this fascinating hybrid in 1890. It marries the simple adobe Territorial box to spindly Victorian woodwork—an architectural metaphor for the cultural revolution that was smoldering in Santa Fe at the time. Now a bank, the Delgado house opens to the public on the first Monday of each month.

Now take the short block west to Grant Street and head northeast (right) to Johnson Street, and then west (left) to the ⑫ **Georgia O'Keeffe Museum** (217 Johnson Street). Established in 1997, this small museum honors one of the region's most eminent painters.

Continue west on Johnson Street, curve south (left) on Guadalupe Street, crossing the sometimes dry Santa Fe River, and continue half a block to the ⑬ **Santuario de Guadalupe,** a late-18th-century church that has twice endured

A screen depicting the Virgin of Guadalupe, in the Santuario de Guadalupe.

"remuddling." Originally a typical New Mexican adobe chapel, it was dressed up as a neo-Gothic New England church in the 1880s, then recostumed yet again as a drab California mission in 1922. But go inside, where an astounding baroque altar screen depicts the Virgin of Guadalupe and a Holy Trinity of three identical men. The painted screen is signed José de Alzibar, 1783.

Head back north up Guadalupe to West San Francisco Street and bear right. The three blocks from Sandoval Street to the Plaza include some of Santa Fe's most intriguing shops and galleries. Woolworth's, the last real people's store on the Plaza, closed in 1998, but some longtime employees leased a sliver of the old space and persevere as the Five & Dime General Store. They still offer the famous Frito chile pie.

Savor the 1931 ⑭ **Lensic Theater** (211 West San Francisco Street), a hybrid of Spanish Renaissance and Moorish architecture. A renovation completed in 2001 has renewed the building's exuberant ornamentation inside and out. (The creatures along the cornice look like a cross between dragons and giant sea horses—a logical Santa Fe theme.) The renovation vastly improved the building's versatility as a

The Lensic Theater is an exuberant fantasy of Spanish and Moorish architecture.

performance space, and it now bills itself as the Lensic Performing Arts Center, serving the Santa Fe Symphony, the Chamber Music Festival, and numerous other groups and performers.

⑮ **La Fonda Hotel,** which sprawls over most of a block at East San Francisco, Shelby, and Old Santa Fe Trail, was designed in the Pueblo Revival style by Rapp & Rapp in 1922, and was enlarged and remodeled in 1928 by John Gaw Meem. Its atriumlike La Plazuela restaurant may be Santa Fe's loveliest room. Wander through the lobby and corridors to see a delightful exhibition of folk-art murals painted by Ernesto Martínez, who has been the in-house artist for more than 50 years. The concierge can arrange tours of the property.

Across East San Francisco Street is the ⑯ **Institute of American Indian Arts Museum** (108 Cathedral Place), housing contemporary Indian artwork—pottery, sculpture, beadwork, basketry, and paintings. As a curator's plaque in one of the museum's exhibits notes, "An attempt has been made to stay away from the stereotypical images made of the American Indian by himself or herself. What has been selected is only a sample of an undercurrent of work that most often has been overlooked—overlooked because they have no feathers, no brave warriors on horseback, no romantic view of tepees or tall seductive women with hair fluttering in the wind."

⑰ **St. Francis Cathedral** closes off the east end of San Francisco Street with an architectural thunderclap; it regards the low adobe neighborhood with the authority of a powerful medieval baron.

The cathedral was designed in Auvergne, France, by French architect Antoine Mouly and his son Projectus, who journeyed together to Santa Fe in 1870 to oversee construction. After a time, Antoine lost his eyesight and Projectus took over. When lack of funds halted construction, Projectus was contracted to build the Loretto Chapel. Before he could resume work on the cathedral he died, in 1879, and a new French architect, François Mallet, was employed. Then in a real-life Romanesque soap opera, Mallet became entwined with the wife of Bishop Lamy's nephew and was shot dead on San Francisco Street, also in 1879. The architect who finally finished the cathedral was the nephew of Joseph Priest Machebeuf. The elder Machebeuf had been in seminary with Bishop Lamy in France and had come with him to the United States. The younger Machebeuf revised and finished the building, which was consecrated in 1886. It is an excellent French cathedral, convincing in every respect except for its perfunctory pipe organ and the odd painted altar screen depicting guitar-playing American saints.

Around the corner on Old Santa Fe Trail is Bishop Lamy's other architectural monument, ⑱ **Loretto Chapel,** whose design and construction were undertaken by Projectus Mouly, son of Antoine Mouly, architect of the St. Francis Cathedral. This was the chapel of the Loretto nuns, the most famous of whom was Lamy's young niece, Marie, who left France with her uncle when she was a child and was educated by the Ursuline nuns in New Orleans. Barely in her teens, she traveled to Santa Fe in 1857, along with her best friend from the convent. Marie entered the Loretto novitiate, becoming Sister Francesca. Legend has it that she played the piano beautifully, and whenever her brother came to Santa Fe, she tried to have a new piano piece ready to play for him.

Finished in 1878, the chapel has a graceful Gothic Revival design that amounts to a pinprick of conscience in the city's skyline, as opposed to the moralist thunder of the cathedral. The chapel is now deconsecrated and privately owned. There is a small admission fee to view it.

A well-worn local legend swirls around the spiral staircase to the choir loft. Somehow the chapel was completed without it, nor was there room to build one, and a mere ladder wouldn't do because modesty for the girls in the nuns' school was a concern. For help with the problem, the Sisters of Loretto decided to dedicate a novena (devotional) to St. Joseph, the patron saint of carpenters. On the ninth and last day of the novena, a man with a toolbox arrived on a donkey and built the "miraculous staircase," which has no central support—it's a rigid wooden spring, a miracle indeed of 19th-century engineering. When the staircase was finished, the sisters looked for the carpenter to offer payment. He had vanished. Some versions of the legend suggest that the miraculous carpenter was St. Joseph himself.

In 2000, however, Santa Fe historian Mary Jean Cook—after 11 years of research and four trips to France—concluded that the builder was François Jean Rochas, a master French craftsman who had inexplicably migrated to a remote canyon in New Mexico to become a rancher. Why he built the staircase remains a mystery, however.

Continue south on Old Santa Fe Trail to De Vargas Street, across the Santa Fe River from the ⑲ **Barrio de Analco,** which after the Plaza is Santa Fe's oldest neighborhood. First occupied by Tlaxcalan Indians from Mexico who accompanied the earliest conquistadors and missionaries as servants, it was resettled by sol-

The "miraculous" staircase of Loretto Chapel.

"The oldest inhabited house in the United States," from Harper's Weekly, *in 1879. (Museum of New Mexico)*

diers after the 1693 reconquest. Several of the private homes on alleylike De Vargas Street date from the 18th century. The many turquoise doors and shutters on this street are an old New Mexico tradition now in revival. Hispanic folklore, which can be traced back to the Moorish occupation of Spain, reveres the color for its ability to ward off evil—the devil, some believe, cannot pass through a turquoise door. Equally magical is the color's radiance in contrast with an adobe wall, especially in low amber sunlight. Try to time your visit to De Vargas Street for early evening, just before sunset.

The ⑳ **"Oldest House in America"** (215 East De Vargas Street) allegedly incorporates part of a puddled-adobe pueblo dating from about A.D. 1250, but its vigas (ceiling beams) date from 1740 to 1767.

Across the street is the ㉑ **Chapel of San Miguel** (401 Old Santa Fe Trail), built around 1626 and destroyed at the start of the Pueblo Revolt. Within the present structure, built in 1710 and much modified over the years, is a carved and painted altar screen installed in 1798. When the chapel was last restored, in 1955, excavators found shards of ancient Pueblo pottery under the floor.

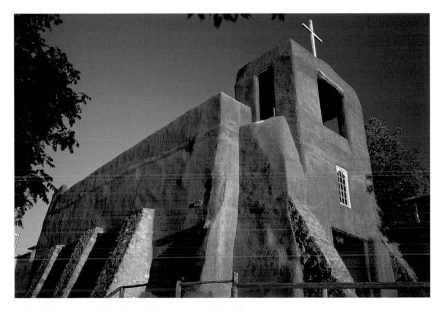

The oldest parts of the Chapel of San Miguel date from 1710.

New Mexico's ㉒ **State Capitol** (Old Santa Fe Trail at Paseo de Peralta) is down the street from the chapel. Interestingly, the town that has, in the Palace of the Governors, the country's oldest public building, also claims one of the newest state capitol buildings. Built in 1966, in a modern style quite unlike Santa Fe's prevailing architecture, it is nonetheless supremely Santa Fean. The round floor plan mimics the sun symbol of the Zia Pueblo on the state flag, and the same symbol—inlaid in gleaming turquoise and brass mosaic on the floor of the rotunda—greets visitors as they enter the capitol. The building is a repository of outstanding art by New Mexican artists, compliments of the Capitol Art Foundation, and the Governor's Gallery on the fourth floor next to the governor's office holds temporary exhibitions.

The state legislature is in session for 60 days in odd-numbered years and for 30 days in even-numbered years, beginning the third Tuesday in January. The Senate and House chambers are below ground and not open to the public, but they're visible from the second floor.

■ WALKING ACEQUIA MADRE/CANYON ROAD

Given the more than 80 galleries flanking historic Canyon Road, the 2-mile walk-ing tour outlined below could take days—and eat your credit card alive. But walking Canyon Road is definitely the way to see it; the street's galleries form the equiva-lent of a vast art museum of extraordinary variety and vitality, and you wouldn't drive through an art museum. Should you not care to walk the road's full length, there is a pay lot in the 800 block across from El Farol (along with very limited street parking).

When walking along Acequia Madre, use caution: the street is narrow and there is no sidewalk. When returning down Canyon Road, pop into as many galleries as time permits. Usually only two or three pieces are visible through the windows, and they may not be representative of what's inside.

Begin at Garcia Street and Acequia Madre. Acequia Madre translates as "mother ditch," which is exactly what this is: constructed in the early 1600s to irrigate the fields south of the chapel of San Miguel, the Acequia Madre served as the southern border of the Santa Fe settlement up until the Pueblo Revolt. Today it forms a lin-ear moat separating the houses on the south from the street, and at certain times of the year, notably autumn, when it's shaded by yellowing elms, the ambiance is nearly brook-like. Every spring for almost 400 years, Acequia Madre residents have gathered to weed and clean the ditch.

Many homes along Acequia Madre date from the middle to late 19th century, and this is one of the best streets in Santa Fe from which to note their quirks and textures and handmade details. The miniature footbridge, sculpted adobe wall, and gate with wrought-iron lanterns at 506 Acequia Madre are a perfect union of archi-tecture and folk art impossible to imagine anywhere but in Santa Fe; note too the unusual adobe archway over the fence at 937 Acequia Madre. The great modernist architect Louis Kahn declared that the brick said, "I like an arch." Well, adobe brick doesn't much like an arch, but it can be tricked into forming one—until it melts back into the earth, which is what adobe likes.

■ ACEQUIA MADRE/CANYON ROAD HIGHLIGHTS

Acequia Madre joins Canyon Road at the 1000 block. Continue up Canyon Road and veer right to visit ① **Cristo Rey Church.** Designed by John Gaw Meem, the prime proponent of Santa Fe's Pueblo Revival style, it was built in 1940 pri-marily by parishioners. It is said to be one of the largest 20th-century adobe buildings on earth. The parishioners, mostly Hispanic, worked five days a week for wages of $2 a day supplied by the archdiocese, and then donated their labor on Saturdays. They laid 180,000 heavy adobe bricks, though as one parishioner, Alfonso "Trompo" Trujillo, recalled later, "Just as hard as we were working, it seemed like it wasn't even working."

I thought the church overbearing on my first visit but later came to appreciate it. Meem indeed evoked the *spirit* of New Mexico's 18th-century Spanish churches here, allowing pure sculptural form to become architecture. The two massive towers express immense strength, but unlike St. Francis Cathedral they embrace earth rather than sky. Inside is a monumental, high-baroque carved-stone altar screen, transplanted from the military chapel of La Castrense demolished long ago on San Francisco Street. It dates from 1760. The front doors of Cristo Rey are usually locked, but you can enter through the second door on the south portal.

Backtrack to Acequia Madre, then take the Canyon Road fork to the right. In Spanish times, this was *el camino del cañón,* a road used to ferry firewood by burro from the mountains east of town. Most houses along the road date from the 18th and 19th centuries and have been pressed into service as restaurants, studios, and galleries. A few of the structures still survive as private homes.

The ② **Rafael Borrego House** is a classic Spanish adobe with a Territorial portal grafted on; the original building dates from the mid-18th century. Geronimo, a classy restaurant, resides within. *724 Canyon Road.*

The nameless house at ③ **602 Canyon Road** contains an art gallery and is well worth a visit inside to experience the radiant color, texture, and emotional warmth of its mud-plastered interior walls. Few Santa Feans use this technique anymore because of the cost and effort involved. You can see how the brilliant sunlight streams through the

Detail from Cristo Rey altar screen.

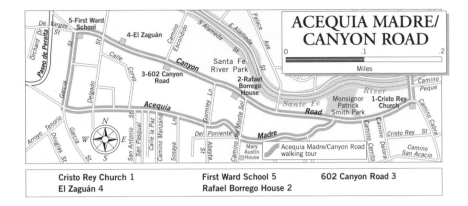

ACEQUIA MADRE/ CANYON ROAD

| Cristo Rey Church 1 | First Ward School 5 | 602 Canyon Road 3 |
| El Zaguán 4 | Rafael Borrego House 2 | |

windows here to counterpoint the much more gently luminous accompaniment of the earth-straw walls. The building was begun around 1760, and rooms were added until about 1900.

The Historic Santa Fe Foundation's *Old Santa Fe Today* guide cites ④ **El Zaguán** as "one of the architectural treasures of New Mexico." No argument here. In afternoon winter light its 300-foot-long dusky pink facade, punctuated by turquoise shutters, seems almost to glow from within its own adobe skin. The structure, which dates from 1849, is now split up into apartments. The pioneering archaeologist Adolph Bandelier lived here around 1890, and he designed the public garden at the building's west end, now maintained by the Historic Santa Fe Foundation. At the cistern is a sign asking for public donations of water to help the garden survive—a classic example of Santa Fe improvisation. *545 Canyon Road.*

The ⑤ **First Ward School,** erected in 1906, is one of those wonderful buildings that drive architectural historians to drink because they can't be filed in any neat stylistic slot. It looks as though one architect drew a dignified neoclassical building, and then, while he was having lunch, a prankster colleague came along and added a Queen Anne witch's hat instead of a pediment. *400 Canyon Road.*

At least a dozen Canyon Road galleries display large-scale sculptures out front or in courtyards, another compelling reason for walking. The northern New Mexico light, particularly in fall or winter, creates striking effects wherever it falls. This surely helps sell the art, but keep in mind: it won't glow like this on the back porch in Michigan.

(preceding pages) Santa Fe's adobe-brick Cristo Rey Church was built the old-fashioned way in 1940 and looks older than its years.

PHOTOGRAPHING SANTA FE

The amateur photographer stepping out in Santa Fe, camera around neck, may in the first flush of euphoria believe that he or she has been delivered to the Promised Land. The heavenly light, constellation of cultures, tawny colors, and ancient architecture are seductive indeed. But the only promise here is that you'll have to work to get memorable pictures. Santa Fe and its environs are more difficult to photograph than many more prosaic places.

Your first problem is contrast. The New Mexico sun frequently creates too much of it—highlights are too brightly lit, shadows too deep. The answer is to shoot in the early morning or late evening light, or pray for a day when high humidity or wispy clouds soften the sun. Eduardo Fuss, who shot most of the photos for this book, prefers evening light. It is warmer, because dust kicked into the air during the day filters the light toward the red edge of the spectrum. Mornings offer the advantage of calmer air, so foreground foliage doesn't dance around.

A second problem is the ghosts of the thousands of professional photographers who have preceded you. It may seem daunting to come up with a fresh image of Santa Fe or Taos, something that hasn't already been done better on a postcard. Here's a little advice: focus on details. A weathered blue window frame on an adobe house, rather than the whole house. The footbridge over the Acequia Madre, encrusted in orange autumn leaves. Shooting the sunset over Santa Fe from Fort Marcy Park is a compelling temptation, but the details tell Santa Fe's story more eloquently.

Indians present a special problem for the photographer. "The moment you raise your camera to your eye, they will turn away, or turn their heads down," says Eduardo Fuss. The reasons are obvious, from their point of view: they don't want to be exploited, nor viewed as exotic objects. Solution: either shoot unobtrusively or ask permission (and perhaps offer a small modeling fee).

Above all, look intently at photo opportunities, imagining what the sunlight might do to scenes at different times of day or in a different season. And be patient. I made the traditional pilgrimage to the San Francisco de Asís church in Ranchos de Taos one evening and was thoroughly depressed to find a dozen amateur and professional photographers jockeying for position around the church's hind end, immortalized by painters as great as O'Keeffe and photographers as untouchable as Ansel Adams. When the last light seemed to fold into the eastern clouds, the clot of photographers dissolved. I hung around, just in case. New Mexico's light is as fickle as the lottery. And I won: right at sunset, the clouds broke and the church's crosses rose in silhouette in a pinkened sky.

In northern New Mexico, the right photo is always worth the wait.

TOWN OF TAOS

I am driving into Taos at the sorcerer's hour. The sun has set at my back over low Carson Mesa, leaving a thin crepuscular strip of pink and yellow light evaporating into the night sky above. Ahead, Taos's lights are blinking on in the valley, huddled feebly below 13,161-foot Wheeler Peak. Above the great mountain, October's full moon is rising, forcing its way through silvered wisps of clouds. Sorcery, indeed. Love at last light.

Taos, and its surrounding countryside and nearby pueblo, have been bewitching otherwise sensible people into writing paragraphs like that for more than a hundred years.

Mabel Dodge Luhan, the New York sophisticate who came to Taos in 1917, first saw the place at about the same time of day I did, and eventually wrote the classic *Edge of Taos Desert:*

> Looking at this definite, sudden, precise earth-form that towered there so still [the mountain], I saw something again that I had never noticed in nature. It seemed to me the mountain was alive, awake, and breathing. That it had its own consciousness. That it knew things. . . . The mountain seemed to smile and breathe forth an infinitely peaceful, benevolent blessing as the light faded away from it.

Author John Nichols, who arrived in 1969, wrote in a modern classic, *If Mountains Die:*

> My eyes, and the eyes of all Taoseños, are forever attracted to the mountain. Nobody can travel the valley without centering off its bold presence. It is the central symbol in our lives to which the eye is always drawn. Some of us may take it for granted, yet in our subconscious it breathes heavily, an exclusively solid shape in the otherwise ever-changing, sometimes ugly, often beautiful, and too often unfortunate landscape through which we travel.

I reach Taos and bunk down for the night in an old but pleasant motel about a quarter-mile from the house where Kit Carson resided from 1843 to 1868. My room has cable TV and a New Mexican beehive fireplace. I build a fire in the req-

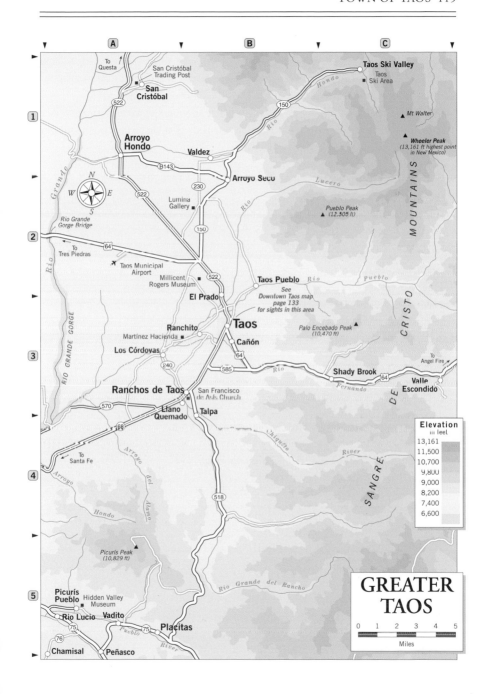

To Questa
San Cristóbal Trading Post
San Cristóbal
522

A

Arroyo Hondo
Valdez
B143
230
Arroyo Seco
Lumina Gallery
522
150

Taos Ski Valley
Taos Ski Area
150
Hondo

B

Mt Walter
Wheeler Peak
(13,161 ft highest point in New Mexico)

Lucero

Pueblo Peak
(12,305 ft)

C

MOUNTAINS

N
W E
S

Rio Grande Gorge Bridge

To Tres Piedras
64

Taos Municipal Airport
Millicent Rogers Museum
522
El Prado

Ranchito
Martínez Hacienda
Los Córdovas
240

Taos Pueblo

See Downtown Taos map page 133 for sights in this area

Taos
Cañón
64

Palo Encebado Peak
(10,470 ft)

Rio Pueblo

CRISTO

To Angel Fire

RIO GRANDE GORGE

Ranchos de Taos
570
Llano Quemado
San Francisco de Asís Church
Talpa
68

585
64
Rio

Shady Brook
64
Valle Escondido

Fernando

DE

SANGRE

Elevation
in feet
13,161
11,500
10,700
9,800
9,000
8,200
7,400
6,600

To Santa Fe
Arroyo del Alamo

Hondo

518

Chiquito

River

Picurís Peak
(10,829 ft)

Rio Grande del Rancho

Picurís Pueblo
Hidden Valley Museum
Rio Lucio
Vadito
75
Pueblo
75
Placitas
River

Chamisal
76
Peñasco

GREATER TAOS

0 1 2 3 4 5
Miles

uisite beehive manner—make a tepee out of three or four split pine logs—and switch on CNN for news of the real world, wondering whether any more inspirational place than the town of Taos, New Mexico, has ever been created.

The late Taos mayor Phil Lovato, in a particularly metaphysical moment, once said that, "Taos is not a city, Taos is not a town, Taos is not even a place. Taos is a state of mind and a power center of the universe."

■ ■ ■

In the morning, clear of head, I decide to drive back south out N.M. 68 to where I saw the moonrise, and return to Taos in daylight.

It's different, predictably. The mountain range is no less of a magisterial presence, but there are now roadside distractions—a blend of low-grade commercial squalor leavened by classic Taos funk and high kitsch.

The first stop is an arresting tepee display. These are real tepees, as real as possible when manufactured by Anglos and sold in a place far distant from the plains, where tepees were used. The Pueblo Indians never dreamed of living in such things. The woman at the counter says they sell for $750 to $6,000, depending on size. "We sell a lot of them."

"What do people do with them?"

"Well, they live in them. Or use them for guest quarters."

Down the road, an old International Harvester truck lies abandoned and overgrown with roadside weeds. In this dry country it takes eons for things to rust away. A legend is painted on it: SPECIAL KNOWLEDGE OF THE DIVINE MYSTERIES COMING 1989—AZTEC—MAYA.

Mobile homes, adrift in an unzoned desert (a Taos city official later laments to me that Taos County has no zoning ordinance). A Kwik Kar Wash. A boutique that sells "Jewelry-Weaving-Skulls-Furs." There is indeed a display of 20 cow skulls, complete with horns, for sale.

Ranchos de Taos, a settlement 4 miles south of the center of town, provides the entrée to Taos's allure. There is a cordon of quaint galleries here, but the real attraction is the mission church of San Francisco de Asís, which presents its back end to N.M. 68. This is fortuitous, because the hand-sculpted adobe-buttressed back of this modest church is one of the purest architectural forms in North America. Its totally blank, brown adobe walls and uneven geometry drink in the sun as it glides

The church of San Francisco de Asís, in Ranchos de Taos.

across the sky, integrating the Spanish concept of *sol y sombra* (sunlight and shadow) into the architecture. G. E. Kidder Smith wrote in *The Architecture of the United States* that "one almost shakes in its presence."

Georgia O'Keeffe reduced the church to near abstraction by stripping away everything but light and form. "I had to paint it," she wrote. "The back of it several times, the front once. I finally painted a part of the back thinking that with that piece of the back I said all I needed to say about the church."

People say that this is the most photographed and painted building in New Mexico, a claim impossible to verify, but we do know that this little church moved Ansel Adams to take up a career in photography. In 1930, Adams and Paul Strand were both staying in Taos with their mutual friend Mabel Dodge Luhan. Adams noticed that whenever something interesting seemed to be happening in the sky, Strand would toss his camera in the car and dash down to Ranchos de Taos to photograph the church. Adams was so impressed with Strand's photos that he gave up his plan of being a concert pianist and dedicated his life to photography.

■ EARLY TAOS

Taos is a corruption of the Tewa Indian words "tua tah," meaning "red willow place." Its Spanish presence is even older than Santa Fe's, with the pioneer explorer Juan de Oñate having appointed a priest, Francisco Zamora, to the mission at Taos Pueblo in 1598. By 1615, a number of Spanish farmers were staking out the valley in the lee of the haunting mountain.

Taos began to assume an important economic role in New Mexico in the 1700s with its annual trade fair, a convergence of convenience in which Puebloans, Comanches, Utes, Apaches, and eventually Spaniards and Americans would all suspend their usual hostilities for a month and meet to trade furs, food, whiskey, and other goods. This was possible only because of Taos's isolation 70 miles north of the capital, where the Spanish governor would have enforced the Spanish crown's ban on commerce with "foreigners."

By the early 1800s, Anglos, the most famous of whom was Christopher "Kit" Carson, had begun settling in Taos in significant numbers. Carson was a fascinating contradiction of a man—a noted killer of Apache warriors who spoke several Indian languages and eventually adopted an Apache orphan, among numerous other foster children. A newspaper profile in 1860 described him a man with "an in-fy-nite small chance of legs [who] sits upon a horse like a king. I have never seen a man presenting a more regal aspect than this veteran mountaineer, when mounted upon his favorite steed, and dashing along like the wind." He married a Taoseña, Josefa Jaramillo, described by a contemporary as having "beauty of the haughty, heart-breaking kind— such as would lead a man with a glance of the eye, to risk his life for one smile." Carson lived with her in a rambling,

Kit Carson in 1850. (Buffalo Bill Historical Center)

The kitchen in Kit Carson's house, where the frontiersman and his wife, Josefa, ate meals with their many children.

12 room house (now the Kit Carson Museum) just east of Taos Plaza from 1843 to 1868, when he died of an aneurysm.

The most famous (and notorious) event in 19th-century Taos was the Revolt of 1847, a bloody footnote to the quiet American seizure of New Mexico the year before. A few months after Stephen W. Kearny had claimed the territory for the United States, a core of Mexican loyalists in Taos allied with some Pueblo Indians and revolted. They stormed Gov. Charles Bent's house, killing him with arrows as his wife and children and Kit Carson's wife, Josefa, desperately tried to cut a hole through the back wall of the house to escape. The revolutionaries then scalped the governor and, after tacking his scalp to a board, paraded it around the Taos Plaza. The revolt lasted less than three weeks, and Indians suffered the severest losses— more than 150 dead in a final, decisive battle at Taos Pueblo on February 3. When the rebel leaders were tried at Taos before a judge whose own son had been killed in the revolt, their accusers included the three women who'd been in the house with Governor Bent: his wife, a Mrs. Boggs, and Mrs. Kit Carson.

■ AMERICAN ARTISTS DISCOVER TAOS

The "discovery" of Taos by artists and intellectuals beginning around 1900 was no fluke, but a reaction to what those people saw as the dehumanizing effects of industrialization, overcrowded cities, and conflict in Europe and the Eastern United States. Taos, in its simplicity and great natural beauty—even given the hardships of its isolation—appeared to be a desert Nirvana. D. H. Lawrence wrote:

> There is something savage, unbreakable in the spirit of the place out here—the Indians drumming and yelling at our camp-fire at evening . . . I am glad to be out here in the south-west of America—there is the pristine something, unbroken, unbreakable. It [is] good to be alone and responsible. But also it is very *hard* living up against these savage Rockies.

(above) Ernest Blumenschein captures the magic of New Mexico light in his painting Sangre de Cristo Mountains. *(Anschutz Collection) (opposite) Blumenschein's studio in Taos.*

Between 1898 and 1942, Taos became a mecca for artists, writers, and intellectuals seeking a new spiritual landing. Two academically trained New York artists, Ernest Blumenschein and Bert Phillips, were the accidental pioneers. On a sketching trip from Mexico to Colorado, their wagon broke down near Taos in 1898 and they decided to stay. Over the next 40 years an astonishing variety of artists followed—impressionists, expressionists, modernists, and traditional "Western" painters. The attractions are: the dramatic New Mexico light, the Spanish and Pueblo cultures, and the magnificent physical environment. It was an environment that for many artists tended to place human beings in appropriate perspective. The painter John Marin wrote from Taos that New Mexico was a land of

Ernest Blumenschein in his Taos studio. (Taos Historic Museums)

"Big Sun heat. Big storm. Big everything—a leaving out of that thing called man." Good description.

During this era, the most influential Taos celebrity was Mabel Dodge, a New York socialite—the term may not be adequate—who arrived in 1917. Wrote historian Roxana Robinson, "Mabel was a rich and frequently married woman from Buffalo who collected people and created situations." These "situations" included divorcing her husband, marrying a Taos Indian, Tony Luhan, and gathering a coterie of artists from D. H. Lawrence to Georgia O'Keeffe.

O'Keeffe didn't stay long in Taos, but she was stunned by New Mexico's high desert sunlight and what it did to the organic material it fell upon. "Its dryness reduced plant and animal life to essential forms, suggestive of the way Georgia

LETTERS FROM GEORGIA O'KEEFFE

Georgia O'Keeffe in Taos, 1929.
(Museum of New Mexico)

Dear Mabel [Dodge Luhan]—
It is 5 a.m. — I have been up for about an hour — watching the moon grow pale — and the dawn come — I walked around in the wet grass by the Pink House — one bright — bright star — so bright that it seems like a tear in its eye — The flowers are so lovely — I came over here to the Studio — so I could see the mountain line — so clear cut where the sun will come — . . . .
—Georgia

My best greetings to you Henry McBride—
. . . .
I have the most beautiful adobe studio — never had such a nice place all to myself — Out the very large window to a rich green alfalfa field — then the sage brush and beyond — a most perfect mountain — it makes me feel like flying   and I don't care what becomes of Art — We wired Marin to come out — and he came — He is having a great time too — Stieglitz says we are being ruined for home — and I feel like saying I am glad of it —

When you say you like Mabel — I must tell you — you really dont even imagine half of what you are liking — Just the life she keeps going around her would be a great deal — but that along with this country is almost too much for anyone to have in this life — However I am standing it well — never felt better — I often think how much it would all entertain you — Do write me that you are having a good summer — and if you are not — just get up and leave it — and go where you will have a good time — or like something or other — Have I painted? I dont know — I hope to — but I really dont care

There are four nice careful paintings — and two — Others —

No — there are five careful ones. . . .

—Georgia O'Keeffe, summer 1929

instinctively simplified her images," wrote Laurie Lisle in *Portrait of an Artist*. O'Keeffe bought a ranch in Abiquiú, 50 miles southwest of Taos. She created abstractions out of reality—the reality of animal skulls and blooming flowers she discovered right around her home—and both mesmerized and pissed off the American art establishment. In the early 1940s, when someone suggested to the director of the Museum of New Mexico that Georgia O'Keeffe was becoming a pretty important artist, and it might be appropriate to commission her to paint a mural for Santa Fe's St. Francis Auditorium, he reportedly replied that he didn't want some "so-called woman artist's bone-littered landscape on the walls."

■ GROWTH AND THE ART MARKET

"I was at the Hog Farm—one of the original communes—for a party last night," says Taos author John Nichols with a laugh. "I've never seen so many old hippies in my life. I would bet you half to two-thirds of them are in real estate today."

Historic Taos is dying, as Nichols sees it. Short version: the hippies swarmed in during the 1960s, eventually became middle-class, made money, and soon land values were escalating.

Says former Taos mayor Fred Peralta, whose family stretches several generations into Taos's past, "Lately, the last seven or eight years, a lot of people have been coming in and buying retirement homes. These are people with substantial money, who don't need to depend on the local economy. We have lots of home offices, people connecting to their businesses with a PC and a modem."

There are few jobs in Taos except in the tourist industry, which pays dismal wages. Consequence: children of families that have lived around Taos for 300 years are moving, typically to Albuquerque, which enjoys a real-world economy.

But Taos's astounding natural attributes continue to make it an artists' community. There are about 80 galleries in town, and some 250 working artists. The Taos Institute of Arts offers two- to five-day classes in everything from "Equine Sculpture" to "Creating Your Creative Life."

"My dad came here as an artist in 1903," says Ouray Meyers, himself an artist and gallery owner, born here in 1938. "I think there's a magic here that either attracts or repels people. We say the mountain either accepts you or it doesn't. It's intangible; a feeling that you belong or you don't. Obviously, I belong. Frederic Remington came here and couldn't do anything and ended up disliking Taos."

The opening of the Ridhwan Sculpture Garden gave Taoseño sculptors a place to exhibit their work within Taos.

Meyers thinks some of the changes Nichols and Peralta regret have been good for Taos. "It makes life easier for an artist, because a lot of art collectors come here, and that puts a lot of us in a position where we can make a living. But we also lose some of our ambiance in the process."

Visitors to Taos will notice some differences between the galleries here and in Santa Fe. The middle-class collector looking for a nice piece of work for $250 or $1,000 may score better in Taos; the collector in search of something on the cutting edge—and probably more expensive—will find more in Santa Fe. Over the years, many artists have complained that Taos is a great place to produce art, but the best of it isn't sold here, traveling instead to New York, Los Angeles, and Europe.

This scenario may be changing. In 1997, Felicia Ferguson, the owner of Lumina Gallery and a native Taoseña, opened an ambitious outdoor sculpture garden on a hillside next to the Mabel Dodge Luhan House. It's no exaggeration to say that with this single extravagant gesture, Taos instantly became a destination for collectors and admirers of large-scale sculpture.

That endeavor, the Ridhwan Sculpture Garden, is now closed, but in late 2003 its successor, Ferguson's Lumina Gallery opened north of town on N.M., 230, near Arroyo Seco. About six dozen sculptures, priced from under $1,000 to more than $300,000, are exhibited in a grove of birch trees bisected by the Rio Lucero. Lumina's pieces tend toward abstract marble totems, whimsical bronze animals, polished steel zigzags blasting toward the sky, and kinetic whirligigs twisting in the breeze. The one common thread is a sensation of joy—this is not sculpture that confronts and baffles you. Browsers will be welcome.

■ VISITING TAOS

The town of Taos, 4 miles north of Ranchos de Taos and 2 miles south of Taos Pueblo, is an enjoyable place to wander on foot, taking in the galleries, small cafés, and the generally funky setting.

Even in the dark of winter, Taos can be filled with light. Brilliantly sunlit snow blankets the rugged peaks of the Sangre de Cristos, forming a spectacular stage set. Stark cottonwood trees guard icy rivulets running through the town. During the Christmas season, as in Santa Fe, thousands of *farolitos* illuminate the Plaza and nearly every building in town.

Tiny Taos is congested because U.S. 64 and N.M. 68 meet in the middle of town, a block from Taos Plaza. Stop where the two highways intersect and take a look at the wonderful mural of a *santero* (carver of saints) painted by local artist George Chacón on the side of a building in 1989. Bristling with symbolism, the anonymous *santero* is carving sculptures representing the Mexican-American family, the individual with a positive outlook, and the struggling single parent. But his santos look eerily like ghosts.

The heart of town looks as though it were trapped in a time warp between the 18th and the 21st centuries. As in Santa Fe, the old brown adobe buildings are mostly protected and preserved—though nothing in Taos has the temerity to rise more than two stories—and the enormous, stately cottonwoods lining the main roads seem to have been there since the dawn of time. And yet the buzz of commerce permeates everything. Taos seems to have been *invented* for tourism. There are several art and historical museums, the world-class Taos Ski Valley, and more boutiques than seem possible in a town of 4,700.

Snowy Taos.

■ **TAOS HIGHLIGHTS**

There are enough historic homes, museums, and art galleries in Taos to keep any visitor busy for several days. Beginning with Taos Plaza, they are listed below and numbered to correspond with the Downtown Taos map and key on page 133. The Museum Association of Taos sells a bargain $20 ticket good for admission to six museums.

① **Taos Plaza**

Just west of the intersection of U.S. 64 and N.M. 68, Taos Plaza, founded in 1790, has a modest charm, even if it was remodeled mainly in brick in 1976. The shops clustered around the Plaza tilt more toward curio than art, especially T-shirt shops. One historic curiosity is the D. H. Lawrence erotic art collection in the cluttered manager's office of La Fonda Hotel on the Plaza's south side. Lawrence lived in Taos from 1922 to 1923 and in 1925, but produced these 10 paintings later. The cops seized them from a London exhibition in 1929. They're hardly lewd by modern-day standards—a few rather vague butts and breasts peek out—but they do demonstrate that Lawrence was a more gifted writer than painter. A small fee paid at the check-in desk gains you admission to the exhibit.

② **Governor Bent Museum**

Charles Bent, a prominent trader along the Old Santa Fe Trail and the first U.S. governor of the territory, lived here until he was scalped in January 1847. The museum displays frontier memorabilia and period furnishings. *117-A Bent Street, a block north of Taos Plaza; 505-758-2376.*

③ **Taos Art Museum at the Fechin House**

Expatriate Russian artist Nicolai Fechin lived in and remodeled this two-story adobe house from 1927 to 1933, investing it with his own distinctive Russian-style furniture, doors, windows, corbels, and beams. The house became home to the Taos Art Museum in 2003 and displays works by many of the early Taos masters, in addition to Fechin. *227 Paseo del Pueblo Norte, a few blocks north of Taos Plaza; 505-758-2690.*

④ **Kit Carson State Park**

A lovely park in the middle of town. Kit Carson is buried in the small graveyard beside his wife and near several other Carson namesakes. Mabel Dodge Luhan is also buried in the same graveyard. *Paseo del Pueblo Norte between Garcia Place and Civic Plaza Drive.*

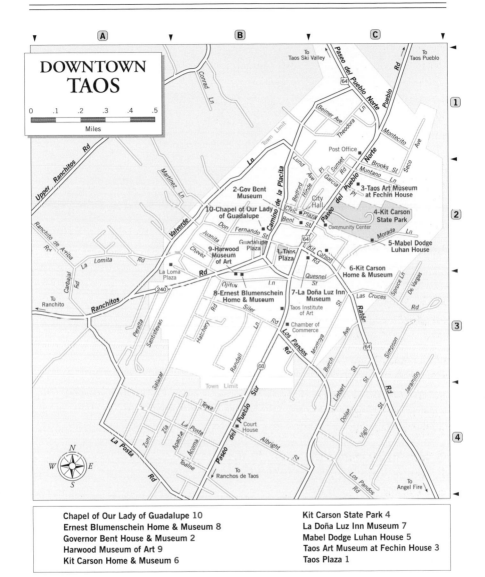

DOWNTOWN TAOS

0 .1 .2 .3 .4 .5
Miles

Chapel of Our Lady of Guadalupe 10
Ernest Blumenschein Home & Museum 8
Governor Bent House & Museum 2
Harwood Museum of Art 9
Kit Carson Home & Museum 6

Kit Carson State Park 4
La Doña Luz Inn Museum 7
Mabel Dodge Luhan House 5
Taos Art Museum at Fechin House 3
Taos Plaza 1

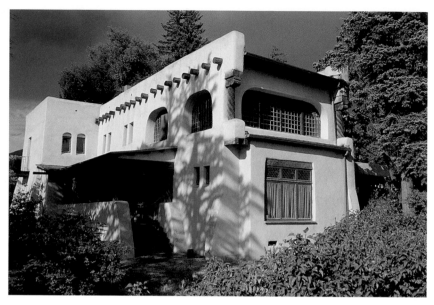

Fechin House, now home to the Taos Art Museum.

⑤ Mabel Dodge Luhan House

Today a bed-and-breakfast inn, Mabel Dodge Luhan's three-story hacienda once hosted such luminaries as Georgia O'Keeffe, Willa Cather, Carl Jung, and Aldous Huxley. Years later, actor Dennis Hopper lived in the house while filming the hippie picture *Easy Rider* in the late 1960s. *242 Morada Lane; 505-751-9686.*

⑥ Kit Carson Home and Museum

Carson bought this 1825 adobe house in 1843 as a wedding gift for his 14-year-old bride, Josefa Jaramillo. The courtyard house holds hundreds of artifacts—guns, furniture, dresses, and contemporary newspaper profiles of Carson. *Kit Carson Road, a half-block east of Taos Plaza; 505-758-0505.*

⑦ La Doña Luz Inn

This small family-owned museum adjacent to La Doña Luz Inn and Gift Shop exhibits Native American and Spanish colonial artifacts and Kit Carson's leather pants. *114 Kit Carson Road; 505-758-4874.*

⑧ Ernest Blumenschein Home and Museum

In 1919, Ernest Blumenschein, one of the six cofounders of the Taos Society of Artists, purchased a rambling house that he shared with his wife, artist Mary Greene Blumenschein, and their daughter, Helen, also an artist. Because the home has been maintained much as it was when they were alive, a visit provides a glimpse into the lifestyle of members of Taos's art colony in its early days. On exhibit, besides the family's personal possessions, are works by all three of the Blumenscheins and by other Taos artists. *222 Ledoux Street; 505-758-0505.*

⑨ Harwood Museum of Art

Operated by the University of New Mexico, this art museum features a permanent exhibit of paintings, drawings, prints, photographs, and sculpture dating from the earliest years of Taos as an art colony (the 1910s). The paintings and photographs testify eloquently to the reasons so many artists have congregated here: the power of the land and the irresistible images of its people, e.g., a painting of Wheeler Peak, brooding in a winter storm as a funeral procession struggles through the snow beneath it. *238 Ledoux Street; 505-758-9826.*

⑩ Chapel of Our Lady of Guadalupe

Worth a look is this inspiring yet subtly conceived adobe chapel built in the 1970s. A large, brilliantly colored portrait of the patron saint adorns a wall inside the chapel. *404 San Felipe Street NW, Patio Escondido.*

■ GREATER TAOS SITES *(see map on page 119)*

Millicent Rogers Museum

The Standard Oil heiress Millicent Rogers was a sophisticated beauty who adopted Taos as her home in 1947 and set about collecting the finest in Southwestern crafts, including jewelry, textiles, and pottery. This museum, founded in 1956, three years after her death, showcases her collections, augmented by more recent additions, among them comprehensive examples of pottery by María Martínez and her family of San Ildefonso Pueblo. Rogers was a jewelry designer in her own right, and in addition to the abundance of outstanding Native American turquoise jewelry on display, some of her own pieces can be seen. *1504 Millicent Rogers Museum Road, 4 miles north of Taos Plaza on U.S. 64; 505-758-2462.*

POWERFUL PEOPLE

Through the months while [D.H.] Lawrence and Frieda hesitated about coming to Taos, I willed him to come. Before I went to sleep at night, I drew myself all in to the core of my being where there is a live, plangent force lying passive—waiting for direction. Becoming entirely that, moving with it, speaking with it, I leaped through space, joining myself to the central core of Lawrence, where he was in India, in Australia. Not really speaking to him, but *being* my wish, I became that action that brought him across the sea.

■ ■ ■

"Come, Lawrence! Come to Taos!" became in me, Lawrence in Taos. This is not prayer, but command. Only those who have exercised it know its danger.

Lawrence hurried over to our house in the morning ready to begin our work together. As I never dressed early in the morning, but took a sun-bath on the long, flat, dirt roof outside my bedroom, I called to him to come up there. I didn't think to dress for him. I had on moccasins, even if my legs were bare; and I had a voluminous, soft, white cashmere thing like a burnous. He hurried through my bedroom, averting his eyes from the un-made bed as though it were a repulsive sight, though it was not so at all. My room was all white and blue, with whitewashed walls, sunny, bright, and fresh—and there was no dark or equivocal atmosphere in it, or in my blue blankets, or in the white chest of drawers or the little blue chairs. But Lawrence, just passing through it, turned it into a brothel. Yes, he did: that's how powerful he was.

■ ■ ■

In that hour, then, we became more intimate, psychically, than I had ever been with anyone else before. It was a complete, stark approximation of spiritual union, a seeing of each other in a luminous vision of reality. And how Lawrence could see!

I won't try to tell you what we said . . . because I can't remember.

—Mabel Dodge Luhan, *Lorenzo in Taos*, 1932

Lumina Gallery
A successor to the Ridhwan Sculpture Garden, this excellent gallery of outdoor sculpture opened in 2003 outside town along the way to Taos Ski Valley. *11 N.M. 230; 877-558-6462.*

Martínez Hacienda
Don Antonio Severino Martínez, the *alcalde* (mayor) of Taos, erected this fortresslike 21-room adobe house in the early 1800s. A testament to the danger of Apache attacks, the hacienda is built around two courtyards and has few exterior openings. Exactingly restored, the home contains fine examples of Spanish colonial furniture and household wares. *Ranchitos Road (N.M. 240), 2 miles south of Taos Plaza; 505-758-1000.*

■ TAOS PUEBLO

One of the most famous architectural monuments in the United States, Taos Pueblo was begun about the year 1200 and has been continuously inhabited by Taoseños for nearly 800 years. The pueblo is described more fully in the "EIGHT NORTHERN PUEBLOS" chapter. *U.S. 64, 2 miles north of town; 505-758-1028.*

EIGHT NORTHERN PUEBLOS

Several years ago, a pottery expert in Santa Fe warned me that I wouldn't save any money driving to the pueblos and shopping for art there, as opposed to the galleries in Santa Fe and Taos.

He was wrong. I was lucky.

On a pleasantly cool spring morning I walked through a creaky screen door into a modest adobe house in Santa Clara Pueblo, about 30 miles north of Santa Fe. Like many buildings in the pueblos, it was both home and shop. Perhaps a hundred bowls and vases were showcased on a series of hand-built shelves. One immediately captured my attention. A small black-on-red Jémez bowl, only 3 inches high, decorated with ancient symbols for feathers, clouds, and lightning, it was exquisite. I bought it without hesitation, for $75.

The proprietor and I had a pleasant conversation. He invited me to Santa Clara's August 12 feast day—a day of dancing and eating on which non-Indian strangers

Feast days, traditional dances, and ceremonies show the strength of Pueblo Indian culture.

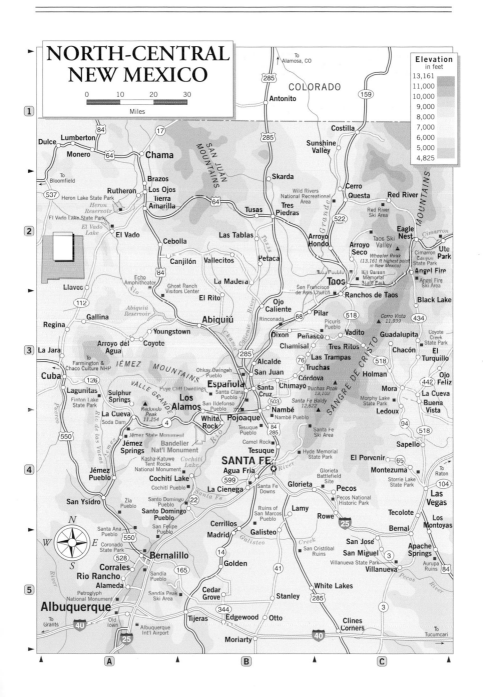

NORTH-CENTRAL NEW MEXICO

0   10   20   30
Miles

Elevation
in feet

13,161
11,000
10,000
9,000
8,000
7,000
6,000
5,000
4,825

COLORADO

To Alamosa, CO

Antonito

Costilla

Sunshine Valley

Dulce   Lumberton

Monero   Chama

Brazos
Los Ojos
Tierra
Amarilla

Rutherford

Heron Lake State Park
Heron Reservoir
El Vado Lake State Park
El Vado Lake

To Bloomfield

El Vado

Cebolla

Canjilón   Vallecitos

La Madera

El Rito

Llaveo

Gallina

Regina

La Jara

Cuba

Lagunitas

Sulphur Springs

La Cueva

Soda Dam

Jémez Springs

Jémez Pueblo

San Ysidro

Corrales
Rio Rancho
Alameda

Albuquerque

To Grants

Old Town
Albuquerque Int'l Airport

SAN JUAN MOUNTAINS

Skarda

Tusas

Tres Piedras

Las Tablas

Petaca

Echo Amphitheater

Ghost Ranch Visitors Center

Abiquiú

Abiquiú Reservoir

Youngstown

Arroyo del Agua

Coyote

JÉMEZ MOUNTAINS

Puye Cliff Dwellings

Española

Santa Clara Pueblo

San Ildefonso Pueblo

Los Alamos

Redondo Peak 11,254

Jémez State Monument

Bandelier Nat'l Monument

Kasha-Katuwe Tent Rocks National Monument

Cochití Lake

Cochití Pueblo

Santo Domingo Pueblo

Santa Ana Pueblo

Coronado State Park

Sandia Pueblo

San Felipe Pueblo

Cerrillos

Madrid

Galisteo

Golden

Cedar Grove

Tijeras

Moriarty

Edgewood   Otto

Sandia Peak Ski Area

Petroglyph National Monument

Wild Rivers National Recreational Area

Cerro

Questa   Red River

Red River Ski Area

Arroyo Hondo

Arroyo Seco

Taos Ski Valley

Wheeler Peak (13,161 ft highest point in New Mexico)

Taos Pueblo

Kit Carson Memorial State Park

San Francisco de Asis Church

Taos

Ranchos de Taos

Ojo Caliente   Pilar

Rinconada

Dixon   Peñasco

Chamisal

Alcalde

San Juan

Santa Cruz

Chimayo

Córdova

Truchas

Las Trampas

Truchas Peak 13,102

Santa Fe Baldy 12,622

Eagle Nest

Cimarron Canyon State Park

Angel Fire

Angel Fire Ski Area

Black Lake

Cerro Vista 11,939

Picurís Pueblo

Vadito   Guadalupita

Tres Ritos

Chacón

Holman

Mora

Ledoux

Coyote Creek State Park

El Turquillo

Ojo Feliz

La Cueva

Buena Vista

Ute Park

SANGRE DE CRISTO MOUNTAINS

Nambé

Nambé Pueblo

Pojoaque

White Rock

Tesuque Pueblo

Camel Rock

Santa Fe Ski Area

Hyde Memorial State Park

SANTA FE

Agua Fria

La Cienega

Santa Fe Downs

Glorieta

Glorieta Battlefield Site

Pecos

Pecos National Historic Park

Rowe

Ruins of San Marcos Pueblo

Lamy

San Cristóbal Ruins

San José

San Miguel

Villanueva State Park

Villanueva

White Lakes

Stanley

Clines Corners

Sapello

El Porvenir

Montezuma

Storrie Lake State Park

Las Vegas

Tecolote

Bernal

Los Montoyas

Apache Springs

Aurupa Ruins

To Raton

To Tucumcari

N
W   E
S

Santo Domingo Pueblo

are frequently invited into Indian homes to dine—and he volunteered a sober opinion about the prime issue among New Mexico's Pueblo tribes at that moment.

"We [Santa Clara] voted not to go into gambling," he said. "It brings in bad blood. And yes, it hurts the artists. Somebody spends $75 at the Pojoaque Pueblo slot machines, that's $75 they don't have to spend for our art."

But times and votes changed, wrenched by the mighty allure of crowded casinos—and more. In 2001, Santa Clara opened a casino and bowling center in nearby Española, joining Pojoaque and about a dozen other New Mexico tribes in building increasingly ambitious casinos, resorts, and even golf courses—Santa Clara's 18-hole course opened for play in 2002. As Santa Clara Gov. Denny Gutierrez succinctly explained, "Revenues from Santa Clara's enterprises will provide resources to revive our culture and language with our children and will allow us to be self-sufficient."

Although one unfortunate effect of the legalization of Indian gaming in New Mexico in 1995 has been a proliferation of garish roadside architecture between Santa Fe and Taos, it is hard to argue with the goal of pueblo self-sufficiency and prosperity. So far, tribal artists seem to be thriving along with the casino operations, and there's a bit of poetic justice in Indian gaming operations taking away dollars from other Americans foolish enough to squander them at a casino.

You might still save on a lovely piece of pottery or jewelry by driving to the pueblos. There's not much artistry in the casinos, and the odds are a lot worse.

■ DURABLE COMMUNITY

The members of New Mexico's numerous Pueblo tribes are the descendants of the participants in the great Anasazi, Mogollon, Sinagua, Salado, and Hohokam migration that took place from about A.D. 1150 to 1450. These people, speaking different languages and coming from different cultural traditions, eventually proved able to live in harmony.

In his remarkable book *Anasazi America,* published in 2000, David E. Stuart, an anthropologist at the University of New Mexico, suggests that from the failed societies of their predecessors, the modern Puebloans learned a great lesson of history, "that survival means establishing a durable community. A durable community is one that balances growth with efficiency and refuses to be seduced by greed and power."

A tourist buys pottery from children at Tesuque Pueblo in 1939. (Library of Congress)

The durable community of pueblos from Santa Fe to Taos is held together in a council called Eight Northern Indian Pueblos. Many visitors from Santa Fe make the one-day trek out to the pueblos expecting to encounter exotic culture, architecture, and art. Some of them return in disappointment. It is difficult to have a conversation of any real depth with a Puebloan until you show a sincere interest in him or her—otherwise most talk will be about the weather. The architecture of the villages, with the exception of Taos, consists of low-roofed homes, usually of adobe or dreary U.S. Department of Housing and Urban Development design, arrayed more or less at random around a large bare-earth courtyard. Many areas are off-limits to the public.

Each pueblo has a scattering of small shops, many of them in peoples' homes, where everything from bolo ties to excellent jewelry and pottery might be sold. It helps, if you're a prospective buyer, to know the subject. "My son makes all these," a very elderly shopkeeper in Taos Pueblo once told me, pointing to a collection of strikingly contemporary necklaces of steel. Then, *sotto voce,* she added, "You have to watch out. Some people around here get their Indian jewelry from factories."

(opposite) Katsina dolls, the one in this case made from a corncob by Barbara Howard, are a much sought-after Indian art form. (above) Indian pots and textiles are also in great demand.

Were it not for the arts, particularly pottery, the pueblos might be less interesting to visit than they are. Each pueblo has developed a distinctive pottery style: glossy black vases for Santa Clara, undecorated micaceous ceramics for Taos, and so on. But there has been so much innovation and cross-fertilization that today it is hard to identify some pieces with certainty. This is one instance, however, when it seems safe to say that tourists and their expectations have influenced native art for the better. The pottery may no longer be functional—nobody buys a $1,000 San Ildefonso jug to pour Beaujolais from it—but the architecture, the intricacy of the painting, the imagination, and the excellence of the designs far surpass that of the pottery being made a century or more ago.

And pottery, unlike pueblo artists' painting, silver jewelry, and sculpture, is the one art that forms a historical thread through the culture. Today's revival, as Stephen Trimble observes in his book *Talking with the Clay,* "is a quiet statement of the worth of the past, of the importance of cultural values." With my modest Jémez bowl, I feel as though I have bought a share in those values.

■ VISITING THE PUEBLOS

The pueblos north of Santa Fe are for the most part strung along a highway traversing magnificent open country—the Jémez Mountains visible to the west, the Sangre de Cristos to the north and east, and a vast, infinitely variable sky overhead. The novelist Willa Cather once wrote of the sky here: "Elsewhere the sky is the roof of the world; but here the earth was the floor of the sky."

If possible, plan your visit to a pueblo for a feast day or dance day; the action will be infinitely more rewarding than wandering around an all-but-deserted plaza.

■ TESUQUE
[*Te Tsu Geh:* Village of the Narrow Place of Cottonwood Trees]

Tesuque's original Tewa name as pronounced by its inhabitants 300 years ago meant "a spotted dry place," an apt description of a creek here that disappears in the sand and periodically emerges in spots. Spanish settlers mispronounced the original Tewa name, and this bungled word was retranslated years later as "cottonwood tree place." In Spanish and English, Tesuque applies to the region around the pueblo.

Tesuque has restored its vast central plaza to its 19th-century configuration and is reviving its agricultural traditions such as organic farming. In the past wary of tourism, the tiny village now is reaching out to visitors with a casino, a flea market, and even a campground. Artists sell their works directly out of their homes. Tribal lands include some intriguing scenery, including Camel Rock—which looks quite like that animal—and "the badlands," striated rock formations set against the backdrop of the Jémez and Sangre de Cristo Mountains. *Off U.S. 285/84, 9 miles north of Santa Fe; 505-983-2667. Photography and video recording prohibited.*

■ POJOAQUE
[*P'o Suwae Geh:* Place to Drink Water]

Most of Pojoaque's original inhabitants died of smallpox imported by the Spanish, and those who survived moved away. Pojoaque was completely abandoned, a ghost pueblo, in the first part of the 20th century, but you'd never know it today. Immense, dazzling signs visible for miles in each direction promise:

POJOAQUE CASINO, MILLIONS WON MONTHLY

Pueblo Etiquette

Each pueblo in the Santa Fe–Taos region celebrates an annual feast day, a remarkable tradition that includes copious food and ceremonial dancing to the accompaniment of drums, rattles, and bells.

Although each celebration honors the Catholic saint for whom the conquistadors named the village, ancient indigenous seasonal ceremonies and rites underlie these festivities. Tribe members will frequently invite non-Indian visitors into their homes to share their meal, although this practice may be endangered because of its expense to the pueblo families and the occasional boorishness of the guests. Some ceremonial events are closed to visitors.

The best single source of information is the Eight Northern Indian Pueblos Council (505-747-1593). The Santa Fe Convention and Visitors Bureau's annual guide to the Eight Northern Indian Pueblos is available free.

There are several rules of etiquette for visiting the pueblos, some of which may be culturally foreign to non-Indian visitors. These apply *at all times,* not just on feast days.

Rules regarding photographing pueblo buildings or ceremonies vary. Before you snap, ask at the pueblo governor's office or visitors center. Some pueblos levy a fee, and video cameras may be prohibited, or the fee assessed may be higher than that for still cameras. Never photograph an individual or private property without asking permission.

Don't talk or move around during dances or other ceremonies. Turn off your cell phone, don't applaud, and don't ask for an explanation of the ceremony. Vernon Lujan of Taos Pueblo told the *Santa Fe New Mexican* that he sometimes responds to requests for explanations by saying, "If I tell you, I'll have to kill you." He's only kidding—but it gets visitors' attention. Most Puebloans simply ignore the requests.

On feast days, don't ask to come into a home for a meal, but graciously accept the invitation if one is offered. The Official Visitors' Guide to the Eight Northern Pueblos advises: "Thank your host, but a payment or tip is not appropriate."

Never enter a pueblo kiva or graveyard.

Never bring pets, firearms, alcohol, or illegal drugs into a pueblo.

Finally, call before traveling to a pueblo to make certain it's open. Some ceremonial days are closed to outsiders.

Nambé Pueblo snuggles in a green level valley with vistas of the Sangre de Cristo Mountains.

The alleged millionaires and the Pojoaqueans may appreciate the signage; New Mexicans who cherish the Rio Grande Valley's scenery aren't so sure. The garish Pojoaque advertisements look straight out of Vegas.

More is to come. The former ghost pueblo runs the 40,000-square-foot "Cities of Gold" casino with a 1,000-square-foot bingo hall, a video game hall, a Homewood Suites Hotel, and a golf course. Plans are under way for an even bigger luxury spread, to be called Buffalo Thunder Resort; Hilton is opening this property in early 2009. Of all the pueblos, Pojoaque most assiduously welcomes visitors. *Off U.S. 285, 15 miles north of Santa Fe; 505-455-3334.*

■ NAMBÉ

[*Nambé:* Mound of Earth in the Corner]

This tiny pueblo with about 600 residents has perhaps the most beautiful setting of any along this route, snuggling in a green, level valley with panoramic vistas of the Sangre de Cristos. First inhabited about A.D. 1300, it contained about 200 structures when the Spanish arrived. About 10 percent of these buildings remain.

The mountains behind Nambé, Nambé Falls, and Nambé Lake provide excellent opportunities for fishing, sightseeing, camping, and hiking. Tribal permits and fees are required for all recreation. Because of the elevation, the site is closed from December to February. An especially colorful day to visit the pueblo would be the Fourth of July, when the Nambé Waterfall Ceremonial takes place at the foot of the falls. *From Santa Fe take U.S. 285 north 15 miles, turn east on N.M. 503, continue 3 miles to the sign at Nambé Falls, then 2 miles north to the entrance; 505-455-4444.*

■ SAN ILDEFONSO
[*Po Woh Ge Oweenge:* Where Water Cuts Down Through]

San Ildefonso is an excellent place to learn about pottery. Though the pueblo's population is only about 700, most families here are involved in making pottery, and many of the artists are descendants of New Mexico's most famous potter, María Martínez, and her husband, Julian. Both were producing pottery in the traditional polychrome style of San Ildefonso before 1918, when Julian developed his famous black-on-black style, in which a shiny background contrasts with a matte-

Festivities at San Ildefonso Pueblo are colorful events that may be viewed by visitors.

black finish. Because María and Julian began signing their pieces early, at a time when this was not common, their remarkable careers can be traced by collectors.

María's sisters—Maximiliana, Desideria, and Juanita—also worked in pottery, as did Clara, the youngest, who did most of the polishing. Santana and Adam Martínez, Maria Poveka, and Juanita's daughter, Carmelita Dunlap, also played key roles in the development of San Ildefonso pottery.

The small San Ildefonso Pueblo Museum sits next to the mission church, which was rebuilt in 1968. (Most of the village buildings are new or reconstructed.) To the village's north lies the natural tabletop fortress of Black Mesa, where in 1694 Pueblo Indians attempted to defend themselves against the Spanish reconquest. *From Santa Fe take U.S. 285 north 15 miles, turn west at N.M. 502. Continue 6 miles to the entrance; 505-455-3549.*

■ **SANTA CLARA**
[*Kha P'o:* Spring Water]

This pueblo is also known for its pottery, in particular that of the Gutiérrez and Tafoya families. According to Margaret and Luther Gutiérrez, pottery-making was passed down through the generations, from their great-great-grandfather, Ta-Key-Sane, who made kitchen utensils for everyday use, to their great-grandfather, who added colors and began making pottery in different sizes. When Margaret and Luther's father, Van, was young, his grandfather would take him into the hills to hunt game and to look for different colored clays, flowers, and roots for paints that would turn into different colors when they were fired. Van and his wife, Lela, were famous for their impressed bear-paw designs on black, polished pots and for their polychrome pots with geometric designs. The Tafoya family's black carved bowls, polished inside and out, have an almost contemporary appeal.

The other compelling attractions here traditionally have been the nearby Puye Cliff Dwellings and Santa Clara Canyon, a recreation area with four lakes, a stream, and canopies of pine, spruce, and aspen. Unfortunately, the devastating Cerro Grande fire of 2000 forced the tribe to close both areas indefinitely. *From Santa Fe take U.S. 285 north to Española. At the second turnoff head west on N.M. 502 across the Rio Grande, then at N.M. 30 travel west 1.3 miles; 505-753-7326.*

A Zuni blanket weaver, ca. 1900. (Library of Congress)

■ OHKAY OHWINGEH

[*Ohkay:* We Are Brothers]

Elements of about 100 homes dating from A.D. 1200 still stand here. In olden times the pueblo's residents practiced dry farming, growing melons, cotton, and corn east of the village.

San Juan Pueblo was Spanish New Mexico's first capital, established by Juan de Oñate in 1598 and named by him San Juan de Los Caballeros ("Gentlemen"). In 2006 the tribe took back its original name, Ohkay Ohwingeh. To their later detriment, the San Juans gave the Spaniards a warm welcome—one of Oñate's friars, according to historian Marc Simmons, "remarked that they were the best infidel people he had ever seen." They certainly were patient. It wasn't until 82 years later that the San Juan medicine man, Popé, led the Pueblo Revolt that drove the Spaniards out of the country.

The pueblo contains one unique curiosity, a New England Gothic–style church that was built in 1899 to replace a crumbling adobe church. The pueblo operates an enormous gaming facility on the highway. *From Santa Fe take U.S. 285 to Española. Continue north along N.M. 68, and turn west on N.M. 74. The entrance is 1 mile past the San Juan Pueblo sign; 505-747-1593.*

■ PICURÍS

[*Picurís:* Those Who Paint]

Once one of northern New Mexico's largest pueblos, with a six-story building rivaling Taos Pueblo's and a population of more than 3,000, Picurís these days is isolated, with only about 250 residents. Exhibits at the pueblo's museum outline the village's history—recent archaeological excavations have unearthed several kivas and storage units more than 700 years old. Like the Taoseños, the people of Picurís make sparkling micaceous pottery. They also own and operate the Hotel Santa Fe in Santa Fe. *From Santa Fe take U.S. 285 north 41 miles (17 miles northeast of Española) to junction with N.M. 75. Turn right and continue 13 miles; 505-587-2519.*

(top) Two people cleaning wheat, 1905, at San Juan Pueblo. (bottom) Zuni woman making bread, 1903. Both photographs by Edward S. Curtis. (Library of Congress)

FEAST DAYS AND DANCES

Call ahead to verify dates and ask for precise directions.

Nambé
Feast day: October 4; Nambé Falls Celebration, July 4. *North and east of Santa Fe off N.M. 503; 505-455-4444.*

Ohkay Owingeh
Feast day: June 24. Deer dance in February. Footraces and arts-and-crafts show in July. *Just north of Española on N.M. 68; 505-747-1593.*

Picurís
Feast day: August 9; dances in February; sunset dance in August. *Northeast of Española off N.M. 75; 505-587-2519.*

Pojoaque
Feast day: December 12. *15 miles north of Santa Fe off U.S. 285; 505-455-3334.*

San Ildefonso
Feast day: January 23. Corn dance in June. *North and west of Santa Fe on N.M. 502; 505-455-3549.*

Santa Clara
Feast day: August 12. Various dances in February and June. *Just west of Española off N.M. 30; 505-753-7326.*

Taos
Feast Day: September 30. Los Comanches dance, February; footraces in May, corn dance in June. *2 miles north of Taos; 505-758-1028.*

Tesuque
Feast Day: November 12. Corn dance in June and July. *9 miles north of Santa Fe on U.S. 285; 505-983-2667.*

(opposite) The Deer Dance is performed at San Juan Pueblo every February.

Taos Pueblo.

◼ TAOS
[*Tua Tah:* Red Willow Place]

Taos Pueblo is the northernmost pueblo, the most famous in literature and art, and architecturally the most ambitious. "It is the extraordinary cellular living and storage units at Taos which most excite the visitor," wrote G. E. Kidder Smith in *The Architecture of the United States:* "the piling of cube on cube coalescing with the splendor of abstract geometry to produce a scale buildup that echoes the hills."

More poetically, the architectural historian Vincent Scully wrote that the pueblo's "syncopated masses clearly dance before the mountain's face. They are active themselves. At the same time, seen from the west, North House rises straight into the sky, and the step-backs of its south face shape the typical Pueblo sky-altar, abstracting the shapes of the clouds. The building is once again the god of sky and mountain alike, no less wholly embodied in it than at Teotihuacán."

The two paeans above might be mere prattle or may truly convey the symbolic meaning of Taos Pueblo's astounding architecture. It's hard to tell. Pueblo life, society, architecture, art, ceremony, and spirituality are so tightly intertwined that—well, the best explanation I have seen is: "Outsiders will never get it."

Whatever Taos Pueblo *means*, it is an achievement by any human standard. The pueblo probably first arose in the 1300s, but what we see today, contrary to popular legend, dates mostly from a reconstruction following the Pueblo Revolt of 1680. This hardly matters. Constructing a five-story apartment building out of mud and straw and maintaining it for several hundred years is no mean feat.

Very few Taoseños live in their ancestral home these days—there are no phones, electricity, or water; most live in modern houses scattered around their reservation. The pueblo is divided into north and south villages with a plaza between them. Walk around the edge of the plaza—walking across it is not considered polite.

Most of the ground-floor apartments have metamorphosed into shops, and *hornos*—outdoor adobe beehive fireplaces—have sprouted around them to produce hot bread for the tourists. Taos Pueblo is not an Indian Disneyland, but it does have that potential—and, increasingly, that inclination. It is the only one of the Eight Northern Pueblos that charges admission (a substantial $10 per person), with additional fees for photographing or sketching. The pueblo traditionally closes to the public for 8 to 12 weeks from February through April and for 10 days from late August to early September. *Off N.M. 68, 2 miles north of the town of Taos; 505-758-1028.*

SIDE TRIPS FROM SANTA FE

The roadside stand was a riot of color—crimson *ristras* of dried chiles, some woven into wreaths; green and orange gourds; bushel baskets of green and red apples; drapes of ornamental corn in red, white, black, yellow. I had been curious about the sign on N.M. 68 for Sopyn's Fruit Stand, between Santa Fe and Taos. It was near the heart of Spanish colonial New Mexico, yet the name on the stand hardly sounded Hispanic.

"I'm Ukrainian," said the proprietor, Anna Sopyn, a compact woman with swirling white hair, gold-capped teeth, a face wizened and bronzed by long days in the New Mexico sun. She held out her hands, proudly displaying thick, strong fingers, two of them sporting bandages. "See, I'm working all the time."

Anna escaped from the Soviet Union in 1942 at the height of what that nation called the Great Patriotic War. She landed in New Mexico in 1950 and has not

Anna Sopyn poses outside her fruit stand, one of the many roadside stands worth visiting along the highways of northern New Mexico.

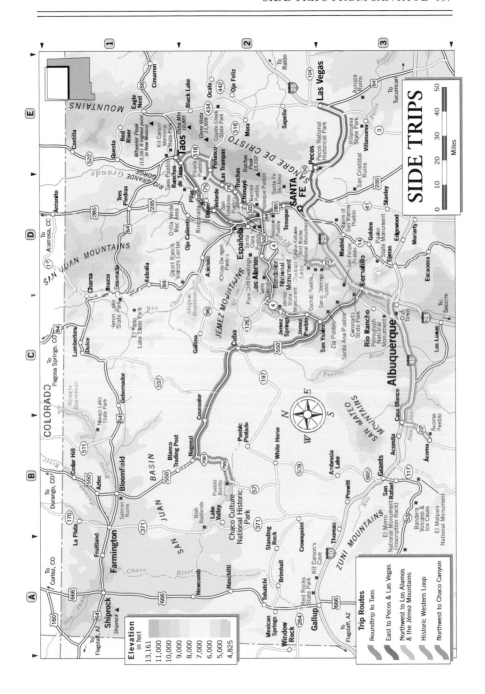

SIDE TRIPS

Miles

Elevation
in feet

13,161
11,000
10,000
9,000
8,000
7,000
6,000
5,000
4,825

Trip Routes

Roundtrip to Taos

East to Pecos & Las Vegas

Northwest to Los Alamos & the Jémez Mountains

Historic Western Loop

Northwest to Chaco Canyon

budged since. She tried farming, eventually opening a stand selling apples and her ornamental arrangements of chiles and corn. We talked for half an hour, partly in her still-fractured English, partly in my nearly defunct Russian. She said she has had a good life in New Mexico. She did not miss or cherish her homeland. "They don't eat, they have nothing," she said, before pausing and smiling. "America is very good."

The chance to meet people like Anna Sopyn is but one reason why you should consider spending time beyond Santa Fe's rarefied world of museums and galleries and restaurants. Within a 130-mile radius of the capital city, you can enjoy at least a week's worth of fascinating one-day excursions through awesome mountain scenery, spooky canyons, prehistoric ruins, and modern pueblos. You'll come across unique and quirky art galleries, often with far lower prices than their counterparts in Santa Fe, and perhaps best of all, you'll experience roadside encounters like the one I had at Sopyn's Fruit Stand. Something about northern New Mexico nourishes creativity and encourages people to reinvent themselves, and they always seem willing to talk about their lives.

I recommend five discovery trips from Santa Fe:

1. North along the main roads (U.S. 84/285 and N.M. 68) to Taos and back along the "High Road" through Truchas and Chimayó.
2. East to Pecos and Las Vegas.
3. Northwest to Los Alamos and the Jémez Mountains.
4. Southwest to Tent Rocks, Albuquerque, and Ácoma.
5. Northwest to Chaco Canyon.

Each of these trips can be done in a day, though the loop to Taos works best if you stay over in one of the towns for a night or two. The expedition to Chaco Canyon makes for a *long* day trip.

Everywhere you go you should invest in some conversation in order to begin to understand the culture of this land, which seems to welcome anyone and any enterprise—the potters of Ácoma; the eighth-generation weavers of Chimayó; the denizens of the solar- and wind-powered Earthship "biotecture," west of Taos; the nude bathers at Spence Hot Springs—and even the creators of atomic weapons. Anything can and does happen in northern New Mexico.

■ ROADS TO TAOS AND BACK

It must be something in the piñon-scented air: New Mexico's most intriguing people and enterprises have congregated along the two routes linking Santa Fe and Taos. They have been doing so for more than three centuries.

This was the farm and ranch country of New Spain. An ancient New Mexican hymn describes the intimate relationship of these people to their land:

> De la tierra fui formado,
> La tierra me da de comer;
> La tierra me ha sostenado;
> Y al fin yo tierra he de ser.

> (From the earth I was made,
> And the earth shall feed me;
> The earth has sustained me;
> And in the end I shall be earth also.)

The quicker route of U.S. 84/285 to N.M. 68 mostly parallels the Rio Grande. The so-called High Road, N.M. 76 to N.M. 518 (to get to N.M. 76, take U.S. 84/285 north to N.M. 503 and head east), winds through the scenic passes of the Carson National Forest and takes you past several delightful little towns, including Las Trampas, Truchas, and Chimayó. A good strategy: do both. Take the Rio Grande route to Taos and return via the High Road.

■ TESUQUE

For the first 20 miles north of Santa Fe, U.S. 84/285 is a four-lane highway that winds and climbs through a wide valley between the Jémez and Sangre de Cristo ranges. The hilly piñon-juniper forests thicken; wealthy Santa Feans' homes peek discreetly—though sometimes flagrantly—out of the low forest canopy. You pass the famous Santa Fe Opera, almost invisible on the west side, and its neighbor, the Tesuque Pueblo Flea Market, which may be the world's ritziest swap meet. Soon afterward come the bustling casinos and roadside businesses both enchanting and strange.

The **Tesuque Village Market,** a deli, wine shop, bakery, sundry store, and café a short detour off U.S. 285 at the Tesuque exit, is a good place to stock up on provisions. Locals come here to savor a good cup of coffee and read the *New York Times*.

■ VELARDE

The next important stop heading north is Velarde and the **Valdez Fruit Stand** (N.M. 68). Running a fruit stand doesn't begin to describe what Herman and Loretta Valdez have done here. Thirty years ago, Loretta quit her secretarial job to raise her children, but she began to miss contact with adults. Herman, her husband, suggested they open a fruit stand to sell produce from their orchard. They did, and it was a success.

A few years later, a line in Helen Hunt Jackson's romantic Victorian-era novel *Ramona* inspired her. The protagonist, Alessandro, left an ear of corn or a gourd at Ramona's window to suggest a liaison. Loretta began weaving gourds, ears of ornamental corn, chiles, garlic, wild grasses, and even pinecones into astoundingly elaborate and beautiful organic sculptures. Under her direction, a large staff now produces the pieces, which are shipped all over the world. They sell for $5 to $5,000. "I don't have any training in designing," she says. "The Man Upstairs just uses my head."

■ DIXON

Just a few miles east of N.M. 68 via N.M. 75, diminutive Dixon has developed a burgeoning arts scene that you'd expect of a town many times larger. A studio tour is held here the first weekend in November, and there's an excellent cooperative gallery attached to **Métier Weaving Shop,** which shows works by some few dozen local artisans.

■ TAOS AND THE RIO GRANDE GORGE

Continuing north on N.M. 68, the road winds through the mountain-rimmed valley where by 1615 Spanish farmers were setting up haciendas. Today, this is unzoned desert land, both beautiful and somewhat disconcerting in its haphazard development. At the settlement of **Ranchos de Taos,** the road passes the mission church of San Francisco de Asís, made famous by the paintings of Georgia O'Keeffe and the photography of Ansel Adams.

Four miles farther lies **Taos** (see the "TOWN OF TAOS" chapter for a full description), with its funky but comfortable plaza, winding streets, and adobe homes. **Taos Pueblo** (see the "EIGHT NORTHERN PUEBLOS" chapter), 2 miles

(preceding pages) A cemetery along N.M. 68 near Embudo.

The Rio Grande Gorge Bridge—don't look down if you're afraid of heights.

north of Taos, is one of the oldest continuously occupied settlements in North America.

For a fascinating detour, drive northwest of Taos on U.S. 64 to the **Rio Grande Gorge.** The valley flatlands, tinted blue-green with stubbly sage and chamisa, suddenly yawn into a black gash 650 feet deep, announced only by a standard highway sign. The Rio Grande Gorge Bridge, a spidery contrivance spanning the chasm, is the second-highest bridge in the U.S. highway system—people with severe acrophobia might want to avoid it.

I decide to walk across the pedestrian lane of the bridge—you'd be loony to drive and gawk. The approach bristles with barbed wire and warning signs in English and Spanish to keep thrill seekers away from the gorge's lip; of course, the fence has been breached in half a dozen places.

On the bridge, a woolly, tentative morning light probes the gorge, softening its sharp angles. Then a medium-duty truck rumbles across, triggering a tremor that persists well after the truck has departed, like a cathedral organ's reverberation. The experience is thrilling, yet unnerving. To challenge this abyss was a feat of civil engineering, but an atavistic nag at the back of my brain wonders at the hubris of it all. Do we really have any business plodding across a log 650 feet above a river?

West of the gorge, watch for the **Greater World Earthship Subdivision** about 1.5 miles farther on your right. This community consists of 30 or so solar- and wind-powered dwellings whose walls are made out of recycled tires stuffed with dirt. The houses catch and reuse all their own water—a big accomplishment in a desert that receives 12 inches of rain in a good year. You can take a tour, book an Earthship for the night, or buy a lot and build one.

The subdivision represents yet another example of New Mexico's wacky dissonance: laudable ecology, architectural blight. The Earthships look like ruined insect hives from the planet Mongo.

For a descent into some quiet natural beauty, continue just beyond Milepost 242 and look for telephone poles on the left. Turn left onto a good, hard-packed dirt road and follow it for 11 miles into the gorge, where another bridge crosses at river level. The **Orilla Verde Recreation Area** begins here with an easy 2.5-mile

For sale or rent: Nautilus model Earthship with mountain view; living room, dining room, kitchen; two kiva fireplaces, no TV, no phone; solar-powered, earth-friendly, sleeps four.

hike on La Vista Verde Trail, which passes by many prehistoric petroglyphs. Wildlife—waterfowl, beaver, cougar, ringtails, and much more—is abundant on the gorge floor.

Beyond here, the gorge gradually widens into a canyon, the road paralleling the slow-moving river lined with salt cedar. The federal Bureau of Land Management has established several picnic grounds and campsites along the riverbank; fees must be paid at the visitors station at Orilla Verde campground. The fishing here is good, with rainbow and German brown trout the customary prizes. Swimming is not recommended because of the shifting currents (and the water's cold). It's possible to return to Santa Fe by continuing farther; the dirt road runs into N.M. 68 at Pilar.

Most travelers return to Santa Fe from Taos on the **High Road,** a route that's a scenic and cultural adventure if you maintain a lazy pace. Because the roads interweave, it's wise to keep a highway map on hand. Take N.M. 68 south of Taos to N.M. 518 and follow signs to Las Trampas and N.M. 76.

During one High Road excursion, my wife and I experienced the adrenaline boost of a lifetime at **Osha Canyon** (off N.M. 518), which we had decided to explore. A few hundred feet down the trail, near a sparkling mountain stream, we heard a vivid baritone snort and gurgle. Staring into the ponderosa forest gloom, we saw nothing, but the vocal signature of a black bear was obvious. Exploration hastily terminated.

A ranger in the Carson National Forest later told us that it had been a dry year, so bears had been trundling down to lower elevations in search of forage. She had not heard of any violent encounters.

■ LAS TRAMPAS

About 25 miles south of Taos on N.M. 76 lies tiny, pastoral Las Trampas, founded in 1751 by a colony of 12 families from Santa Fe. There's little commerce in the village, whose prime attraction is the church of San José de Gracia, built circa 1760–1776. The beautifully restored mission has broad adobe shoulders capped with delicate wooden pyramids with crosses, almost suggesting the steeple on a New England church, though in Roman Catholic rather than Protestant dress. The church is open to visitors from June to August. Interesting modern santos, carved in juniper and aspen by local artists, are sold at La Tiendita, a store across the parking lot from the church.

■ TRUCHAS

At first view—from an overlook along the highway—Truchas appears to float across a grassy valley below the snow-capped Truchas Peak, a spectacular mountain soaring up to 13,101 feet. The village was founded in 1749 and changed little until the late 20th century. Many generations of residents made a living by small-scale farming, and even today the village's main street retains the air of an isolated Mexican village snoring away the centuries.

Truchas's isolation ended dramatically, though, when Robert Redford brought a crew to film *The Milagro Beanfield War* in 1986. All the celebrities and commotion put the town on the map. Since then, some gift shops, galleries, and B&Bs have opened. Ray Tafoya, whose family has owned the Truchas General Store for more than 60 years, said strangers still come to see the town and ask about the movie.

"Pretty good movie, huh?" Tafoya remarked. I mumbled agreement even though I hadn't seen it. Weeks later I rented the tape. It's a *spectacularly* bad movie, with little of the humor and humanity that filled the John Nichols book on which it was based. Moreover, it shows little of Truchas—Redford and company built sets outside the town rather than using existing buildings.

Like most of the little towns within the orbit of Taos and Santa Fe, Truchas is in the throes of enormous cultural change. Artists fleeing the high cost of living in

(opposite) Harry Córdova at work on his textiles in Truchas. (above) Truchas lies in a verdant valley of the Sangre de Cristo Mountains.

EURALIA VIGIL:
THE TEACHER AND HER APPLES

"When we were growing up here," says Euralia Vigil, "we would never go to dances or the movies like the other kids, because we were always working. My mother would say, 'Don't worry—when they grow up they won't know how to do anything, and you will.'"

Mother's wisdom was profound. Euralia, now 74, farms a 12-acre orchard in Chimayó, 40 miles north of Santa Fe, selling her apples, jellies, pies, and chile powder at farmers' markets in Santa Fe and Los Alamos. She also has a master's degree in education; she taught school for 33 years. Her six surviving brothers and sisters also are or were teachers, and they know ranching or farming as well.

Their father, Severo Martínez, had three months of schooling. Their mother, Julianita, had none; she never even learned to read. But both were determined that their children not only would get college degrees, but would use their degrees to give future generations the education they had never had.

When Euralia was born in 1928, Chimayó was an isolated Hispanic farming community without a school, without any connections, really, to contemporary America. When Euralia started school she spoke no English, and she was not taught it in today's gentle, politically correct manner. "The teachers would hit us for speaking Spanish," she recalls. "It was a very bad way to teach."

There were 13 Martínez children, but a diphtheria epidemic took five of them. There was no doctor in Chimayó. "My father tried to take the children on the wagon to Española [10 miles away], but they wouldn't make it—they would die on the way. Two of my sisters died on the same day."

The survivors went to a private boarding school in Albuquerque because there was no bus to ferry them back and forth to the public school in Española. There wasn't enough money for tuition, so Severo paid the school in apples. "We were poor," Euralia says, "but in a sense we were also rich, because we always had everything we needed. We had close to 100 acres, and we grew everything. Apples, corn, chile, sugarcane, wheat. We had horses, cows, pigs. We never had to buy anything. And we knew how to work! The young kids do not know how to work nowadays."

Not the kind of work that matters most to her, anyway. The old ways are evaporating. "The families give their orchards to their children, and the children just let the trees die," she says. "They get work in Los Alamos—some get good jobs at the lab, others are cooks and janitors. But they're not interested in farming."

Her love for the land is profound. "Even when I was teaching, I always had a garden. The land is life to me. It is a lot of work, but work is also life to me."

It still seems a hard life. In a good year Euralia can make $1,000 a week selling produce at the farmers' markets alone. In a bad year a late freeze kills all the apple buds and she has nothing. No sign of frustration clouds her explanation. "You just have to be patient and do it all over again."

She is a short, sturdy woman, her square-cornered face weathered and arroyoed by decades in the New Mexico sun. She wears a farmer's fashions: jeans, heavy plaid shirt, a trace of earth under her nails. The rural home she shares with her husband, Victor Vigil, is small and warm and immaculate. The living room is choked with flower-print pillows and green plants and pictures of her extended family—two daughters, two grandchildren, dozens of nieces and nephews and in-laws.

Nearly all are college graduates; most are teachers.

"It's a happy life," Euralia Vigil says, "because I know I have done my part."

Santa Fe have settled here, as have immigrants from around the country who have been charmed by Truchas's pastoral quietude and scenery.

Nearly all the newcomers are Anglo; nearly all the natives are Hispanic. I talked to an aging hippie who came to Truchas 25 years ago. "I stuck it out, and I'm finally accepted as a native," she said. "But for a long time they were terrified of us. I raised two kids here, and there was a lot of hostility toward them."

Weaver Harry Córdova brooks no hostility, but he's not thrilled with the way the town is changing. "People move out of the city because they want to live here in the country," he says. "But then they think somehow their quality of life has gone down, and they want to bring all the things from the city with them. Suddenly septic tanks aren't good enough, and we've got to incorporate, and all that."

The **Córdovas' Handweaving Workshop** is one of two essential stops in Truchas. Harry and his father, Alfredo Córdova, produce beautiful custom-woven rugs and sell them much too cheaply. Harry is cheerful and always willing to take a few minutes away from the loom to talk about his family's work.

The other important stop is Bill Franke's **Hand Artes Gallery,** one of northern New Mexico's most interesting and eclectic galleries. Franke sells furniture, folk art, fine art, religious art, Hispanic art, and provocative art, such as a painting of the Virgin Mary holding a live bullet.

Santuario de Chimayó.

■ CHIMAYÓ

From Truchas, the High Road descends into the drier and warmer piñon–juniper scrubland of the Chimayó Valley. Of all the villages strung along the High Road, Chimayó is the most interesting. It has a venerated family of weavers that has maintained its business for eight generations; a historic and (according to believers) miraculous chapel; and a famous restaurant, Restaurante Rancho de Chimayó.

Before the Spanish town was founded around 1700, there was a Tewa-speaking pueblo in this fertile valley. According to Indian legend, a pool here, perhaps a hot spring, held water or mud with healing properties.

The present **Santuario de Chimayó** may have inherited that very site. Archaeologically interesting remnants have been found here, and some historical accounts have the chapel's interior smelling of an "earthen dampness," rather than dry earth and dust.

More mystery swirls about the chapel's origins. On the night of Good Friday in 1810, says another legend, a Chimayó settler named Bernardo Abeyta was performing the customary penances of the Society of Penitentes when he saw a bright light shining from a hole in the ground near the Santa Cruz River. He walked over and picked up, incredibly, a crucifix of the Black Christ, similar to that in the Cathedral of Esquípulas in Guatemala—a shrine 2,000 miles away that was believed to have miraculous powers to heal the sick.

As the story goes, the crucifix was taken to the church in nearby Santa Cruz, but would not remain there. Twice it returned—of its own accord—to the place where it had been found.

Abeyta got the message: he petitioned the priest in charge of New Mexico missions for permission to build a private shrine on the site. Completed in 1816, the Santuario remained in the Abeyta family until 1929, when it was turned over to the Archdiocese of Santa Fe.

Each year, more than 300,000 people visit the Santuario, which is sometimes called "the Lourdes of America." Some visitors come out of curiosity, some to relish its architectural beauty, and many because they believe in its curative powers. During Holy Week, more than 50,000 believers undertake a pilgrimage to Chimayó. Some struggle to carry heavy wooden crosses.

The secular miracle of Chimayó is its chile, usually dried and ground into powder. Nowhere else in the country, or probably in the world, does the chile attain such a beautiful balance of fire and flavor. Several markets in Chimayó sell bags of ground chile; one near the Santuario opportunistically markets it as "holy chile." Holy or hellish, to preserve the flavor store it in an airtight container when you get home.

(above) The Easter pilgrimage to Santuario de Chimayó attracts thousands of worshipers every year. (following pages) A kiva at Pecos National Historical Park.

■ EAST TO PECOS AND LAS VEGAS

The great Sangre de Cristo range yields to the Great Plains on this 130-mile (round-trip) excursion that passes through a pueblo and a small city with a fine collection of Victorian architecture. To get to the first stop, head east from Santa Fe on I-25 to N.M. 63.

■ PECOS NATIONAL HISTORICAL PARK

Pecos Pueblo, now a national park, was founded sometime around A.D. 1300. The Pecos River is close at hand, and the location was on the very edge of the Pueblo world, bordering the territory of the nomadic Plains Indians—which made it a crossroads for trade. Rings made by tepees set up for extended swap meets are still visible in the area.

The Pecos traders must have been nervous, however. Over time the settlement took on the look of a fortress, with a high perimeter wall and a five-story pueblo with no outside doors or windows. An invader would have had to drop through a roof hatch into a darkened room, where he could reasonably expect to be greeted with a spearhead or hatchet.

The first conquistadors appeared at Pecos in 1590. They were not welcomed, so they decided to seize the pueblo by force. Pecos had 500 determined defenders, but it did not have rifles and cannon.

In 1598, Juan de Oñate, the leader of the Spanish settlers in the area, assigned a missionary to attend to the surly Pecosans, but he had scant success in seeding the Gospel among them. In 1621 a more experienced friar, Andrés Juárez, arrived and supervised the building of a mammoth mission church, **Nuestra Señora de los Ángeles.** The ruins visible today are not of this church, but of a smaller replacement finished in 1717. The original was destroyed, along with the local priest, in the Pueblo Revolt of 1680.

After Spanish rule resumed, Pecos slid into a slow decline. By the 1830s, it had become a ghost pueblo, the victim of Comanche attacks, European-introduced diseases, and its abandonment by residents hoping for a life elsewhere, principally Jémez Pueblo, 80 miles to the west.

Only the pueblo's low walls remain. One kiva has been reconstructed and the adobe shell of Fray Juárez's church still stands. The arches on either side of the chancel are very rare in New Mexican missions.

■ LAS VEGAS

Las Vegas, 45 miles east of Pecos on I-25, was New Mexico's territorial capital—for a day or so. When Gen. Stephen Watts Kearny marched into New Mexico in 1846 to claim it as a U.S. territory, he did so from a rooftop in this little Mexican village. The crowd that assembled in the plaza to hear Kearny must have been perplexed, for though he promised to respect their religion and property rights and said he would protect them from Apache raids, he warned, "He who promises to be quiet, and is found in arms against me, I will hang."

When the first train steamed into Las Vegas in 1879, the town boomed almost overnight, attracting not only merchants and entrepreneurs but also hustlers and hoodlums. The outlaw Billy the Kid slept here—in jail—and the gambler "Doc" Holliday briefly ran a dental practice before shooting a man and moving on to greater notoriety in Tombstone, Arizona. Law enforcement was so deficient that some Las Vegans eventually formed a vigilante committee, shooting suspected criminals or hanging them from a windmill in the plaza. As the 19th century came to a close, civilization began to catch up with Las Vegas. A state university opened in the 1890s, and by 1900, Victorian homes as stately and imposing as those in Albuquerque had been constructed in the now-prosperous town.

Downtown Las Vegas, New Mexico, has eclectic architecture and a comfortable Old West, small-town environment.

More than 900 buildings survive from the Victorian era, most of them on the National Register of Historic Places. The Citizens' Committee for Historic Preservation has assembled two self-guided walking tours, outlined in free brochures available at many downtown businesses. One tour surveys the **Douglas– Sixth Street and Railroad Avenue Historic District,** which is mainly commercial. The other takes in the residential **Library Park Historic District.** Don't miss the **Plaza Hotel** (230 Old Town Plaza), a three-story Italianate Victorian decorated with a curved or triangular pediment over every window. A grand broken pediment crowns the parapet. To the Victorian mind, excess was never wretched.

The **Old City Hall of 1892** (626 Sixth Street), is built in the Richardsonian Romanesque style and would look perfectly at home in Boston. Unlike Santa Fe, Las Vegas never tried to build on its Hispanic architectural heritage, but instead dressed itself in the popular styles of the East—a way of announcing that prosperity and American style had arrived in the territorial hinterlands.

Six miles north of Las Vegas on N.M. 65 is **Montezuma Castle,** an astonishing 1886 Victorian hotel restored and reopened in 2000 as centerpiece of the Armand Hammer United World College of the American West. Student-led tours (call 505-454-4200 for information) are conducted on many Saturday afternoons in summer.

■ Los Alamos and the Jémez Mountains

"Peace is still controversial in Los Alamos," reported the *Santa Fe New Mexican* in 1994. A coalition of 41,000 children from 50 states and 53 nations had proposed a "Peace Park" at the entrance to this town, birthplace of the atomic bomb. The Los Alamos city council rejected the idea, fearing that the park would become a magnet for protests against nuclear arms.

"Couldn't you just once let them [the children] be idealistic?" an adult supporter begged the council. A foe responded: "This is the kind of peace that ultimately sees nothing as worth dying for, nothing worth going to war over. This is a peace that expresses itself in a sentimental view about human nature. . . ."

The council voted no. There will be no Peace Park in Los Alamos, 35 miles northwest of Santa Fe, though you will find a provocative nuclear-energy museum with a very rich lode of history for a town founded during, and because of, World War II. Los Alamos is also a gateway to Bandelier National Monument and the Jémez Mountains, and the three destinations can add up to an edifying, if long, day trip from Santa Fe.

■ LOS ALAMOS

The genesis of Los Alamos was a letter from Albert Einstein to President Roosevelt in August 1939. The physicist wrote, "It may be possible to set up a nuclear chain reaction, by which vast amounts of power and large quantities of new radium-like elements would be generated . . . extremely powerful bombs of a new type may thus be constructed."

The race to create that chain reaction took place in Los Alamos. Until 1943, the town, on a 7,410-foot-high mesa northwest of Santa Fe, consisted of nothing more than a boarding school for boys. About halfway through World War II, the U.S. government condemned the school and created a top-secret company town to develop the bomb.

The site was the third choice. Maj. John H. Dudley, who was assigned the task of finding a place for the Manhattan Project, had first proposed a site in Utah, but it would have taken too much farmland out of production. Dudley then suggested Jémez Springs, 30 miles west of Los Alamos, but physicist J. Robert Oppenheimer vetoed it—Jémez Springs is in a canyon, and Oppenheimer wanted a place with expansive horizons for his team.

For the wartime families assigned to live in Los Alamos, though, the horizons were fiercely contained by security. They were forbidden to mention the name of the town in correspondence. When babies were born, birth certificates carried a post office box number rather than "Los Alamos." There were no in-laws, no jails, no poor, no idle rich, no sidewalks. The apartments hastily thrown up for the scientists and their families frequently caught fire from their primitive coal-heating stoves—a bit of a paradox in the nation's highest-tech town. The Los Alamos scientists referred to the weapon they were developing as "the gadget." Manhattan Project supervisor Gen. Leslie Groves referred to the scientists as "the greatest collection of crackpots ever assembled."

Los Alamos today remains a company town, and the majority of its 18,800 residents work at Los Alamos National Laboratory. The facility continues nuclear-weapons development, but has also branched into peacetime research in fields such as superconductivity.

Controversy continues, not surprisingly. One room of the **Bradbury Science Museum** in downtown Los Alamos is dedicated to citizens' opposition, such as posters protesting "LANL's Deadly Legacy," 12 million cubic feet of buried radioactive waste. The museum, which has more than three dozen interactive exhibits

The atomic age dawned at Trinity Site in New Mexico on July 16, 1945, following years of research at Los Alamos National Laboratory. The familiar mushroom cloud begins to develop about five seconds after detonation. The Army released these photographs on August 17, 1945, shortly after the bombing of Hiroshima and Nagasaki. (Los Alamos National Laboratory)

about the Manhattan Project and other defense-oriented research, is definitely worth visiting. Einstein's prescient letter to Roosevelt, along with the casing of a bomb identical to "Fat Man," which destroyed Nagasaki with vast amounts of power, is on display. A short film documents the building of the first atomic bomb. *15th Street and Central Avenue; 505-667-4444.*

The **Los Alamos Historical Museum** covers everything from the Cenozoic Period to the Atomic Age, including an impressive display on the changing of attitudes toward nuclear power—from optimism to cynicism. *1921 Juniper Street; 505-662-4493.*

Antoine Predock, New Mexico's most prominent architect, designed the **Mesa Public Library,** a quarter-mile west of the historical museum. The structure ignited great controversy when it was finished in 1994. Said one county council member, "When you build sculpture like this, it is hard to know if you have something that is going to bite you in the rear end." Like all of Predock's buildings, this library is intellectually challenging, laden with symbolism—such as a circular "kiva" that serves as a children's reading room and gathering place—but ultimately beautiful. The library's western wall features a curving window with stunning views of the Jémez Mountains. *2400 Central Avenue; 505-662-8240.*

Another Los Alamos attraction is the **Larry R. Walkup Aquatic Center,** an Olympic-size indoor swimming pool. The Italian, Canadian, and Australian swim teams have trained here, appreciating the high elevation of Los Alamos for its contribution to lung endurance. Amateur swimmers are welcome every day; there is a small admission fee. *2760 Canyon Road; 505-662-8170.*

■ **BANDELIER NATIONAL MONUMENT**
Extraordinary pueblo ruins are accessible 11 miles south of Los Alamos at Bandelier National Monument, and about 75 miles of hiking trails invite exploration.

The ruins were discovered in 1880, when a Swiss-born geologist named Adolph Bandelier peered over the rim of **Frijoles Canyon,** 20 miles northwest of Santa Fe, and saw something that would change the course of his life: the ruins of stone houses at least half a millennium old. Southwestern archaeology did not then exist, but over the next two decades Bandelier, along with a Swedish naturalist named Gustaf Nordenskiold and a Colorado cowboy named Richard Wetherill, would invent it. Thirty-six years later the forested Pajarito Plateau and the dramatic canyon that so captivated Bandelier would become a national monument named in his honor.

Something new and something old in architecture: (above) Mesa Public Library and (opposite) a reconstructed pueblo in Bandelier National Monument.

This was evidently a good place to live in prehistoric times; there is evidence of human presence on the plateau and in the canyon since 9500 B.C. The canyon's year-round creek was obviously its key attraction throughout the millennia. The pueblo ruins of Frijoles Canyon, however, date from about A.D. 1175 to 1500.

There is no way to guess whether the ancient people who lived here were also enchanted by the canyon's stunning natural beauty, but modern visitors certainly are. In fall the box elder and narrow-leaf cottonwood trees flanking the stream explode with color. In summer the canyon is a moist, green, cool oasis. In winter— well, at an elevation of 6,066 feet, the shivering residents of Frijoles Canyon would have anxiously awaited the first signs of spring.

The canyon's largest ruin is **Tyuonyi,** an oval-shaped pueblo built of rough volcanic tuff stones. Its construction took about a century, beginning around 1350. At its peak it had 400 rooms on several levels. It would have had a defensive, forbidding attitude: the rooms completely encircle the large central plaza, and there

was only one ground-floor entrance, which had large poles installed in it in a zigzag pattern, suggesting a maze. Today, though, the ruin is oddly beautiful, its remaining walls a muted rainbow of salmon, auburn, gray, and black stones. Several cliff dwellings cling to the south-facing canyon wall along a 1.5-mile self-guided trail. Visitors in good physical condition also should climb the ladders 140 feet up to Ceremonial Cave, a reconstructed kiva in a large natural alcove in the canyon wall. It's wise to call ahead before you visit Bandelier, which was licked by forest fires in 1996 and 2000, because auto travel into the canyon is sometimes banned. *N.M. 4 off N.M. 501; 505-672-0343.*

■ JÉMEZ MOUNTAINS
From Bandelier, you can continue west on N.M. 4 into the Jémez (pronounced HAY-mes) Mountains. On the right, about 10 miles from Bandelier, you'll reach **Valles Caldera National Preserve,** which is anchored by one of the world's largest calderas—a crater formed by a volcano's collapse. The preserve is a popular spot for all sorts of recreational activities, including hiking, horseback riding, hunting, and fishing (you must call to make a reservation to visit). Fourteen miles across, it looks like an immense meadow in the shape of a saucer. *505-661-3333 or 866-382-5537.* Nearby is **Jémez Falls,** where the Jémez River squeezes through a rocky chute and tumbles about 30 feet into a miniature canyon, widening into a wonderful bridal-veil spray as it falls.

Bares in the woods: the Forest Service is squeamish about publicizing this, but there are half a dozen hot springs in the Jémez Mountains that are popular with bathers—who customarily are nude. The most popular is **Spence Hot Springs,** 6.5 miles north of the Jémez Springs ranger station. There is no sign. If you're driving from Bandelier, watch for the Dark Canyon sign, then continue a quarter mile and look for a large dirt parking area on the left.

The trail descends about 150 feet to the Jémez River, then up about 100 feet to a cauldron of natural hot water elegantly embraced by boulders. Most bathe in the buff, but more modest people can simply strip off their shoes and relax their feet in the hot water—nobody seems to care. In response to reports of a rare "brain-eating" amoeba in the hot springs, signs now warn bathers to avoid immersing their heads in the water.

A rainbow spans a valley in the Jémez Mountains.

Kasha-Katuwe Tent Rocks National Monument in the Jémez Mountains provides one of the most spectacular environments for hiking in the region.

Thirty miles west of Los Alamos are **Jémez Springs** and **Jémez State Monument,** a ruined pueblo and mission church. Jémez Springs, the town, has a health spa that mixes massage therapy and long baths in the hot mineral waters of the springs. There are private and group tubs, and the water includes natural traces of acid carbonate, calcium, potassium, and several other minerals said to contribute to a bather's well-being.

The monument is not compelling. All that remains of the 14th-century pueblo of Giusewa is earthen mounds and a kiva. Walls of the 1621 church of San José de los Jémez are also visible. One fascinating observation is that the stone masonry of the Indian kiva and the Catholic church are almost identical. A Jémez Pueblo Indian working at the monument told me that the same people—the women and children of the pueblo—constructed both. "We used to have a sign that said that," he said, "but some women objected and we took it down."

To complete this round-trip, continue south on N.M. 4. At San Ysidro, follow U.S. 550 south and east, and then head north on I-25 to return to Santa Fe.

■ HISTORIC WESTERN LOOP

This excursion conveniently combines an easy hike in an unusual canyon, a visit to petroglyphs, a spin through an old historic town, a tour of one of the Southwest's most remarkable historic pueblos, and a visit to a dry, eerie landscape that eons ago was a sea. The drive to see these sights is fairly long, about 300 miles, so you might consider an overnight stay in Albuquerque.

■ KASHA-KATUWE TENT ROCKS NATIONAL MONUMENT

A million years ago, give or take a few, a volcanic eruption created Tent Rocks, a formation of soft pumice and tuff. Some of the rock eroded into conical tentlike formations that now poke into the sky, forming the walls of an intimate canyon. Some of the formations are almost comical: where caprock remains atop the softer cones, the effect is like a giant mushroom skewered by a tepee. The hike is most spectacular, though, where the canyon narrows into a slot as little as 3 feet wide and 100 feet deep. The trail hugs the canyon floor, and on a windless day the stillness inside the canyon is breathtaking. The one sound you may periodically hear is the tuff and pumice eroding, a pebble or two at a time. Watch for snakes and stay out of the canyon if a thunderstorm threatens. This is a bad place to be in a flash flood. The trail demands no climbing, and it's only a 3-mile round-trip—an ideal introduction to hiking in New Mexico. *Southwest of Santa Fe off N.M. 22; 505-761-8700.*

■ PETROGLYPH NATIONAL MONUMENT

Off I-25 heading south toward Albuquerque, Petroglyph National Monument preserves 15,000 or so images pecked into a lava escarpment by members of early Indian cultures. Some petroglyphs are suspected to be Archaic, as old as 2,000 to 3,000 years. But the most vivid ones are startlingly clear and refined images of birds, other animals, humans, and abstractions left by Puebloans after A.D. 1300. Three easy, self-guided trails pass by the best rock art in the monument.

Interpreting prehistoric art is a risky enterprise. Theories abound, and even modern Pueblo Indians who "read" their ancestors' rock art differ in their interpretations. Some signs almost surely track clan migrations and some might have been engraved prayers or curses, solar calendars, or even abstract art or casual graffiti. A visit here resolves no mysteries, but it is like touring a prehistoric art museum. *Unser Boulevard at Western Trail Rd. (from Santa Fe take I-25 south about 56 miles, and then take I-40 west to the Coors Road north); 505-899-0205.*

■ OLD TOWN ALBUQUERQUE

Albuquerque's Old Town section is a terrific arts shopping center and a mecca for sharp-eyed architecture buffs. Most of the buildings date from the 19th century, and several of them illustrate how Anglo pioneers struggled to reconcile their Greco-Roman architectural heritage with the adobe building blocks of Hispanic New Mexico.

Old Town is easy to find. Exit I-40 at Rio Grande Avenue and drive about half a mile south. Street parking is available in Old Town, and there are municipal lots to the north and east.

La Villa de San Francisco de Alburquerque was founded in 1706. Christened after a Spanish viceroy, the Duke of Alburquerque, the city's name has been mis-spelled for at least a hundred years. Although movements are afoot to rectify the situation, undertaking to spell the duke's name properly on maps, official docu-ments, and public buildings would be a formidable task.

Through most of the 18th century, Albuquerque was just a loose string of farms and ranches flanking the Rio Grande, but in 1779 Santa Fe ordered the residents to begin forming a compact community, defensible against Apache attacks, around the church of San Felipe de Neri. This was the genesis of Old Town.

Old Town failed to become downtown Albuquerque because in 1880 the rail-road passed a mile and a half to the east to avoid the nuisance of curving the track. Downtown blossomed around the railroad. Old Town briefly became a saloon and red-light district, but in the 1930s a renaissance occurred. Today the area is delightful, if not thoroughly authentic.

Not authentic? Well, a few buildings have suffered "Puebloization" for the sake of touristization. Check the **Antonio Vigil House,** built in 1879. Notice the vigas protruding from intersecting walls: if real, they would collide at right angles inside the house. But they're fake. Real vigas jut north and south, or east and west, but never intersect. *413 Romero Street NW.*

Some other buildings poignantly illustrate the Anglo pioneers' yearning to make New Mexico look like home. **Our Lady of the Angels School,** built in 1877 as Albuquerque's first public school, mates Greek Revival to adobe vernacular. Several

(opposite) The Bisti Badlands, 30 miles south of Farmington, are a wilderness of sand punctuated with what looks like a giant chess set of red and gray pieces sculpted by a mad surrealist. (following pages) Albuquerque's church of San Felipe de Neri, built in 1793.

other buildings express little classical details, like modest carpenter's pediments over the windows. Spotting these architectural oddments in Old Town is a fascinating game. *320 Romero Street NW.*

Old Town Plaza still serves its ancient civic function. Neighborhood residents relax on the benches, read newspapers, and feed pigeons. This feels like the spiritual center of Albuquerque, much more than its anonymous downtown.

Facing the plaza is Old Town's centerpiece, the 1793 church of **San Felipe de Neri,** which replaced an earlier structure on the site. The church's style is best described as French Carpenter Gothic executed, amazingly, in adobe. It is said to be the third-oldest church in the United States that has had continuous services since its founding. The parish has about 800 families today. *Old Town Plaza; 505-243-4628.*

About two dozen galleries operate in Old Town, along with many more boutiques, jewelry stores, and restaurants. **Agape Southwest Pueblo Pottery** is one of the most comprehensive Indian pottery galleries in the Southwest. *414 Romero Street NW.*

The **Albuquerque Museum of Art and History** is adjacent to Old Town and is decidedly worth a visit, especially since it underwent a dramatic expansion in 2004. It focuses mainly on New Mexico art, culture, and history. Old Town walking tours start from the museum daily except Mondays from mid-March to mid-December. *2000 Mountain Road NW; 505-243-7255.*

■ Ácoma Pueblo

Ácoma Pueblo, about 65 miles west of Albuquerque off I-40, is romantically but not inaccurately termed the "Sky City" for its dramatic pose atop a 367-foot-high mesa. It also is sometimes called the oldest continuously occupied settlement in America, a distinction challenged by the Hopi village of Old Oraibi in Arizona. Actually, neither village can be dated to the precise year of its founding; published dates for Ácoma range from A.D. 1150 to the late 1200s.

The site evidently was chosen for defense. One of Coronado's parties came across it in 1541 and reported, "The natives . . . came down to meet us peacefully, although they might have spared themselves the trouble and remained on their rock, for we would not have been able to disturb them in the least."

Half a century later the Spaniards were to disturb these Pueblo people in a shockingly cruel fashion. Juan de Oñate's party marched up the mesa in 1598 and extracted the usual pledge of allegiance from the residents to the king. Later that year, as another Spanish party camped below the Sky City, a battle ensued and the

A hand-tinted photograph of Ácoma Pueblo, ca. 1900. (Underwood Photo Archives)

Ácomas prevailed. A furious Oñate dispatched a larger force to teach the Indians a lesson. That they did. Hundreds of Indians were killed and hundreds more were taken prisoner. The Spaniards then cut off one foot of each captive man to serve as a "deterrent" to any future rebelliousness, and sentenced all the prisoners, male and female, to 20 years as slaves to Oñate's soldiers.

The pueblo in modern times welcomes visitors, although they must be escorted by an Ácoma guide. There are 465 houses atop the mesa, but only 13 families still live here—most Ácomas occupy more convenient houses scattered across the valley floor.

The architectural centerpiece of the town is the mission church of **San Esteban del Rey,** completed in 1640 and another of those wonderful New Mexican missions that is almost more sculpture than architecture. Pure, bold, unadorned form, it is the adobe Parthenon of this desert Acropolis. Inside, the church walls feature not only the traditional Stations of the Cross, but also symbolic native art, such as an ear of corn growing under a benevolent rainbow.

The Sky City's houses may not delight historic-preservation purists. Although they still lack contemporary amenities such as electricity, plumbing, and phones, they have been adapted with screen doors and milled casement windows. A few of the houses, incongruously, have second stories of concrete block set over adobe first stories. There are seven square kivas, all built above, rather than below, ground— which, our guide said, was a ruse to fool the Spaniards into thinking they were mere houses so the Ácomas could carry on their religion in secret.

In May 2006, Ácoma opened the spectacular new Sky City Cultural Center and Haak'u Museum, a stately facility at the foot of the mesa, containing a museum with rotating exhibits, a café, and a theater showing a film on the Ácoma people. The pueblo known for its feast-day rooster pull, which involves Ácoma horsemen galloping past roosters buried in sand up to their necks and reaching down to pull them up by their heads. *Exit 102 off I-40; 505-470-4967 or 800-747-0181.*

■ NORTHWEST TO CHACO CANYON

Chaco Culture National Historical Park is a long drive from Santa Fe. As the crow flies this incredible collection of ruins is 112 miles to the west. Unfortunately, all the road routes snake roundabout, none less than 180 miles, and more than 20 miles of them are unpaved. Leave Santa Fe before dawn, arrive early at Chaco, and plan to spend all day, but preferably not overnight. Pack lunch and plenty of water; there are no concessions.

The prehistoric ruins of Chaco Canyon are the most monumental, perplexing, and controversial anywhere in what we now call the United States. At least a dozen books have been written about them, each proposing different answers to the question that keeps Anasazi archaeology swirling in turmoil: What *was* Chaco?

We know this much: it was a terrifically inhospitable place for a prehistoric metropolis. In modern times the U.S. Park Service has recorded a high of 106° F, a low of -38° F, and an average of 8.7 sparse inches of rain a year. Yet between A.D. 900 and 1130, a march of monumental buildings—the largest, Pueblo Bonito, had between 600 and 800 rooms and 40 kivas—rose from the canyon floor. Archaeologists figure that the structures could have housed up to 5,000 people, but the meager natural resources available near the desert canyon could not have supported more than a thousand. Moreover, these "great houses" were architect-designed in precise geometric forms (Pueblo Bonito is an immense "D" 500 feet long) and built with sandstone shaved into remarkably precise bricks. Nothing like this had appeared anywhere in the American Southwest before. Who or what inspired it? Still more: Absolutely straight dirt "roads," most a uniform 30 feet wide and visible today from the air when the sun is low in the sky, radiated from Chaco to outlying communities up to 42 miles distant. Why would people who had no draft animals or wheeled vehicles need freeways?

The honeycomb of rooms and kivas of Pueblo Bonito are exposed to the desert elements and tourists' eyes in Chaco Canyon.

An 8-mile loop road visits seven of the 11 great houses in the canyon, including Pueblo Bonito, the most spectacular. I strongly recommend the trail ascending to the canyon rim behind the ruin of Kin Kletso, which provides crow's-eye floor-plan views of three of the great ruins. The trail is only mildly strenuous, but carry water and watch out for rattlesnakes.

In 1999, a maverick Arizona anthropologist named Christy Turner published *Man Corn: Cannibalism and Violence in the Prehistoric American Southwest,* a scholarly but explosive book that opened up even more dramatic questions surrounding Chaco: was it the nerve center of a culture that practiced cannibalism?

Turner had been studying the evidence for 30 years: bones with sawing and chopping marks on them, bones with marrow scraped from them, bones that had been boiled—all *human* bones. In his book, Turner argues vigorously that the culture centered at Chaco was a totalitarian regime that used cannibalism as a form of social control—not mere nutrition. Many other anthropologists dispute Turner's opinions, and Native Americans who consider themselves descendants of the Anasazi are livid. The furor is certain to boil for years.

From Santa Fe take I-25 south 41 miles to U.S. 550, follow U.S. 550 north about 120 miles to County Road 7900 (3 miles east of Nageezi), and then head south along County Road 7950; 505-786-7014.

Farther afield, but well worth a visit, are the **Bisti Badlands,** a 3,968-acre sandstone wilderness in the San Juan Basin. Abandon hope, all ye who enter here, if you've neglected to bring food, water, and especially a compass. This is maybe the most desolate and remote of all the West's badlands: no roads, no rangers, no trails, no campsites, no evidence of earthly life except the fossil recollections of Upper Cretaceous dinosaurs. The landscape is fine gray, orange, and pink sand, punctuated with a giant chess set of red and gray sandstone and shale hoodoos. The chessmen, sculpted by wind (and maybe a mad surrealist), take the shapes of toadstools, teardrops, gnomes, domes, harbor seals, Panama hats, and Hershey Kisses. They defy gravity and reason. You would assume that since the forms are so distinctive, it would be easy to memorize landmarks and plot a path back to your starting point. But since they are without precedence in your experience on this planet, they prove reluctant to lodge in memory. The day after a trek into the Bisti—you brought that compass, so you made it back—it will seem like a vaguely remembered dream, a hike into a wilderness of another world. *From Chaco Canyon, drive south on N.M. 57 and then head west on Navajo Road 9 and north on N.M. 371; 505-599-8900.*

Dinosaurs once roamed the desolate Bisti Badlands.

CUISINE ❖ RESTAURANTS

"Salmon," suggests the dinner menu at Santa Fe's La Fonda hotel. Then come the details that the fish is "marinated in achiote and orange juice and then roasted in banana leaves, served with Chihuahua cheese mashed potatoes."

What, New Mexican salmon? Lost, somehow, 1,200 miles up the Rio Grande? No, what's lost here is New Mexican food, now spawning offshoots as exotic as buffalo sausage and blue crab, bathed in sauces incorporating everything from papaya juice to pureed piñon nuts and served with polenta or risotto and accompanied by chile-spiked beer or margaritas made with tequila and Grand Marnier. Don't believe it? Here's a sampler from contemporary Santa Fe menus:

> Shiitake and cactus spring rolls with green chile salsa (from
> Santacafé).
> Pork tenderloin medallions with Zinfandel-braised onions, sweet
> potatoes with piñon nuts, and a red chile-bourbon reduction (Inn
> of the Anasazi Restaurant).
> Spicy grilled tamarind shrimp with sweet rice banana tamal and
> green-papaya salad (Cafe Pasqual's).
> Idaho ruby red trout stuffed with poblano chile and grilled
> Portobello mushrooms baked in adobe clay (La Casa Sena).
> Seared Hudson Valley foie gras with candied ginger, sugared pecans,
> and sundried-cranberry compote (Geronimo).

Nowhere but Santa Fe will the diner encounter such wild and crazy permutations—some will say perversions—of traditional Latino food. At the same time, nowhere else has the nova of New Southwestern cuisine burned so brightly. Not all the culinary experimentation has been successful, but one thing every foodie can agree on: Santa Fe is an outrageously interesting place to eat.

The choices here are as varied as in any big city—Spanish tapas, Chinese dim sum, French, Italian, Thai, American Indian, Asian Indian, Pacific Rim fusion, *world* fusion—and even New Mexican.

"I think regionalism is almost a thing of the past, unfortunately," says Katherine Kagel, owner of the very popular Cafe Pasqual's, "but at the same time, there's much more openness to different cuisines. I think that's terrific, especially in a xenophobic world."

HARD WORK ON THE HACIENDA

Behind the style of the big river households there was much work, for the men out of doors, for the women within. . . . Food and drink took much work to produce. The women made spiced wine, simmered in an earthen pot for a day with spices and sugar, sealed with a ring of fresh dough. Sweet cookies were made with twenty-four egg yolks. On a heated metate stone, dense chocolate was made by grinding cocoa beans, stick cinnamon, pecans and maple sugar—all imported—into a paste which was dried and cut into cakes. Cooked with thick whole milk, these made the black chocolate drink which was served at breakfast, and at four in the afternoon with cookies. The finest tortillas—large, thin, round corncakes—were made from blue corn meal. Three of these, layered with slices of pink onion and curls of yellow cheese and sprinkled with green lettuce and swimming in cooked red chili pepper sauce, made a favorite dish. . . . Pork fat was diced and fried in deep fat to make cracklings which were used in place of bacon. A soupbone was used not once but many times, and was even passed from one poor family to another to boil with beans. In the fall . . . the hacienda women cut up sweet pumpkins and melons, setting the pieces out on stakes to dry.

—Paul Horgan, *Great River: The Rio Grande*, 1954

Despite all the experimentation, there are still dozens of thoroughly traditional New Mexican restaurants in town—no salmon spawn in their kitchens—and there are some mothers who patiently pat out damp corn masa into thin disks and make their own tortillas before every meal. Santa Fe's supermarkets routinely carry ingredients that are difficult to find even in other Southwestern cities. The local Albertson's, for instance, carries canned *menudo* (tripe soup), *camarón* (dried and shredded shrimp), and, of course, powdered Chimayó chile. Chile is not just an ingredient here, but a passion, and Santa Feans eat it *hot*. Incidentally, nothing will draw more derision around Santa Fe than to spell it or pronounce it *chili*, as in Texas. *Nuevomexicanos* use the correct Spanish spelling; it is a signature of the state.

It is also declassé to refer to the traditional dishes of Santa Fe such as *picadillo* and *carne adovada* as "Mexican food." The preferred term is *New Mexican* food. Santa Fe isn't just being snooty. There are discernible differences between the traditional Hispanic cooking of northern New Mexico and that elsewhere in the Southwest. The reason is that until recently, Santa Fe and its environs remained relatively isolated, so its cuisine developed distinctive characteristics. Even as Anglos began streaming into the region in large numbers in the mid-20th century, the American "melting pot" didn't find its way to the stove here. "Simply put, the New Mexicans refused to melt," writes historian Marc Simmons.

The Spaniards of the *Entrada* encountered a semiarid land that yielded precious little natural bounty when compared to southern Mexico or southern Europe. Sixteenth-century Puebloans subsisted on a diet of corn, beans, and squash, supplemented with occasional wild game—much the same as their Anasazi and Mogollon forebears had done for a millennium. The Hispanic settlers introduced two important improvements: ranching, to provide a reliable source of meat; and chile, to flavor it. Still, until Mexican independence opened New Mexico to Yankee trade in 1821, Santa Fe cooking would have been fairly spare and primitive.

■ SANTA FE FARMERS MARKET

To get some insight into the farming traditions of the Rio Grande Valley, visit the Santa Fe Farmers Market, which from late April through early November takes place at the corner of Cerrillos Road and Guadalupe Street on Tuesday and Saturday mornings. A smaller indoor version is held at nearby El Museo Cultural in winter on Saturday mornings. *505-983-4098.*

Some of the families selling produce out of pickups and campers have been working the same New Mexico land for six or seven generations. In one stall, a man roasts hundreds of green chiles in a rotating steel mesh drum heated by roaring propane jets made from recycled tin cans. The aroma is delectable. Another is selling miniature decorative corn in a mosaic of white, yellow, cherry, and purple kernels. Also for sale are apple cider (100 percent organic, made last night), homemade salsas and chutneys, apples, squashes, tomatoes, lettuce, onions, and herbs. Free samples abound, and they definitely generate sales.

Family farming is a tradition in jeopardy: all across northern New Mexico, family farmers are under pressure because of higher taxes, developers, and a new generation largely uninterested in this line of work.

Produce from the Santa Fe Farmers' Market includes many varieties of freshly baked bread.

SANTA FE SCHOOL OF COOKING

Janet Mitchell is plopping red chiles into her *carne adovada* sauce, tuning the ensemble like a composer choosing among saxes, bassoons, and trombones, looking for the exact mixture of finesse and snarl the music needs. Her basic instrument is Chimayó chile, grown around the town of the same name 40 miles north of Santa Fe. "You can use more Chimayó for more flavor without increasing the heat," she says. "*Caribe* chiles turn up the heat. *Anchos* add richness and smokiness.

"It's like wine," she adds, as the aroma from the open saucepan storms the room. "You can talk about chiles in terms of smoke, or licorice, or plum. I think there are about 300 adjectives to describe the flavors of chiles."

This is a weekday morning class at the Santa Fe School of Cooking, and 17 of us from assorted parts of the country have assembled to learn some of northern New Mexico's traditional culinary secrets. It operates in a sunny second-story room in a retail marketplace a block from Santa Fe's four-centuries-old Plaza. Owner Susan Curtis started the school in 1989, reasoning that a lot of people come to Santa Fe mainly to eat, and a lesson or two would give visitors a way to take the city's flavors home.

The school began with one instructor and one class, and now there are several instructors and myriad classes—some in traditional New Mexican cuisine, and others in contemporary Southwestern cuisine, Mexican cuisine, Native-American dishes, tapas, and various low-fat and vegetarian permutations. In summer, the high season, well over 100 people take the classes every week.

The operation includes a retail store, which manager Nicole Curtis Ammerman, Susan's daughter, says is a perfect complement to the classes. Participants typically leave the store with armloads of spices and herbs like *epazote* (which cuts the antisocial after-effects of pinto beans), as well as chile varieties such as *guajillo, chipotle, moritas,* and *cascabeles,* all as easily available as moon rocks in most of the country. (New Mexican food fanatics stranded without such supplies order them by mail from the store.)

Our class menu today covers a lot of culinary ground: *carne adovada, calabacitas* (corn and squash), *chiles rellenos,* homemade tortillas, refried beans, and sopaipillas. This is definitely not a feast approved by the American Heart Association, but Mitchell does compromise by subbing vegetable oil for lard—which in *adovada,* with its pervasive red chile sauce, will make no difference in flavor.

Carne adovada translates best as "cured meat," and it dates from New Mexico's pre-fridge days. Strips of pork are marinated in the chile sauce for 24 hours, then stewed in the same sauce. The marinating not only flavors the meat, but keeps bacteria at bay. Not every organism loves chile.

As she cooks, Mitchell tosses out helpful hints and chile lore. "Hispanic cooks believe that if you cut the meat with the grain it will absorb more of the sauce, which will tenderize it." On *chiles rellenos:* "The Anaheim you get everywhere else is the same variety as the New Mexico Hatch, but California's mild climate doesn't develop the intense flavor in the chile." On making tortillas. "They don't have to be perfectly round. They should look like they were made by the human hand." That's reassurance for her assistant, who is new to the tortilla craft. Some of his are coming out shaped like Nevada. "Just don't overcook them,

Janet Mitchell of the Santa Fe School of Cooking.

or they'll taste like Frisbees. Basically, you only want to dry them out."

The whole demonstration takes two hours—much of the instructors' prep work is done in advance—and then we all prepare to eat what we've made. The aromas alone could arouse de Anza from his grave; even the humid scent of freshly griddled tortillas evokes warmly satisfying images of mom, hearth, and home. Factory-prepared Mexican foods don't even come close. These dishes are trouble to cook, but the results are worth it.

And when we eat, we are warmed (in more ways than one) and gratified. It isn't just the lingering tang of the chile concerto on our tongues. It's also the echo of history, the notion that we visitors are learning traditions perpetuated by people whose roots in New Mexico stretch back to the 16th century.

"The traditional New Mexican cuisine has been here forever," declares Susan Curtis. "It will never die."

Santa Fe School of Cooking, 116 West San Francisco Street, Santa Fe; 505-983-4511 or 800-982-4688. Classes offered year-round. Reservations are advised.

■ New Trends in New Mexican Cuisine

Through the first three-quarters of the last century, the glory of Santa Fe food was basic but delicious traditional New Mexican dishes: enchiladas, *chiles rellenos,* tamales, *carne asada, carne adovada,* simmered beans, *posole.* Nobody fretted about cholesterol, or about which chile might best flavor a papaya-tangerine sauce for pheasant breast. Local sources dispute exactly when and how the nuevo New Mexican (or nuevo Latino, nouvelle Numex or New Southwestern) era began, but Mark Miller's Coyote Cafe, born in 1987, certainly had something to do with it. Miller conjoined ingredients and techniques from Mexico, New Mexico, France, and Berkeley, drew a gush of national publicity and the suspicion of local traditionalists, and inspired a rash of innovation. The sting of chile spread through cuisines that no one could have imagined. Shrimp tempura with red chile sauce? Green chile vichyssoise? You can eat them in Santa Fe.

The fire of chile-spiked innovation still burns brightly, but lately some chefs have been returning to Mexican or New Mexican roots to build on them. Lane Warner, the executive chef of La Fonda hotel's La Plazuela restaurant, says his menu is essentially Mexican with an upscale twist. Other trends in restauranting are a surge in high-end bistros that focus squarely on classic French or Mediterranean food, and places serving food with Asian influences.

■ Chiles

There are more than 300 varieties of chiles and a universe of things one can do with them. They can be used fresh, pickled, dried, smoked, crushed, or powdered. A whole pod or several can be simmered all day in a stew to impart a distinctive flavor—and different varieties do have different flavors. A *chipotle,* which is a smoked jalapeño, will invest the pot with both smoke and fire, while an *ancho* has a plumlike flavor. Even greater differences exist in the fire quotient, which comes from an alkaloid chemical called capsaicin that develops naturally in the chile. This is measured scientifically in Scoville Units, a scale developed by a chemist for the Parke-Davis pharmaceutical company in 1912. The drug-maker was marketing a chile-based ointment for arthritis sufferers, and while some patients were enjoying relief, others were getting blisters, so a test was needed to quantify the relative power of different chiles.

An everyday bell pepper will rate close to zero Scoville Units, a jalapeño typically will score about 5,000, and a *habanero* up to *300,000!* Eating a *habanero,* a brilliant orange chile about the size of a stubby thumb, is like grabbing a mouthful of live killer bees. Carelessly rub your eye after fingering one, and it will put an end to productive work for the rest of the day.

New Mexicans, unlike Texans, seldom eat their chiles straight. Instead, they're commonly incorporated into salsas, or sauces.

The first thing an outlander needs to know is the meaning of the question "Red or green?" which usually follows any order of a traditional New Mexican plate. It means red or green sauce, which is slathered over burritos, *chiles rellenos,* enchiladas, omelets—practically everything but salmon. Order a "Christmas" plate and you'll get a sampling of both. Red is made with dried chiles, green with fresh. Before freezers and trucks from California, green was the summer sauce, and red warmed New Mexico's palates through the winter. Both now are made year-round.

CHILE SCORCH SCALE

Chiles enhance taste, are intriguing to look at, and can scorch the unsuspecting. How is chile heat measured? In 1912 a Mr. Scoville gave us a guide to chile heat by testing a range of chiles on some non-chile eaters (how they later fared is unrecorded). Some common chiles and their heat levels are recorded below.

CHILE	SCOVILLE HEAT UNITS	RATING
Mild Bell	0	0
R-Naky, Mexi-Bell	100–500	1
NuMex Big Jim	500–1000	2
Pasilla, Española	1000–1500	3
Sandia, Cascabel	1500–2500	4
Jalapeño, Mirasol	2500–5000	5
Serrano	5000–15,000	6
Cayenne, Tabasco de Arbol	15,000–30,000	7
Aji, Piquin	30,000–50,000	8
Santaka, Chiltepin	50,000–100,000	9
Habanero, Bahamian	100,000–300,000	10

Green tends to be hotter. It is made mostly or entirely with Hatch chiles, grown in southwestern New Mexico. Hatches are the same species as the familiar Anaheims from Southern California, but New Mexico's cool summer nights urge the chile to develop more capsaicin.

Chiles find their way onto New Mexican breakfast plates, which isn't strange at all. New Mexican breakfasts are infinitely better than the bowls of steaming limp gray stuff that greet too many American palates in the morning. *Huevos rancheros* are one popular staple: eggs poached in a red chile sauce, served over corn tortillas and dripping with melted cheese. Breakfast burros (burritos) are made many ways, nearly always delicious. You might find a mild bacon-and-egg scramble swaddled in a flour tortilla or something more aggressive like shredded potatoes and bacon wrapped in a flour tortilla and drenched in an eye-opening green chile sauce.

■ TORTILLAS

Visitors also need a reverent appreciation of the tortilla, the staff of life from northern New Mexico all the way to Central America. Indians made tortillas long before the arrival of Columbus and Coronado, grinding dried corn with a *mano* and *metate* (essentially a stone mortar and pestle), mixing in a little water and heating it. Tortillas made from wheat flour are a relatively modern invention, probably issuing from northern Mexico in the 19th century. Blue corn tortillas may or may not have been made in prehistoric times, but they have become a virtual symbol of trendy Santa Fe cuisine in the last decade.

And now come a plethora of *flavored* tortillas from Leona Medina-Tiede, whose little burrito stand next to the Santuario de Chimayó is a veritable Baskin-Robbins of tortillas. "One of the B&Bs wanted something besides toast and croissants to serve for breakfast," she said, "so I tried making cinnamon tortillas and it kind of went crazy from there." Crazy? Try more than 25 flavors.

The tortilla's uses are even more varied than leavened bread's. They can be eaten plain with butter or salsa, filled with cheese and heated (a *quesadilla*), rolled around a filling of meat or beans (a burrito), fried and wrapped around a filling (a taco), or cut into triangles and fried as chips to dip in salsa. They take the place of pasta in Mexican chicken soup. When they are served plateside in a covered basket,

Green, red, and orange peppers provide color and flavor to a meal, not to mention heat— eating an orange habanero *is like feasting on live killer bees.*

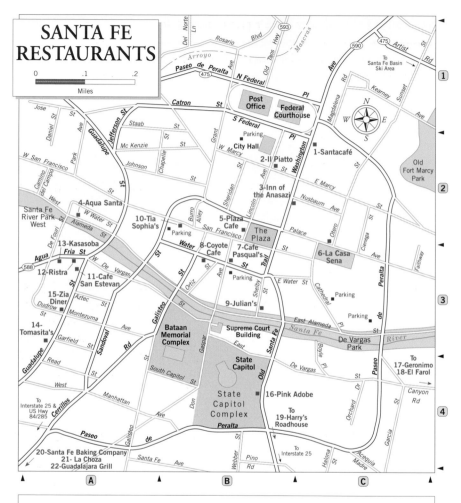

SANTA FE RESTAURANTS

0   .1   .2
Miles

Aqua Santa 4	Inn of the Anasazi 3	Ristra 12
Cafe Pasqual's 7	Il Piatto 2	Santacafé 1
Cafe San Estevan 11	Julian's 9	Sanfe Fe Baking Company 20
Coyote Cafe 8	Kasasoba 13	Tia Sophia's 10
El Farol 18	La Casa Sena 6	Tomasita's 14
Geronimo 17	La Choza 21	Zia Diner 13
Guadalajara Grill 22	Pink Adobe 16	
Harry's Roadhouse 19	Plaza Café 5	

you should tear them into smaller pieces, dump a lump of stew or beans inside, and use the tortilla to ferry food to mouth. As with leavened bread, freshness is everything. A tortilla that's been snoring in the refrigerator for three days might as well be a compact disk. If you stumble across a restaurant that's making its own tortillas in the kitchen several times a day, forget the New Mexican scallops in *ancho*-garlic-cilantro butter over at La Maison del Rio Grande, and savor the tortillas. They're for real.

■ Santa Fe Area Restaurants

Prices per person, excluding tax, tip, and drinks: $ = under $10; $$ = $10–$25; $$$ = over $25; ★ = Recommended by author

■ Santa Fe

★ Inn of the Anasazi
Both the decor and cuisine would make a prehistoric Anasazi think he had passed on to another world. Modern foodies may think they've gone to heaven. Celebrated chef Martin Rios creates complicated, innovative, and beautifully prepared New Southwestern dishes that may mingle, for example, pork medallions, sweet potatoes, and red chile-bourbon reduction. Elegant, but nobody demands you dress up. Generally regarded as one of Santa Fe's very best restaurants. *113 Washington Avenue; 505-988-3030.* $$$

Aqua Santa
Talented chef Brian Knox helms the open kitchen in this very small, very special restaurant on the edge of downtown. Try the boneless lamb loin with crispy polenta and a green peppercorn sauce, and you'll see why it can be very hard to score a table here on summer evenings and weekends. *451 West Alameda Street; 505-982-6297.* $$–$$$

★ Cafe Pasqual's

The outrageously eclectic menu at one of Santa Fe's most inspired small restaurants draws inspiration from New Mexican, Chinese, and Thai cuisine—not to mention owner Katherine Kagel's Jewish grandmother's cooking. The sunny dining room is decorated with cheerful hand-painted tiles. *121 Don Gaspar Avenue; 505-983-9340.* $$–$$$

★ Cafe San Estevan

"The angels have inspired me to elevate these beans and chiles to a new cuisine based on native cooking methods," says the cafe's owner-chef Steve Garcia, a former Franciscan monk. The menu isn't that unconventional, but the enchiladas, among Santa Fe's best, are indeed heavenly. *428 Agua Fria; 505-995-1996.* $–$$

★ Coyote Cafe

Very popular. Very noisy. And very controversial. Some conservative Santa Feans resent the fame Mark Miller's restaurant has drawn, because it caused the eclipse of traditional New Mexican cuisine, at least in the national consciousness. Rabbit enchiladas with mole *poblano* and orange-jicama salsas? Radical indeed, but Coyote's food is superb. *132 West Water Street; 505-983-1615.* $$$

★ El Farol

The specialty at "The Lantern" is tapas—appetizer-size plates of Spanish specialties such as shrimp sautéed with garlic, sherry, and lime juice. The selection of Spanish wines is good; entertainers perform nightly. *808 Canyon Road; 505-983-9912.* $$

★ Geronimo

No connection to the famed Apache warrior here, but a man named Gerónimo López did own this house for a time around the mid-18th century. There's nothing historic about the cuisine, however, which chef Eric DiStefano calls "global fusion." Expect the world. *724 Canyon Road; 505-982-1500.* $$$

Guadalajara Grill

The Solís family comes from close-by-the-coast Guadalajara, so half the menu at their restaurant is shrimp in various Jalisco styles: *camarón al mojo de ajo* (shrimp in garlic juice), *a la parrilla* (grilled), *a la diabla* (in a sauce spawned by the devil himself). The food is simple, traditional, and fresh, and the grill is always busy. *3877 Cerrillos Road; 505-424-3544.* $–$$

The Coyote Cafe is one of Santa Fe's most popular restaurants.

Harry's Roadhouse

A quirky, always-jumping adobe spread with several dining rooms and patios, this festive local favorite is on the southeast side of town, a 15-minute drive from the Plaza. The menu is eclectic—green-chile cheeseburgers, grilled salmon tacos, creative pastas, and amazingly tasty desserts. *Old Las Vegas Highway, 1 mile south of Old Pecos Trail; 505-989-4629.* $–$$

★ Il Piatto

A thousand kitchen implements hang on the walls here, which correctly focuses diners' minds on what's important: the food. *Esquire* rated this one of America's best new restaurants in 1996, and the dishes—pastas, roast chicken, grilled seafood—continue to earn plaudits. *95 West Marcy Street; 505-984-1091.* $$

★ Julian's

The owner's name is Gustafson, but the cuisine here is contemporary Milanese—and inspired. Sea bass braised with garlic, tomatoes, mustard, pine nuts, and raisins might sound unlikely, but it's a symphonic blend. Julian's consistently turns up as the "most romantic" restaurant in local polls, but the food is really what's to love here. Julian's is open for dinner only. *221 Shelby Street; 505-988-2355.* $$$

Kasasoba

An increasing number of very good Asian restaurants has invaded Santa Fe, and this hip space specializing in innovative small plates of Japanese fare leads the pack. Sake-steamed striped bass with enoki mushrooms is one of the more tempting items. *544 Aqua Fria; 505-984-1969.* $$

★ La Casa Sena

There are two restaurants here: a stylish and expensive place serving northern New Mexican crossed with *nuevo,* and a crowded cantina with simpler and cheaper food and superb young musicians who sing Broadway show tunes and wait tables. Try an alfresco lunch in the courtyard and the cantina for a fun evening. *125 East Palace Avenue; 505-988-9232.* $$–$$$

★ La Choza

A relatively untouristy spot for superb, completely authentic New Mexican food, this rambling adobe on the edge of the Guadalupe District turns out terrific pork *carne adorada,* and wonderful *huevos rancheros. 905 Alarid Street; 505-982-0909.* $

Pink Adobe

Rosalea Murphey opened the doors to landmark "the Pink" 50 years ago, planting the seeds for Santa Fe's culinary excellence. The fare is standard: steaks, lamb, pork, and traditional New Mexican dishes. *406 Old Santa Fe Trail; 505-983-7712.* $$$

Plaza Café

This lively storefront restaurant on the west side of the Plaza has a cheerful Art Deco–inspired dining room, complete with an old-fashioned soda fountain. Since 1918, it's been a reliable source for New Mexican and American food. Try the spicy tortilla soup, followed by home-style meat loaf. *54 Lincoln Avenue; 505-982-1664.* $–$$

Ristra

An elegantly minimalist restaurant known for creative Franco-Southwestern meals, this local favorite in the Sanbusco Market complex serves a traditional blend of French sauces perked up with New Mexican flair. Try the black Mediterranean mussels in chipotle mint broth or the stuffed chicken breast with piñon nuts, raisins, spinach, and nopalitos. *548 Agua Fria Street; 505-982-8608.* $$$

★ Santacafé

This elegant restaurant has eclipsed the Coyote Cafe in national fame, offering a cuisine that fuses Asian, European, and New Mexican influences. One example: ginger-cured salmon on crispy won tons with tequila-citrus aioli. The setting is the historic Padre Gallegos House, the private, and palatial, residence of one of the priests Bishop Lamy defrocked. *231 Washington Avenue; 505-984-1788.* $$$

★ Tia Sophia's

This is the best place to eat breakfast in Santa Fe. A good strategy is to arrive at 7 A.M. (you can park right outside without fear of a ticket until 8) and order the breakfast burrito, huevos rancheros, or cheese enchiladas. Tia Sophia's is open for breakfast and lunch only. *210 West San Francisco Street; 505-983-9880.* $

★ Tomasita's

"Chile is a main ingredient of our dishes and we serve it hot. If you are new to the taste please ask for a sample before ordering. . . ." So warns the menu at this traditional New Mexican restaurant. This is some of the hotter New Mexican food in America. Tomasita's is hot commercially too: it's one of Santa Fe's more popular restaurants. The crowds can be huge, so go at an odd time like 4 P.M. Reservations are not accepted. *500 South Guadalupe Street; 505-983-5721.* $

Zia Diner

A longtime Santa Fe favorite, Zia has a quirkiness that seems completely in tune with the city's. The classic American-diner menu has, of course, Santa Fe touches such as chile-infested meatloaf. If diner fare isn't for you, pasta and fresh fish are also served. Zia has a soda fountain *and* a full bar. *326 South Guadalupe Street; 505-988-7008.* $

■ NEAR SANTA FE

★ Embudo Station Restaurant

This beautiful place is nestled under ancient cottonwoods on the west bank (literally) of the Rio Grande. The succulent smoked meats come from the restaurant's own smokehouse. Embudo is only open from May through November. *N.M. 68, 16 miles north of Española; 505-852-4707.* $–$$

Gabriel's

Come here for expertly prepared Mexican and Southwestern cuisine—the guacamole, made fresh at your table, is sheer genius. If you arrive around sunset, ask for a table on the outdoor patio, order a fabulous margarita, and take in the spectacular views of the Sangre de Cristo Mountains. *Off U.S. 85/284, 13 miles north of Santa Fe; 505-455-7000.* $$

■ CHIMAYÓ

★ Restaurante Rancho de Chimayó

The Jaramillo family settled around present-day Chimayó in 1695; nine generations later their descendants run this popular restaurant in a rambling hacienda. How popular? Well, it serves 300,000 meals a year. Try not to arrive at lunchtime in summer, when tour buses disgorge diners by the hundreds. Strike at an odd hour, and you'll find less commotion as you dine on excellent traditional New Mexican food. *N.M. 520, a mile south of Chimayó; 505-351-4444.* $$

■ TAOS

See Taos Lodging and Restaurants map, page 225, for restaurant locations.

Apple Tree

A popular and pleasant restaurant with cozy fireside tables in winter and a breezy patio to enjoy when it's warmer. The menu offers a range of dishes from curried chicken to shrimp quesadillas. *123 Bent Street; 505-758-1900.* $$$

Bent Street Café

Close to Taos Plaza, this long-running spot with a cheery patio serves tasty and affordable American standards. Try the smoked turkey sandwich at lunch, and finish things off with a chocolate-nut brownie. *120 Bent Street; 505-758-5787.* $

Joseph's Table

Few restaurants in the Southwest have garnered more kudos than this elegant, romantic space inside La Fonda Hotel. One culinary showstopper is peppercrusted elk tenderloin with a rich foie gras and truffle demiglace. Order a side of duck-fat-french fries. *108-A South Taos Plaza, 505-751-4512.* $$–$$$

Momentitos de la Vida, a touch of L.A. swank in Taos.

★ Lambert's of Taos

This cottagelike restaurant serves superb new American cuisine such as grilled lamb chops with mushrooms, occasionally slipping in a New Mexican accent with smoky chipotle sauces. *309 Paseo del Pueblo Sur; 505-758-1009.* $$–$$$

Sabroso

A chic, relatively new spot in Arroyo Seco, en route to Taos Ski Valley, Sabroso opened in 2006 to raves. At this mid-19th-century hacienda, enjoy such Mediterranean-inspired fare as wood-grilled shrimp skewers in a savory clam broth, or have a glass of wine in the intimate piano bar. *470 N.M. 150; 505-776-3333.* $$–$$$

★ Trading Post Cafe

The name conjures visions of a cowboy watering hole, but this is a sophisticated bistro. The Italian-accented menu includes items such as lamb chops with tomato mint salsa and shrimp Creole. The food is excellent, the atmosphere informal and convivial. *4179 N.M. 68, Ranchos de Taos; 505-758-5089.* $$

(following pages) The kitchen at Martínez Hacienda.

L O D G I N G

Santa Fe is *expensive*. No, *outrageous*. This is the first reaction of every cost conscious visitor who tries to book a room and has his ears battered with a flurry of three-figure-a-night quotes.

Santa Fe is *full*. This is the dismayed realization of would-be July-through-September visitors who wait until the last few days to book reservations. Rooms during the opera season, Indian Market, and Albuquerque's Balloon Festival may seem unavailable at any price.

But there are almost always places to stay in Santa Fe—even somewhat reasonably priced accommodations. Finding them takes personal initiative, not a travel agent. And planning well ahead of your visit is essential.

■ ■ ■

Santa Fe accommodations fall into four basic categories: hotels, motels, B&Bs, and privately owned "vacation rentals."

Hotels

The hotels are clustered in or very near downtown, and their rates range from mildly to very expensive. A powerful argument for staying in a hotel is that you'll have a parking space downtown. All the lodgings cultivate a relaxed atmosphere, however stratospheric their rates. "We're informal even at dinner," said a clerk at the Inn of the Anasazi, which *Condé Nast Traveler* has named to its American "Gold List" of hotels. "We might discourage a Metallica T-shirt."

Motels

Most of the motels line Cerrillos Road, the unromantic commercial strip that runs for several miles south from the central city. Traffic on Cerrillos is often congested in summer, and driving downtown to find parking—well, head out at 7 A.M. But the price differential is substantial. In a recent summer survey, the New Mexico Hotel and Motel Association found the average daily rate for a hotel room in downtown 87 percent higher than that for a room on Cerrillos Road.

The Inn at Loretto.

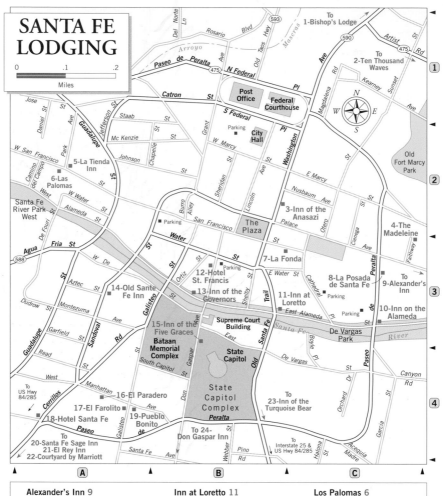

SANTA FE LODGING

0   .1   .2
Miles

To
1-Bishop's Lodge

To
2-Ten Thousand
Waves

Post Office
Federal Courthouse
City Hall
Parking

5-La Tienda Inn
6-Las Palomas
Santa Fe River Park West

Old Fort Marcy Park

3-Inn of the Anasazi
4-The Madeleine

The Plaza

7-La Fonda
12-Hotel St. Francis
13-Inn of the Governors
11-Inn at Loretto

8-La Posada de Santa Fe
9-Alexander's Inn
10-Inn on the Alameda

14-Old Sante Fe Inn
15-Inn of the Five Graces
Bataan Memorial Complex

Supreme Court Building

State Capitol

De Vargas Park

16-El Paradero
17-El Farolito
18-Hotel Santa Fe
19-Pueblo Bonito

State Capitol Complex

23-Inn of the Turquoise Bear

To US Hwy 84/285
To
20-Santa Fe Sage Inn
21-El Rey Inn
22-Courtyard by Marriott

To 24-
Don Gaspar Inn

To
Interstate 25 &
US Hwy 84/285

Alexander's Inn 9	Inn at Loretto 11	Los Palomas 6
Bishop's Lodge 1	Inn of the Anasazi 3	The Madeleine 4
Courtyard by Marriott 22	Inn of the Five Graces 15	Old Santa Fe Inn 14
Don Gaspar Inn 24	Inn of the Governors 13	Pueblo Bonito 19
El Farolito 17	Inn of the Turquoise Bear 23	Santa Fe Sage Inn 20
El Paradero 16	Inn on the Alameda 10	Ten Thousand Waves 2
El Rey Inn 21	La Fonda 7	
Hotel St. Francis 12	La Posada de Santa Fe 8	
Hotel Santa Fe 18	La Tienda Inn 5	

B&Bs

About three dozen B&Bs operate in Santa Fe, many of them in adobe or Victorian houses within walking distance of downtown. Most provide sumptuous breakfasts. The rates tend to fall between those of Cerrillos motels and downtown hotels.

Rentals

Many Santa Fe residents rent out their homes or adjoining "casitas" for much of the year. Several local agencies specialize in booking the high-priced rentals (from $1,000 to $2,000 per week). If you're on a budget, look in the classified section of the *Santa Fe New Mexican* (www.santafenewmexican.com) and search under the Vacation Rentals heading. Rentals are available by the day, week, or month. Several private reservation services can also help you find accommodations:

New Mexico Bed & Breakfast Association. *800-661-6649; www.nmbba.org.*
New Mexico Central Reservations. *505-766-9770 or 800-466-7829; www.nmtravel.com.*

The "high season" for most lodgings stretches from May through October. The rates at other times are from 15 to 30 percent less. Some hotels kick their rates back up around Thanksgiving and Christmas, when Santa Fe again becomes a popular, if frosty, destination. Hotel, motel, and sometimes even B&B rates are negotiable in all but times of peak occupancy. If you are not a member of a discount plan (such as AAA, AARP, or Encore), ask for the corporate rate and describe your business in Santa Fe.

Some visitors stay in nearby towns and commute into Santa Fe. Española (505-753-2831 for lodging information) and Los Alamos (505-661-4844) are both an easy 30-mile drive away, and the motels there are substantially less expensive than Santa Fe's. Los Alamos is more scenic than Española.

■ LODGING LISTINGS

Chains. Many major hotel and motel chains are well represented in Santa Fe. To find out what is available and where, use the national toll-free numbers listed below, but for the best rates make your reservations at the local number; the reservations clerk is frequently authorized to quote discounted rates.

Best Western. *800-528-1234; www.bestwestern.com.*
Comfort Inn. *877-424-6423; www.choicehotel.com.*
Doubletree. *800-222-8733; www.doubletree.com.*
Hilton Hotels. *800-445-8667; www.hilton.com.*
Holiday Inn. *800-465-4329; www.6c.com.*
La Quinta. *800-531-5900; www.laquinta.com.*
Marriott Hotels. *800-228-9290; www.marriott.com.*
Quality Inns. *800-228-5151; www.qualityinn.com.*
Ramada Inns. *800-272-6232; www.ramada.com.*

Price designations for accommodations:
$ = under $100; $$ = $100–$200; $$$ = over $200

■ CENTRAL SANTA FE

Alexander's Inn
This 1903 Craftsman-style house with seven rooms has gardens and a backyard hot tub. The inn is a short walk from the Plaza. *529 East Palace Avenue; 505-986-1431 or 888-321-5123.* $–$$

Don Gaspar Inn
The three small houses that make up this dapper B&B south of the Plaza represent three Common Santa Fe styles: Arts and Crafts, Pueblo Revival, and Territorial. Some suites have fireplaces, and beautiful gardens surround the property. *623 Don Gaspar Avenue; 505-986-8664 or 888-986-8664.* $$–$$$

El Farolito
Here there are seven adobe casitas with fireplaces, private baths, and charming Southwestern features such as flagstone floors, exposed vigas, and skylights. *514 Galisteo Street; 505-988-1631 or 888-634-8782.* $$–$$$

El Paradero
Six blocks from the Plaza, El Paradero is one of Santa Fe's first B&Bs and it remains among the most pleasant. Its 12 rooms and two suites are in a rambling 1800s adobe farmhouse remodeled in Territorial style. *220 West Manhattan Avenue; 505-988-1177.* $–$$

Hotel St. Francis
This Spanish Colonial Revival hotel was built in 1923. Most rooms are small by modern standards, but there is a grand lobby where afternoon tea is served daily (or, in season, on the veranda). *210 Don Gaspar Avenue; 505-983-5700 or 800-529-5700. $–$$$*

Hotel Santa Fe
The only Native-American owned hotel in town is six blocks from the Plaza and a little less expensive than ones closer in. The modern Pueblo Revival structure contains 131 large, warmly decorated rooms. *1501 Paseo de Peralta; 505-982-1200 or 800-825-9876. $$–$$$*

Inn at Loretto
Adjacent to the Loretto Chapel, this five-story Pueblo-style inn is decorated with handmade furnishings and Native-American artwork. Reasonably priced for the location, it has a swimming pool and a restaurant. *211 Old Santa Fe Trail; 505-988-5531 or 800-727-5531. $$$*

Inn of the Anasazi
A beautiful, very expensive, and acclaimed small hotel. All 57 rooms have gas fireplaces and ceilings of vigas and *latillas* (sticks laid between the vigas). Don't expect views; rooms are squeezed into a long, narrow downtown block between another hotel and a burrito shop. *113 Washington Avenue; 505-988-3030 or 800-688-8100. $$$*

Inn of the Five Graces
A highly distinctive, enchanting boutique hotel on Santa Fe's oldest street, Five Graces contains 22 sumptuously furnished suites with fascinating East-meets-West antiques and artwork. Rates include all kinds of perks, from refrigerators stacked with gourmet goodies to lavish afternoon margarita spreads. *150 East DeVargas Street; 505-992-0957 or 866-992-0957. $$$*

Inn of the Governors
Some rooms in this downtown attractive, warmly furnished hotel three blocks south of the Plaza have wood-burning fireplaces. *101 West Alameda Street; 505-982-4333 or 800-234-4534. $$–$$$*

Inn of the Turquoise Bear

This rambling adobe B&B six blocks from the Plaza is the former home of poet Witter Bynner. D.H. Lawrence slept here, as did Igor Stravinsky. This lodging is especially popular with gay travelers. *342 East Buena Vista Street; 505-983-0798 or 800-396-4104.* $–$$$

Inn on the Alameda

This intimate 66-room lodging is four blocks east of the Plaza by River Park. The "Breakfast of Enchantment" buffet is included in the room rate. Some rooms have fireplaces and views. *303 East Alameda Street; 505-984-2121 or 888-984-2121.* $$–$$$

La Fonda

John F. Kennedy, Errol Flynn, Raymond Burr, and Diane Keaton have all slept here. Guest rooms and most of the public spaces are graced with murals or painted furnishings by Ernesto Martínez, La Fonda's resident artist for 50 years. This is a grand, comfortable, colorful hotel whose art, architecture, and history make it worth the price. *100 East San Francisco Street; 505-982-5511 or 800-523-5002.* $$$

La Posada de Santa Fe

Parts of this famous inn date from the 1930s. The 149 rooms sprawl across 6 landscaped acres. Some rooms have Southwestern decor, others Victorian. Ask about views. The cheaper rooms overlook parking lots. *330 East Palace Avenue; 505-986-0000 or 866-331-7625.* $$–$$$

La Tienda Inn and Dusan House

A funky but charming pair of inns a short walk west of the Plaza, this B&B comprises 11 rooms done with natty Victorian, Southwestern, and folk furniture. Enjoy Continental breakfast on a sunny courtyard patio in warm weather. *445-447 West San Francisco Street; 505-989-8259 or 600-889-7611.* $$

Las Palomas

The 38 luxurious, stunningly decorated casitas that make up this secluded but centrally located compound contain handcrafted furnishings and full kitchens. *460 West San Francisco Street; 505-982-5560 or 877-982-5560.* $$–$$$

A room at La Fonda.

The Madeleine

This 15-room Queen Anne–style inn was built in 1886. It has serene gardens, stained-glass windows, lace curtains, and an in-house masseuse. *106 Faithway Street; 505-982-3465 or 888-877-7622. $–$$$*

Old Santa Fe Inn

One of the better values within walking distance of the Plaza, this charming adobe motel has 43 elegantly decorated rooms and suites. Tile bathrooms, CD stereos, and kiva fireplaces are common to the top units. *320 Galisteo Street; 505-995-0800 or 800-745-9910. $$*

Pueblo Bonito

Narrow brick paths wind amid adobe archways and huge shade trees on the grounds of this century-old adobe compound. The decor includes old Santa Fe–style furnishings and modern local artworks. *138 West Manhattan Avenue; 505-984-8001 or 800-461-4599. $–$$*

Bishop's Lodge.

■ GREATER SANTA FE

Bishop's Lodge

This luxury resort began as the mountain retreat of the first bishop of Santa Fe—Bishop Lamy bought the land in the 1860s and built himself a "lodge" of two rooms and a chapel that are still on the property. The 111 rooms here are in 15 separate "lodges" spread over 450 hillside acres that contain a restaurant, a pool and spa center offering everything from massage to acupuncture to yoga and Pilates classes, a stable of horses and riding trails, tennis courts, and a summer children's program. The setting is quiet and forested; the views are beautiful. *Bishop's Lodge Road (N.M. 590), 3 miles north of Santa Fe; 505-983-6377 or 800-419-0492. $$$*

Camel Rock Suites

An affordable, modern all-suites hotel about 3 miles south of the Plaza, Camel Rock has 120 suites, with full kitchens. It's ideal for longer visits. *3007 St. Francis Drive; 505-989-3600 or 877-989-3600. $*

Courtyard by Marriott

The sprawling Marriott has 213 rooms done in standard chain-hotel style. There's an indoor pool. *3347 Cerrillos Road; 505-473-2800 or 800-777-3347. $–$$*

El Rey Inn

More than a basic motel, this inn, a good value, has guest rooms beautifully decorated in Pueblo, Spanish, or Victorian styles. Many rooms have fireplaces. *1862 Cerrillos Road; 505-982-1931 or 800-521-1349. $–$$*

Santa Fe Sage Inn

This unpretentious place is probably the least expensive accommodation within walking distance (six blocks) of downtown, and a significant makeover in the mid-2000s greatly improved it. *725 Cerrillos Road; 505-982-5952 or 866-433-0335. $*

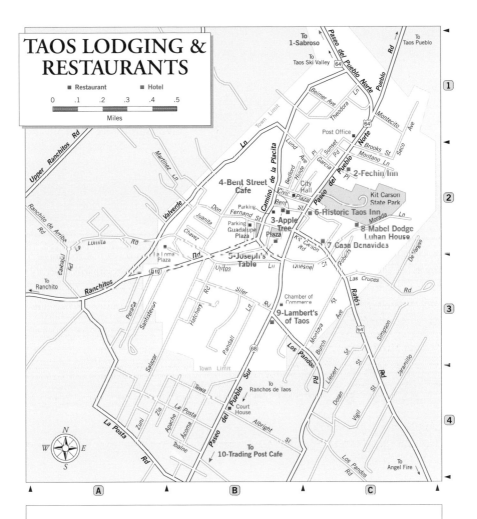

TAOS LODGING & RESTAURANTS

■ Restaurant   ■ Hotel

0   .1   .2   .3   .4   .5
Miles

LODGING

Casa Benavides 7

Fechin Inn 2

Historic Taos Inn 6

Mabel Dodge Luhan House 8

RESTAURANTS

Apple Tree 3

Bent Street Cafe 4

Joseph's Table 5

Lambert's of Taos 9

Sabroso 1

Trading Post Cafe 10

Ten Thousand Waves

Unusual for Santa Fe, this is a Japanese-style health spa offering private and communal hot tubs outdoors in the woods, massage therapy, herbal wraps, and upscale rooms in sleekly furnished cottages. It's especially popular with sore skiers returning from the mountains. *3451 Hyde Park Road, 3.5 miles north of Santa Fe; 505-982-9304. $$$*

■ BEYOND SANTA FE

Algodones

Hacienda Vargas. A stagecoach stop in the late 1700s, an Indian trading post in the 1900s, today the hacienda is a cozy B&B with a friendly staff and a pleasant garden and courtyard. All seven of its rooms have kiva fireplaces, antique furnishings, and contemporary Southwestern art. *1431 N.M. 313, 35 miles south of Santa Fe off I-25; 505-867-9115 or 800-261-0006. $$*

Hacienda Rancho de Chimayó.

Chimayó

Hacienda Rancho de Chimayó. A lovely B&B in an old adobe across the road from the famous Restaurante Rancho de Chimayó, the hacienda has seven rooms surrounding a courtyard. Much peace and quiet. *County Road 98 off N.M. 503, about 40 miles north of Santa Fe; 505-351-2222. $–$$*

Española

Rancho de San Juan. This exquisite Relais & Châteaux compound a few miles north of Española ranks among the most romantic and attractive in the state. The inn's restaurant serves first-rate contemporary fare. *U.S. 285; 505-753-6818. $$$*

■ TAOS

Taos probably has more B&Bs per capita than any other town in the Southwest. For referrals, consult the **Taos Chamber of Commerce** (505-758-3873 or 800-732-8267; www.taoschamber.com). You can also try the **Taos Association of Bed and Breakfast Inns** (800-939-2215; www.taos-bandb-inns.com). Best Western, Quality Inn/Comfort Suites, Hampton Inn, and Ramada Inn (see chain numbers and Web addresses in "Lodging Listings," above) have motels in Taos.

Casa Benavides

In this modern and colorful B&B, the spacious rooms are adorned with Navajo rugs, Native-American pottery, flagstone floors, and other Southwestern trappings. *137 Kit Carson Road; 505-758-1772 or 800-552-1772.* $$–$$$

Fechin Inn

This elegant hotel embraces the Russian artist Nikolai Fechin's nearby home both physically and spiritually; the lobby furniture is hand-carved in Fechin's distinctively rustic style. *227 Paseo del Pueblo Norte; 505-751-1000 or 800-811-2933.* $$–$$$

Historic Taos Inn

Taos's famous old downtown hotel opened in 1936, but parts of the building date from the 1600s. Most rooms have fireplaces. The lobby bar, where there is live entertainment, is known as "Taos's living room" because it appeals to locals as much as to visitors. Much local art is on display. *125 Paseo del Pueblo Norte; 505-758-2233 or 888-518-8267.* $$–$$$

Mabel Dodge Luhan House

Early in the century, Mrs. Luhan coaxed many literati, including D. H. Lawrence and Willa Cather, to come west and stay in her rambling old house. Even in its present incarnation as an 11-room B&B, the tradition continues with artists' workshops and writers' conferences. The place has a casual, rustic flavor. *240 Morada Lane; 505-758-9456 or 800-846-2235.* $–$$

PRACTICAL INFORMATION

■ AREA CODE

All New Mexico answers to the 505 area code. Calls from Santa Fe to Tesuque, Los Alamos, and White Rock are local; everything else is long distance.

■ METRIC CONVERSIONS

1 foot = .305 meters
1 mile = 1.6 kilometers
Centigrade = Fahrenheit temperature minus 32, divided by 1.8
1 pound = .45 kilograms

■ CLIMATE/WHEN TO GO

October is the best month to visit northern New Mexico. Summer's mad crowds have diminished—at least slightly—and the native cottonwoods, aspens, and alders are turning a brilliant gold. Brisk mornings and evenings call for sweaters, but winter's occasional blizzards are still well in the distance.

If your aim is to enjoy Santa Fe with the smallest possible crowds, try November, the first three weeks of December, or January. Avoid times that coincide with the big annual events: Christmas, Spanish Market (July), Indian Market (August), and the opera season (July and August). Snow falls mainly December through March, which may make day trips into the Jémez or Sangre de Cristo Mountains rather adventurous: you'll learn firsthand why so many Santa Feans have four-wheel drive.

Particularly in summer, apply a sunscreen if you're going to be spending time outdoors. It may not be hot, but ultraviolet radiation at these 7,000-foot elevations is very hazardous to the skin.

The one bit of sensible advice regarding dress is to anticipate a wide range of temperatures. Even in summer, the nighttime mercury will almost always fall into the 50s.

Climate Averages

MONTH	FAHRENHEIT	CENTIGRADE	RAINFALL IN INCHES
	High/Low	High/Low	(25 mm=1 inch)
January	40°/19°	4°/-7°	.61"
February	44°/22°	7°/-6°	.79"
March	51°/28°	11°/-2°	.76"
April	60°/35°	16°/2°	.92"
May	69°/43°	21°/6°	1.18"
June	79°/52°	26°/11°	1.11"
July	82°/57°	28°/14°	2.41"
August	80°/56°	27°/13°	2.31"
September	74°/49°	23°/9°	1.65"
October	63°/38°	17°/3°	1.10"
November	50°/27°	10°/-2°	.72"
December	41°/20°	5°/-7°	.71"

■ Getting There

By Air

Most visitors coming to Santa Fe from substantial distances rent a car and drive to the city after flying into **Albuquerque International Sunport** (ABQ, Sunport Boulevard off I-25), 65 miles south of Santa Fe. Albuquerque's airport receives flights from a number of major carriers.

Santa Fe Municipal Airport (SAF, Airport Road/U.S. 284 west of N.M. 14) has very expensive and limited commuter service (usually propeller planes) from Denver.

By Shuttle

A convenient way to make the Albuquerque–Santa Fe connection is to use **Sandia Shuttle Express,** a bus service with several daily round-trips between the Albuquerque airport and any Santa Fe motel or hotel (with advance reservations). Phone: 505-243-3244 or 888-775-5696. You can make phone reservations with a credit card.

By Train or Bus

Amtrak provides passenger train service to Albuquerque and Lamy, 15 miles south-east of Santa Fe, the latter with a bus shuttle into the city. **Greyhound Bus Lines** provides service to Albuquerque, Santa Fe, and Taos.

■ GETTING AROUND

A detailed street map of Santa Fe will help you negotiate Santa Fe's 17th-century tangle of asphalt linguine.

By Car

Do you need a car in Santa Fe? Admittedly, it can seem more of a nuisance than a convenience when you're trying to find a parking space. But unless you plan to confine your sightseeing to downtown and Canyon Road, it is hard to get by with-out wheels. One possibility: Take the Albuquerque–Santa Fe shuttle to your down-town hotel, spend the first couple of days on foot, and then rent a car for day-tripping. There are rental agencies downtown.

By Bus

Santa Fe has a comprehensive city bus service, **Santa Fe Trails** (505-955-2001).

On Foot

For walkers, Santa Fe is much safer than any large American city. However, in recent years there has been a disconcerting surge in late-night muggings on down-town streets. Police presence has been increased.

Vehicular traffic within Santa Fe is slow because of the narrow streets and con-gestion. Traffic on the highways practically everywhere in New Mexico is very fast, which is surprising considering the state's reputation as one vast speed trap. The speed limit on I-25 between Albuquerque and Santa Fe is 75 miles per hour, but drivers travel at 80-plus—on the theory that the State Police can't nail *everybody*. Be especially wary of speeding on Indian reservations, however: the posted speed limits are tortoise-slow (e.g., 35 mph), the tribal police presence is high, and pets and children are likely to dart into the roadway.

(preceding pages) The sun sets over the rugged landscape of northwest New Mexico.

■ OUTDOORS

With more than 300 days of sunshine a year and usually mild weather, northern New Mexico presents opportunities for outdoor recreation of all sorts. One caveat: Santa Fe and Taos both lie at around 7,000 feet, so don't expect to replicate the level of strenuous activity you're accustomed to in the lowlands.

■ HIKING

Scores of maintained hiking trails wind through the desert and forests around Santa Fe; the sheer variety of scenery is astounding. A useful guide, available at many Santa Fe bookstores, is *Day Hikes in the Santa Fe Area,* published by the Santa Fe Group of the Sierra Club. The club, a gregarious and thoroughly pleasant bunch, usually schedules two or three day hikes every weekend, and visitors are always welcome, whether Sierra Clubbers or not. Check the left-hand column on the first page of the "Outdoors" section of the *Santa Fe New Mexican's* Thursday edition for announcements.

When hiking in New Mexico, be careful of overexertion and overexposure to sun (always apply a sunscreen). Rattlesnakes are about, but they are easy to avoid. Don't put hands or feet anywhere you haven't looked, don't sit down to rest on a rock or log without looking around it, and never, ever torment a snake. Veteran hikers in the Southwest swear to this aphorism: Don't be the third hiker in a group. Why? "The first one wakes the snake up, the second one ticks him off, and the third one gets the fangs." They're just kidding—probably.

The forests around Santa Fe also are home to a fair number of black bears. Avoiding trouble is mostly a matter of knowing what *not* to do:

> Don't panic—you won't remember the rest of these rules.
> Don't run. It triggers the bear's chase instinct, and bears are much
>   faster than you.
> Don't climb a tree. Black bears, unlike grizzlies, are terrific climbers.
> Don't lie down and play dead.
> Don't throw anything, shout, or growl at it.

Just back slowly away, keeping a wary eye on the bear but not trying to stare it down, which could be interpreted as a contest for dominance.

If the bear charges anyway, you probably still don't need a Plan B. Usually it will be a bluff charge. If not, well, there really isn't a Plan B.

■ **SKIING**

Northern New Mexico has seven ski areas within a two-hour drive of Santa Fe, an embarrassment of slippery riches if ever there was one, and the dry climate makes for the kind of snow skiers dream of. Taos Ski Valley is the undisputed king, a world-class mountain rated second in challenge among American ski resorts by readers of *Ski* magazine. Santa Fe Ski Area, only 16 miles from town, offers a wider range of beginner, intermediate, and advanced slopes, and spectator events such as the January Celebrity Ski Classic.

The ski areas peak at about 12,000 feet and average 110 to 350 inches of snow every year. Yet the weather is unlikely to be bitterly cold; meteorologists calculate the chance of skiing under sunshine to be 70 to 80 percent on a given day. The ski season, on average, stretches from the third week of November into late April. Most of the areas, Taos in particular, have nearby accommodations to offer

Road conditions statewide are available from the New Mexico State Police at 505-827-5594. Ski packages, including transportation, accommodations, and ski tickets, can be booked through New Mexico Central Reservations, 800-466-7829.

NORTHERN NEW MEXICO SKI RESORTS

Ski Area	Area Phone	Snow Phone	Peak Elev.	Avg. Snowfall	Runs
Angel Fire	505-377-6401	505-377-4222	10,650'	210"	70
Pajarito	505-662-5725	505-662-5725	10,441'	140"	37
Red River	505-754-2223	505-754-2220	10,350'	214"	58
Sandía	505-242-9133	505-242-9052	10,378'	125"	28
Santa Fe	505-982-4429	505-983-9155	12,000'	225"	44
Sipapu	505-587-2240	505-587-2240	9,065'	110"	19
Taos	505-776-2291	505-776-2916	11,819'	320"+	72

The Santa Fe Ski Area, a 30-minute drive from the Plaza, has a peak elevation of 12,000 feet.

■ Rafting

The brochure of one of several Taos- and Santa Fe–based river rafting companies begins thus:

> Our full-day Taos Box trip, on the Rio Grande Wild and Scenic River, traverses 16 miles of wilderness gorge, encountering demanding rapids guaranteed to get you wet. This, our most exciting trip, is NOT for the timid.

Watching the Big River wind its stately course through gardens of great cottonwoods beside N.M. 68 south of Taos, it's hard to envision the thrills, or terrors, of Class IV rapids a few miles upstream—but they're there, at least in the Rocky Mountains' spring runoff season. Not all the rafting trips are suitable only for the intrepid, though. Many others are placid, pastoral recreational floats, with some of them also including fishing, visits to petroglyph sites, or a twilight dinner on the riverbank. For the most part, the rafting season stretches from April through September. Whitewater enthusiasts will most appreciate April, May, and June. If you do go rafting, don't be surprised if you get dirty looks from some of the more militant locals, who are trying to create "rafterless days" so the Rio Grande habitat can get a much-needed rest.

To get wet on the Rio Grande or the smaller Rio Chama, check the Santa Fe or Taos yellow pages under "River Trips." A sampling:

Kokopelli Rafting Adventures. *Santa Fe, 505-983-3734 or 800-879-9035.*
Los Rios River Runners. *Taos, 505-776-8854 or 800-544-1181.*
New Wave Rafting. *Santa Fe, 505-984-1444 or 800-984-1444.*

■ Tours

Walking tours, flying tours, historic church tours, pueblo tours—all are available in Santa Fe, and given the richness and complexity of northern New Mexico's culture and history, an expert's guidance can be very helpful. Reservations should always be made. A sampling of tours:

Aboot About. Two-hour walking tours of downtown Santa Fe, led by opinionated local historians; ghost tours in the evening. *505-988-2774 or 866-614-8404.*

Custom Tours by Clarice. These open-air tram tours last 90 minutes and cover the city's top landmarks. *505-438-7116.*

Rafting in the Taos area.

Great Southwest Adventures. This company conducts van tours to nearby areas, from Bandelier to Abiquiu to Taos. *505-455-2700.*

■ OFFICIAL TOURIST INFORMATION

New Mexico. *800-733-6396; www.newmexico.org.*
Santa Fe. *505-955-6200 or 800-777-2489; www.santafe.org.*
Taos. *505-758-3873 or 800-732-8267; www.taoschamber.com.*

■ USEFUL WEB SITES

The Collectors Guide. Guide detailing northern New Mexico's superb art and gallery scene. *www.collectorsguide.com.*
Eight Northern Pueblos. Touring and other advice. *www.eightnorthernpueblos.com.*
Lensic Performing Arts Center. Santa Fe's premier performing-arts venue. *www.lensic.com.*
National Park Service. For information about Bandelier National Monument, Chaco Culture National Historical Park, and other parks. *www.nps.gov.*
Santa Fe Gallery Association. Show information and the gallery scene scoop. *www.santafegalleries.net.*
Santa Fe New Mexican. Daily newspaper's site has news and events information. *www.santafenewmexican.com.*
Santa Fe Reporter. Weekly newspaper carries news and culture coverage and has annual "Best of Santa Fe" guides. *www.sfreporter.com.*
Taos Gallery Association. Show information and the latest on the Taos art scene. *www.taosgalleryassoc.com.*
Taos Museums. Discount passes for visits to multiple museums, plus other information. *www.taosmuseums.org.*
Taos News. Weekly newspaper. *www.taosnews.com.*
Taos Ski Valley. Ski reports and other news. *www.skitaos.com.*

Art for sale at the Spanish Market held each summer in Santa Fe.

Santa Loucia (Saint Loucy).
Martyred because of her Christian beliefs,
Lucia was an extremely popular saint
from Mexico to Chile found in Mexican and
New Mexico. Saints known as *retablos* painted
as a woman holding a platter with her eyes.

20th Conquistadora
one of this statue, for many centuries has

SPANISH

EXHIBITOR Frank

CATEGORY re

■ FESTIVALS AND EVENTS

Northern New Mexico almost always has some sort of festival going on. The Santa Fe Opera season is perhaps the best known, but Indian Market draws the largest crowds—more than 100,000 lookers and shoppers. For schedules contact the state and local tourist boards (see page 238). Most of the pueblos have feast days and dances that are open to the public. The Eight Northern Indian Pueblos Council (505-747-1593; www.eightnorthernpueblos.com) has information about the dates.

■ MARCH–APRIL

Chimayó Pilgrimage. Thousands march to Santuario de Chimayó on Good Friday. *505-351-4889.*

■ MAY

Taos Spring Arts Celebration. A community-wide celebration incorporating gallery and museum shows, performances, and an arts-and-crafts fair. *800-816-1516; www.taoschamber.com.*

■ JUNE

Rodeo de Santa Fe. *505-471-4300; www.rodeodesantafe.org.*

Santa Fe Opera. Five operas presented in repertory from late June to late August. *505-986-5900; www.santafeopera.org.*

■ JULY

Contemporary Spanish Market. In conjunction with the traditional Spanish Market, this arts festival includes works by many contemporary Hispanic artisans. *505-992-0591.*

Eight Northern Indian Pueblos Arts & Crafts Show. Ohkay Ohwingeh Pueblo. *505-747-1593; www.eightnorthernpueblos.com.*

Santa Fe Chamber Music Festival. In July and August. *888-221-9836; www.santafechambermusic.org.*

Spanish Market. Traditional Spanish colonial arts such as carved santos presented in a juried show. *505-982-2226; www.spanishmarket.org.*

Smoking Cigars at a Ball

Susan Shelby Magoffin left her native Kentucky in 1846 as an 18-year-old bride and set out for Santa Fe and Mexico on a trading expedition with her husband Samuel Magoffin and his brother James. The Magoffin brothers had been trading in the Southwest for nearly two decades, establishing themselves as well-known figures in the Mexican-ruled territory. In 1846, however, James Magoffin undertook the journey with more political intentions; he had secret instructions from President James Polk to negotiate Governor Armijo's peaceful surrender of New Mexico. As a member of this influential party, Susan Magoffin recorded her impressions of the fledgling Santa Fe society during the time of the American conquest.

Friday 11th [September 1846]
First the ballroom, the walls of which were hung and fancifully decorated with the "stripes and stars," was opened to my view—there were before me numerous objects of the biped species, dressed in the seven rain-bow colours variously contrasted, and in fashions adapted to the reign of King Henry VIII, or of the great queen Elizabeth, my memory cannot exactly tell me which, they were entirely enveloped, on the first view in a cloud of smoke, and while some were circling in a mazy dance others were seated around the room next the wall enjoying the scene before them, and quietly puffing, both males and females their little cigarritas a delicate cigar made with a very little tobacco rolled in a corn shuck or bit of paper. I had not been seated more than fifteen minutes before Maj. Soards an officer, a man of quick perception, irony, sarcasm, and wit, came up to me in true Mexican style, and with a polite, "Madam will you have a cigarita," drew from one pocket a handfull of shucks and from an other a large horn of tobacco, at once turning the whole thing to a burlesque.

—Susan Shelby Magoffin, *Down the Santa Fé Trail and into Mexico*, written 1846–47, published in 1926

Taos Pueblo Powwow. Colorful dances performed by Native Americans from many tribes. *505-758-1028; www.taospueblopowwow.com.*

■ AUGUST
Indian Market. Native American artists from all over the country present juried work at this two-day event in the Plaza. It's the most popular event of the year; accommodations must be booked early. *505-983-5220; www.swaia.org.*

■ SEPTEMBER
Las Fiestas de Santa Fe. The oldest continuously celebrated community festival in the country, established in 1712 to commemorate the reconquest of Santa Fe by Don Diego de Vargas in 1692. The highlight is the ceremonial burning of Zozobra, Old Man Gloom. *505-988-7575; www.santafefiesta.org.*

New Mexico Wine Festival. The more than 30 wineries in the state present music, food, and tastings in Bernalillo. *505-867-3311; www.newmexicowinefestival.com.*

Wine and Chile Fiesta. Luncheons, tours, demonstrations, and tastings. *505-438-8060; www.santafewineandchile.org.*

■ OCTOBER
Albuquerque International Balloon Fiesta. Hot-air balloons from around the world fill the sky. *505-821-1000; www.balloonfiesta.com.*

■ DECEMBER
Winter Market. A smaller affair than the summer's Spanish Market but still the same idea: Spanish colonial artwork, furniture, and crafts. *505-982-2226; www.spanishmarket.org.*

Christmas in Santa Fe. *Farolitos* tours, art-and-crafts fair, dance performances, and a Canyon Road Christmas Eve party. *800-733-6396; www.santafe.org.*

Festivals are held throughout the year at the living-history museum El Ranchos de las Golondrinas, 15 miles southwest of Santa Fe.

RECOMMENDED READING

■ PERIODICALS

The *Santa Fe New Mexican* has been published continuously since 1849, which makes it the West's oldest newspaper. Its reporting is mainstream and its commentary fairly tepid, but it does a solid job of reporting Santa Fe's local news and ever-intriguing New Mexican politics. "Pasatiempo," the paper's excellent Friday arts and entertainment tabloid, is particularly useful to the visitor.

The *Santa Fe Reporter,* published on Wednesdays, is Santa Fe's free "alternative" weekly. Its columnists are a good deal livelier and less predictable than the *New Mexican's*. It also has comprehensive arts and entertainment coverage.

Palacio, the excellent magazine of the Museum of New Mexico, has been published since 1895. Its authoritative and usually well-written articles deal in depth with New Mexican art, culture, history, and personalities. *Subscriptions: P.O. Box 2087, Santa Fe, NM 85704; 505-476-5055.*

The *Santa Fean,* a slick magazine, leans heavily toward arts coverage, naturally, but it also includes some quirky essays such as "Learning to Love Cerrillos Road." *Subscriptions: 444 Galisteo Street, Santa Fe, NM 87501; 800-770-6326.*

New Mexico, a state-owned magazine published by the Tourism Department, has been a fixture since 1923. Coverage includes history, scenery, arts, and personalities throughout the state. *Subscriptions: P.O. Box 12002, Santa Fe, NM 87504; 800-898-6639.*

■ FICTION

Bradford, Richard. *Red Sky at Morning.* Philadelphia: Lippincott, 1968. A charming novel about a 17-year-old named Josh who spends World War II in a New Mexican town called Sagrado, which strongly resembles Taos.

Cather, Willa. *Death Comes for the Archbishop.* New York: Knopf, Inc., 1927. A thinly disguised and idealized historical novel about the life of Jean Baptiste Lamy. A classic and a good read, but had Cather acknowledged Lamy's flaws of character—he had a few—it would have been better.

La Farge, Oliver. *Behind the Mountains*. Los Angeles: Charles Publishing, 1984. The writing is elegant in this keenly detailed story of a family's life on a northern New Mexico sheep ranch.

Nichols, John. *The Milagro Beanfield War*. New York: Henry Holt, 1976. A profound, brilliant, and funny novel about New Mexican Hispanic families rebelling against a rich gringo developer. All the humanity of *The Grapes of Wrath* and the fantasy of Gabriel García Márquez's *One Hundred Years of Solitude,* and more fun to read than either. Don't bother to rent the movie.

■ HISTORY

La Farge, John Pen (editor). *Turn Left at the Sleeping Dog: Scripting the Santa Fe Legend, 1920–1955*. Albuquerque: University of New Mexico Press, 2001. Rich and revealing oral histories of Santa Feans from the era before the great tourist flood.

Magoffin, Susan Shelby. *Down the Santa Fé Trail and into Mexico*. New Haven, Connecticut: Yale University Press, 1926. The diary of Susan Shelby Magoffin, from 1846 to 1847. A lively first-person account of the Southwest, its people and customs, during the American conquest of New Mexico.

Noble, David Grant. *Pueblos, Villages, Forts & Trails: A Guide to New Mexico's Past*. Albuquerque: University of New Mexico Press, 1994. A thick book of short articles, laced with historical anecdotes, on all the state's historic attractions—much more informative than the brochures handed out by the state parks, pueblos, and towns.

——— (editor). *Santa Fe: History of an Ancient City*. Santa Fe: School of American Research Press, 1989. One can never have too much Santa Fe history.

Old Santa Fe Today. Albuquerque: University of New Mexico Press, 1991. The Historic Santa Fe Foundation's well-documented and illustrated guide to Santa Fe's historic houses, churches, and plazas.

Santo, Joe S. *Pueblo Nations: Eight Centuries of Pueblo Indian History*. Santa Fe: Clear Light Publishers, 1992. By a Native American from the Jémez Pueblo, this respected insider's view covers Pueblo history and contemporary land, water, and economic and cultural survival issues.

Simmons, Marc. *New Mexico: An Interpretive History.* Albuquerque: University of New Mexico Press, 1988. Simmons, a transplanted Texan, is New Mexico's most respected historian, and he writes in a bright, clear, nonacademic voice.

Stuart, David E. *Anasazi America.* Albuquerque: University of New Mexico Press 2000. Stuart, a University of New Mexico archaeologist, is one of the leading authorities on the prehistoric Southwest and one of the rare archaeologists who writes in an engaging and readable style.

Wilson, Chris, *The Myth of Santa Fe: Creating a Modern Regional Tradition.* Albuquerque: University of New Mexico Press, 1997. A big and boldly researched book on how Santa Fe consciously invented itself as a unique (and profitable) tourist destination.

■ COOKING

Curtis, Susan. *The Santa Fe School of Cooking Cookbook.* Salt Lake City: Gibbs-Smith, 1995. Huntley Dent's *The Feast of Santa Fe* has long been the definitive Santa Fe cookbook, but this newer volume by the owner of the Santa Fe School of Cooking is easier to use. Traditional dishes such as *chiles rellenos* and *nuevo* concoctions with salmon and cornish hens get equal billing.

■ ART

Lisle, Laurie. *Portrait of an Artist: A Biography of Georgia O'Keeffe.* New York: Simon & Schuster, 1980. The definitive chronicle of the life and work of this celebrated and fascinating artist.

Mather, Christine, with Sharon Woods. *Santa Fe Houses.* New York: Clarkson Potter, 2002. With the color photography of Jack Parsons, this book takes you behind the doors of its subjects and shows you what a houseproud Santa Fean can achieve. Every detail of Santa Fe style is here.

Trimble, Stephen. *Talking with the Clay: the Art of Pueblo Pottery.* Santa Fe: School of American Research Press, 1987. Trimble is perhaps the most authoritative writer on Southwestern Native Americana today. This beautifully illustrated small book not only explains techniques and differences in pottery styles among Pueblo artists, but also explores their lives and their feelings toward their unique art.

■ ESSAYS AND MEMOIRS

Crawford, Stanley. *A Garlic Testament.* New York: HarperCollins, 1992. Crawford is an eloquent writer and a real-life garlic farmer in Dixon, 40 miles north of Santa Fe. This meditation on life, land, and garlic is engaging and luminous in its quiet wisdom.

Luhan, Mabel Dodge. *Edge of Taos Desert.* Albuquerque: University of New Mexico Press, 1987 (reprint of 1937 edition). In Taos Pueblo, the author, a disaffected New York sophisticate, discovers an idealized new world. "I finished it in a state of amazed revelation," testified her friend, Ansel Adams.

Nichols, John. *If Mountains Die.* New York: Norton, 1979. A Taos memoir by northern New Mexico's finest contemporary writer, bursting with love, outrage, and humor.

Reid, Robert Leonard. *America, New Mexico.* Tucson: University of Arizona Press, 1998. If you buy just one book about New Mexico, this should be the one. Reid's essays probe deeply and bite hard into New Mexico's history, cultures, and landscapes. His sentences practically glow in the dark. A fine example is his wry observation on boutique-ful Santa Fe: "Many New Mexicans feel that in its present incarnation, Santa Fe would be better off in California, or Colorado at least, to be welcomed home when it is ready to rejoin the community of struggle and pain."

■ TRAVEL AND DESCRIPTION

Mahler, Richard, *New Mexico's Best.* Golden, Colorado: Fulcrum Publishing, 1996. An eccentric but useful potpourri of information that will surprise natives and travelers. Best Navajo rug auction, best place to see a lava flow, best Victorian hotel—it's all here, and much more.

Preston, Douglas. *Cities of Gold.* Albuquerque: University of New Mexico Press, 1992. An amazing chronicle of a Santa Fe author and his friend who try to retrace Coronado's route on modern horseback from the Mexican border to Pecos, New Mexico. History, adventure, and commentary weave together in a strong and seamless narrative.

G L O S S A R Y

Spanish words abound on northern New Mexico's maps, menus, street signs, and in everyday conversations—even among Anglos. An ordinary Spanish-English dictionary is not of much help because so many of the words are uniquely New Mexican. Bookstores have dictionaries of regional Spanish. Here is a guide to some of the more common *palabras de Nuevo México*.

■ FOOD

Many Santa Fe menus provide helpful explanations of each dish. When you're marooned with one that doesn't . . .

carne adovada Literally "cured meat." A pork stew marinated in red chile sauce for 24 hours, then simmered in the same sauce. Pronounced "CAR-neh ah-do-VAH-dah."

chilaquiles Lightly fried tortilla strips baked in a casserole with chile sauce, onions, cheese, chicken and anything else that comes to the cook's mind. A traditional way to use leftovers at breakfast, lunch or dinner. Pronounced "chee-lah-KEE-lehs."

chiles rellenos Mild to moderately hot Hatch chiles stuffed with cheese, coated with egg batter, then fried in lard or oil. Pronounced "CHEE-lehs ray-YEH-nos."

enchiladas Corn tortillas stuffed with cheese or meat, bathed in red or green chile sauce, and baked.

fajitas Literally "little skirts." Originally a Mexican stir-fry of onions, chiles, and thin strips of skirt steak, this now can be made with chicken, seafood, and even tofu. Pronounced "fa-HEE-tahs."

frijoles Beans, usually pinto or black. Frequently served as *frijoles refritos* (refried beans), where the boiled beans are mashed into a soft paste and cooked in hot lard or oil. Pronounced "free-HO-lehs."

guacamole A dip made of mashed avocado, onion, garlic, tomato and spices. Pronounced "wah-kah-MO-ley."

picadillo Finely chopped beef or pork, sautéed with chiles, spices and sometimes raisins and almonds. Pronounced "pee-cah-DEE-yo."

piñon The nut of a native New Mexican pine, which has a delicately sweet, smoky flavor. Pronounced "peen-YOHN."

posole Hominy, often cooked with salt pork or tripe and red or green chiles. The classic northern New Mexican side dish or stew. Pronounced "po-ZO-ley."

salsa (Literally "sauce") May refer to the appetizer dip usually served with fried tortilla chips, or to the red or green sauce ladled over a burrito—or to a *salsa nueva* as sophisticated as anything French.

sopaipillas Common New Mexican dessert. Airy puffs of sugared white flour, deep-fried and served with honey. Occasionally served as a main course, filled with a meat stuffing—a perversion. Pronounced "so pie PEE yas."

tamales Spiced meat (usually beef or pork) and chile swaddled in corn *masa* (moist ground corn) and dried corn husks, then steamed. The proper singular is not tamale, but tamál.

tacos In chain restaurants, ground beef, lettuce, tomatoes, and cheese stuffed into a folded and crisp-fried tortilla shell. In traditional New Mexican cuisine, better quality spiced meat grilled and swaddled in a soft tortilla.

tortilla In New Mexico, the staff of life is a disc. Traditionally made from ground corn and salt and lightly fried. Flour tortillas are equally common today.

■ OTHER WORDS

arroyo A normally dry riverbed, subject to flash flooding.

corbels Architectural brackets serving to support and redistribute the weight of a roof.

farolitos Candles or electric lights placed in paper sacks and used to outline walkways, ledges, and rooftops at Christmas. Literally, "little lanterns."

horno An adobe oven, generally shaped like a beehive. Pronounced "OR-no." (Spanish *H* is silent.)

latillas Small sticks used to fill in the spaces between the *vigas* in the ceiling of a traditional Santa Fe house.

nicho A nook in the wall of a traditional Santa Fe house, used to hold a santo or other artwork.

plaza The central square or park around which Spanish and Mexican towns were built.

portal A porch-like extension from the front or sides of a Spanish or Territorial-era building.

posada Inn. Very common name for hotels, motels, and B&Bs in New Mexico.

rio River.

ristra A bunch of dried red chiles tied together, generally for inside or outside decoration. Literally, "string."

santero A professional carver of santos. Fem. *santera*.

santo An image of a Christian saint, traditionally carved in wood.

vigas Round wooden beams, usually of pine, that stretch across the entire length of a traditional Santa Fe building and support the roof. Normally left exposed to view inside and protruding through the wall outside. Frequently faked, non-functional stubs on the exteriors of modern Spanish-Pueblo Revival buildings.

Vigas protrude from this house's adobe walls; carved corbels support and decorate its portal.

INDEX

Abeta, Bernardo 170–171
Abiquiú 128
Acequia Madre 63, 112–116
Ácoma Pueblo 28, 33, 34, *34, 96,* 190–191, *191,* 193; pottery 82
Adams, Ansel 117, 121, 162
adobe architecture 93–97
Agape Southwest Pueblo Pottery 190
Agresto, John 68
agriculture 21–22, 44, 198
air travel 229
Albuquerque 78, 128, 187–190
Albuquerque International Sunport 229
Albuquerque Museum of Art and History 190
Alburquerque, Duke of 187
Alexander's Inn 220
Algodones 226
altar screens 46, *46,* 113, *113*
Alvarado, Hernando de 33
Alzibar, José de 106
Ammerman, Nicole Curtis 200
Anasazi 21, 22, 26, 28, 29, 30, 31, 140, 180, 193–194, 198; pottery 24, *24,* 26, 28, 80
Anasazi America (Stuart) 140
Antonio Vigil House 187
Anza, Juan Bautista de 45, 47
Apaches 45, 47, 51, 122, 137, 175, 187
Apple Tree 212
Aqua Santa 207
Aragón, Ray John de 57
Archaic 21
architecture 93–97
Architecture of the United States (Smith) 121, 154

Armand Hammer United World College of the American West 176
Armijo, Manuel 53, 241
art museums 87–90
arts 70–97; architecture 93–97; art museums 87–90; Hispanic art 85–86; Indian arts 78–84; jewelry 76; Pueblo pottery 81–84; Santa Fe Opera 90–92; shopping for art 77–78
atomic bomb 40, 176, 177–179, *178*

B&Bs 219
Bandelier, Adolph 116, 179
Bandelier National Monument 29–30, *32,* 176, 179–182, *181*
Barceló, Gertrudis 51–52
Barrio de Analco 108, 110
bears 45–46, 233
Becknell, William 38, 48
Benavides, Alonso de 42
Bender, Madeline *91*
Ben-Hur (Wallace) 39, 101
Bent, Charles 123, 132
Bent Street Café 212
Billy the Kid 39, 175
Bisti Badlands *186,* 194, *195*
Bishop's Lodge 224
Black Mesa 148
Black Mesa Landscape, New Mexico/Out Back of Marie's II (O'Keeffe) *74*
Blake, Ernie 40
Blumenschein, Ernest 39, 104, *124, 125,* 126, *126,* 135
Blumenschein, Helen 135

Blumenschein, Mary Greene 135
Bobrick, John 207
Borrego, Rafael 113
"boutiquery" 61
Bradbury Science Museum 177, 179
Burro Alley 51
bus travel 232
Bynner, Witter 222

Cafe Pasqual's 196, 208
Cafe San Estevan 208
Camel Rock 144
Camel Rock Suites 224
Camino Real 16–17
cannibalism 21, 194
Canyon Road 112 116
car travel 232
Carlos I 34
Carson, Christopher "Kit" 118, 122,
    122–123, 132, 134
Carson, Josefa Jaramillo 122–123, 134
Carson National Forest 159, 165
Casa Benavides 227
Cather, Willa 55, 134, 144, 227
Catholicism 36, 44, 47, 55
Catron Block 102
Ceremonial Cave 182
Cerro Grande fire 148
Chaco Canyon 8, 21, 22, 22, 158, 192,
    193–194
Chaco Culture National Historical Park
    26–27, 29, 193–194
Chacón, George 131
Chapel of Our Lady of Guadalupe 135
Chapel of San Miguel 110, 111
chiles 171, 197, 200, 202–205
Chimayó 75, 168, 170–171, 205; lodging
    226; restaurants 212

Chino, S. 82
City Hall 28
Civil War 39, 98, 101
cliff dwellings 22, 26, 148, 182
climate 228–229
Cochití Pueblo 76, 84
College of Santa Fe 95
Comanches 44, 47, 122, 174
Commemorative Walkway Park 103
Commerce of the Prairies (Gregg) 9, 48, 51
Condé Nast Traveler ranking 58, 62
Confederate Army of New Mexico 39
Contemporary Hispanic Market 86
Cook, Mary Jean 52, 108
Cordero, Helen 84
Córdova, Alfredo 169
Córdova, Harry 166, 169
Córdovas' Handweaving Workshop 169
corn 21–22
Coronado, Francisco Vásquez de 33, 36–37,
    38, 81, 190
Courtyard by Marriott 224
Coyote Cafe 202, 208, 209
Cristo Rey Church 46, 46, 112–113, 113,
    114–115
Crosby, John 40, 90, 92
cuisine 196–215; chiles 202–205; restaurants
    206, 207–215; Santa Fe Farmers' Market
    198, 199; Santa Fe School of Cooking
    200–201; tortillas 205, 207; trends 202
Curtis, Edward S. 22, 31, 34, 150
Curtis, Susan 200

Death Comes for the Archbishop (Cather) 55
Deer Dance 152
Delgado, Felipe 104
DiStefano, Eric 208
Dixon 162

Dodge, Mabel. *See* Luhan, Mabel Dodge
Domínguez, Francisco Atanacio 45
Don Gaspar Inn 220
Doss, Mark *91*
Douglas--Sixth Street and Railroad Avenue
    Historic District 176
Down the Santa Fé Trail and into Mexico
    (Magoffin) 241
downtown walking tour 98–111
Downum, Christian 26
Dudley, John H. 177
Duke of Alburquerque 187
Dunlap, Carmelita 148

Edge of Taos Desert (Luhan) 118
Eight Northern Indian Pueblos 34, 141, 145
Einstein, Albert 177, 179
El Camino Real de Tierra Adentro 51
El Farol 208
El Farolito 220
El Paradero 220
El Rancho de las Golondrinas *16–17, 242*
El Zaguán 116
Embudo *160–161*
Embudo Station Restaurant 211
Entrada 36, 94, 102, 198
Ernest Blumenschein Home and Museum 135
Española 75, 140, 168, 226

Farmington 187
feast days 145, 153
Fechin House 134
Fechin Inn 227
Fechin, Nicolai 132, 227
Federal Courthouse 104
Felipe Delgado House 104
Ferguson, Felicia 129, 131
festivals and events 240, 243
Fiorina, Tom 67

Fire Station No. 7 97
First Ward School 116
fishing 165
Five & Dime General Store 106
Freeman, Michael 97
Frijoles Canyon 179, 180
furniture 85, 162
Fuss, Eduardo 117

Gabriel's 212
Gaddes, Richard 92
Galisteo 31, 43, 75
Gallegos, José Manuel 103–104, 211
gambling 51–52, 140
Garcia, Steve 208
Genoveva Chavez Community Center 97
Georgia O'Keeffe Museum 87, *87,* 104
Geronimo 196, 208
Gislimberti, Carlo 213
Giusewa Pueblo 184
Godoy, Francisco Lucero de 43
Gorman, R.C. 79
Governor Bent Museum 132
Great River: The Rio Grande (Horgan) 197
Greater World Earthship Subdivision 158,
    164, *164*
Gregg, Josiah 9, 48, 51
grito de dolores 47–48
Grosshenney, Francis X. *39*
Groves, Leslie 177
Guadalajara Grill 208
Gutierrez, Denny 140
Gutiérrez, Margaret and Luther 148
Gutiérrez, Van and Lela 148
Gutiérrez family 82, 148

Hacienda Rancho de Chimayó 226
Hacienda Vargas 226
Hand Artes Gallery 169

Harry's Roadhouse 209
Hartley, Marsden *71,* 75
Harwood Museum of Art 135
Hawikuh Pueblo 37
Hazen-Hammond, Susan 15, 63, 64
Henderson, William Penhallow 104
Henri, Robert 39
Hewett, Edgar Lee 58
Hidalgo y Costilla, Miguel 4*7*–48
High Road 159, 165, 170
highway names 159
hiking 233
Hispanic art 85–86
Hispanic Santa Fe 36–57
historic district 63–64
Historic Taos Inn 227
history time line 38–40
Hohokam 24, 28, 140
Holliday, "Doc" 175
Hopi 33, 190
Hopper, Dennis 134
Horgan, Paul 57, 197
hot springs 182, 184
Hotel St. Francis 221
Hotel Santa Fe 221
hotels 216, 219–220
Houser, Allan 79
Howard, Barbara *142*

If Mountains Die (Nichols) 118
Il Piatto 208
Indian arts 78–84
Indian dances *52,* 153
Indian Market 79
Indian pottery 81–84, 190; buying 80
Indians 36–37, 45–46, 49, 94, 98, 117, 134,
    135, 140, 185, 190–191, 232. *See also*
    specific tribes; map 20
Inn at Loretto *217,* 221

Inn of the Anasazi 221
Inn of the Anasazi Restaurant 196, 207
Inn of the Five Graces 221
Inn of the Governors 221
Inn of the Turquoise Bear 222
Inn on the Alameda 222
Institute of American Indian Arts Museum
    87, 107

James, Thomas 49
Jaramillo, Debbie 19, 62, 67
Jaramillo, Josefa 122–123, 134
Jémez Falls 182
Jémez Mountains 63, 144, 159, 176,
    182–184, *183, 184*
Jémez Pueblo 28, 83, 84, 174, 184
Jémez River 182
Jémez Springs 177, 182, 184
Jémez State Monument 184
jewelry 76, *76*
Jewish settlers 44
Joseph's Table 212
Juan Carlos I 40
Juárez, Andrés 174
Julian's 209

Kagel, Katherine 196, 208
Kahn, Louis 112
Kasasoba 210
Kasha-Katuwe Tent Rocks National
    Monument *184–185*
Katsina dolls *142,* 143
Kearny, Stephen Watts 38, 53, 98, 103,
    123, 175
Kin Kletso 194
Kit Carson Home and Museum 123, 134
Kit Carson State Park 132
Klah, Hastiin 90
Koshare clowns *40*

La Casa Sena 196, 210
La Castrense chapel 46, 113
La Choza 210
La Conquistadora 44
La Doña Luz Inn 134
La Fajada Butte *22*
La Farge, John Pen 69
La Farge, Oliver 50
La Fonda Hotel 107, 132, 196, 202, 222, *223*
La Plazuela Restaurant 202
La Posada de Santa Fe 222
La Tienda Inn and Dusan House 222
La Villa de San Francisco de Alburquerque 187
La Villa de Santa Fé 38
Laguna Pueblo 28, 81
Lambert's of Taos 213
Lamy, Jean Baptiste 38, 52, *54*, 54–57, *57*,
    104, 107–108
Lamy, Marie 108
*Landscape No. 3 (Cash Entry Mines, New
    Mexico)* (Hartley) *71*
Larry R. Walkup Aquatic Center 179
Las Campanas 62
Las Palomas 222
Las Trampas 165
Las Vegas *175*, 175–176
Lawrence, D.H. 39, 69, 124, 126, 132, 136,
    222, 227
Lecompte, Janet 50, 53
Legorreta, Ricardo 95
Lensic Performing Arts Center 107
Lensic Theater 40, *106*, 106–107
Letters from the Southwest (Lummis) 96–97
Library Park Historic District 176
Lisle, Laurie 128
lodging 216–227; Algodones 226; B&Bs
    219; central Santa Fe 220–223; Chimayó
    226; Española 226; greater Santa Fe

223–224; hotels 216, 219–220; maps 218,
    225; rentals 219; Taos 226–227
López, Gerónimo 113, 209
Lorenzo in Taos (Luhan) 136
Loretto, C.G. 84
Loretto Chapel 108, *109*
Los Alamos 40, 168, 176, 177–179, *178*, 184
Los Alamos Historical Museum 179
Los Alamos National Laboratory 177
Lovato, Phil 120
Luhan, Mabel Dodge 39, 118, 121, 126, 127,
    129, 132, 134, 136, 227
Luhan, Tony 126
Lujan, Vernon 145
Lumina Gallery 129, 131, 137
Lummis, Charles 96–97

Mabel Dodge Luhan House 129, 134, 227
Machebeuf, Joseph Priest 57, 107
Madeleine, The 103, 223
Magoffin, James 241
Magoffin, Samuel 241
Magoffin, Susan Shelby 241
Mallet, François 107
*Man Corn: Cannibalism and Violence in the
    Prehistoric American Southwest* (Turner)
    21, 194
Manhattan Project 177–179
maps: Acequia Madre/Canyon Road 116;
    central Santa Fe 99; greater Santa Fe 7;
    lodging 218, 225; Native Americans 20;
    New Mexico 139; Pueblos 139; restaurants
    206, 225; side trips 157; Taos 119, 133, 225
Marin, John 126, 127
Martínez, Adam 148
Martínez, Antonio José 57, 137
Martínez, Ernesto 107, 222
Martínez Hacienda 137, *214–215*

Martínez, Julian 78, 83, 147–148
Martínez, María 78, *78*, 83, 135, 147–148
Martínez, Severo and Julianita 168
Mazria, Ed 97
McBride, Henry 127
Means, John 49
Medina-Tiede, Leona 205
Meem, John Gaw 90, 107, 112
Melgares, Facundo 49
Mesa Public Library 179, *180*
Métier Weaving Shop 162
metric conversions 228
Mexican War 52
Meyers, Ouray 128–129
Milagro Beanfield War, The 167
Miller, Mark 202, 208
Millicent Rogers Museum 135
Mimbres 80
Mission Church 38
Mitchell, David Dawson 52
Mitchell, Janet 200–201, *201*
Mogollon 28, 140, 198
Móntez, Rey 85–86
Montezuma Castle 176
motels 216
Mouly, Antoine and Projectus 107, 108
murals 131
Murphey, Rosalea 210
Museum of Fine Arts 89, *89*, 104
Museum of Indian Arts and Culture 89
Museum of International Folk Art *88*, 89
Museum of New Mexico 128
Museum of Spanish Colonial Art 89–90
museums 87–90. *See also individual*
    museums

Nambé Falls 147
Nambé Lake 147
Nambé Pueblo *146*, 146–147

Naranjo family 82
Native Americans, map 20
Navajo Woman, The (Gorman) 79
Navajos 22, 76
New Buffalo Commune 40
New Mexico 36, 38, 39; map 139
N.M. 68 *160–161*
Nichols, John 118, 128, 167
Ninth Cavalry Band *101*
Nordenskiold, Gustaf 179
Nuestra Señora de los Ángeles 174

Oden, Loretta Barrett 208
Ohkay Ohwingeh 151
O'Keeffe, Georgia *14*, 39, 40, 74, *74*, 87, *87*,
    89, 104, 121, 126–128, *127*, 134, 162
Old City Hall of 1892 176
Old Fort Marcy Park 103
Old Santa Fe Inn 223
Old Town Albuquerque 187–190
Old Town Plaza 190
Oldest House in America 110, *110*
Oñate, Juan de 38, 41, 51, 122, 151, 174,
    190–191
Only in Santa Fe (Hazen-Hammond) 15
opera 40, 90–92, *91, 92*
Oppenheimer, J. Robert 177
Ordóñez, Isidro 41
Orilla Verde Recreation Area 164–165
Ortega family rugs 71
Osha Canyon 165
Otermín, Antonio 43
Our Lady of the Angels School 187, 190
outdoors 233–236; hiking 233; rafting 236;
    skiing 235

Padilla, Carmella 64
Padre Gallegos House 103–104, 211
Pajarito Plateau 179

Palace of the Governors 28, 38, 43, *78,* 94,
    98, 101–102, *102*
Paleo-Indians 21
Pecos National Historical Park *172–173,* 174
Pecos Pueblo 174
Pecos River 174
Penitente societies 44, 170
Peralta, Fred 128
Peralta, Pedro de 38, 41
Petroglyph National Monument 30, 185
petroglyphs 30, *30,* 165, 185
Phillips, Bert Geer 39, 104, 126
photographing Santa Fe 117
Picurís Pueblo *35,* 151
Pike, Albert 50
Pike, Zebulon 38
Pilar 165
Pink Adobe 210
Plains Indians 76, 174
Plaza, the 38, *39,* 79, 98, *100,* 101, *101*
Plaza Café 210
Plaza Hotel 176
Pojoaque Pueblo 31, 140, 144, 146
Polk, James 241
Popé 43, 151
population 8, 45
Portrait of an Artist (Lisle) 128
pottery 24–25, *24–25,* 78–79, 81–84, 143,
    147–148, 190; Á]coma 82; Anasazi 24, *24,*
    26, 28, 80; buying 80; Pueblo 71, 81–84,
    81–84
Poveka, Maria 148
Predock, Antoine 179
Preston, George Cuyler 103
Prince, L.B. *102*
Pueblo Bonito *26–27,* 29, *192,* 193, 194
Pueblo Bonito (inn) 223
Pueblo culture 31–35
Pueblo Indians 22, 28–29, 30, 31–35, 37, 38,

41–44, 47, 78–79, 101–102, 110, 120, 122,
    123, *138,* 148, 174, 185, 198; pottery 71,
    81–84, *81–84*
*Pueblo Nations: Eight Centuries of Pueblo
    Indian History* (Sando) 28–29
Pueblo Revolt 98, 103, 110, 112, 123, 151,
    155, 174
pueblo ruins 179–182, *181*
pueblos 28, 34, *138,* 138–155, *142, 143;*
    community of 140–143; Eight Northern
    Indian Pueblos 34, 141, 145; etiquette 145;
    feast days and dances 153; map 139;
    Nambé 146–147; Picurís 151; Pojoaque
    144, 146; San Ildefonso 147–148; San Juan
    151; Santa Clara 148; Taos 154–155;
    Tesuque 144; visiting 144–151
Puye Cliff Dwellings 148

Quiros, Arias de 103

Rafael Borrego House 113
rafting 236
Rake's Progress, The (Stravinsky) 90
Ramona (Jackson) 162
Rancho de Chimayó Restaurante 170, 212
Rancho de San Juan 226
Ranchos de Taos 117, 120–121, 131, 162
Redford, Robert 167
Remington, Frederic 128
restaurants 207–215; Chimayó 212; maps
    206, 225; near Santa Fe 211–212; Santa Fe
    207–211; Taos 212–213, 225
Ridhwan Sculpture Garden 129, *129,* 131
Rio Chama *72–73,* 236
Rio Grande Gorge 163–165
Rio Grande Gorge Bridge *163,* 163–164
Rio Grande highway 159
Rio Grande River, rafting 236
Ristra 210

Robinson, Roxana 126
Rochas, François Jean 108
Rodríguez, Anita 86
Rogers, Millicent 135
Romero, Orlando 93, 95
Romero, Pedro 86
Roosevelt, Franklin D. 177, 179
Royal Road to the Interior 51
rugs 71

St. Francis Auditorium 128
St. Francis Cathedral 39, 44, 55, 107
St. John's College 68
Sabroso 213
Salado 25, 28, 140
San Esteban del Rey church 104, 191
San Felipe de Neri church 187, *188–189*, 190
San Francisco de Asís church 117, 120–121, *121*, 162
San Francisco de Asís Church of Ranchos de Taos (O'Keeffe) *14*
San Ildefonso Pueblo 78, 79, 83, 135, *147*, 147–148
San Ildefonso Pueblo Museum 148
San José de Gracia church 165
San José de los Jémez church 184
San Juan Basin 194
San Juan Pueblo 38, *40*, 41, *150*, 151, *152*
San Ysidro 184
Sandía Pueblo 41
Sando, Joe S. 28–29
Sangre de Cristo Mountains *10–11*, 63, *64*, 131, 144, 159, 174
Sangre de Cristo Mountains (Blumenschein) *124*
Santacafé 196, 211
Santa Clara Canyon 148
Santa Clara Pueblo 28, 82, 138, 140, 143, 148

Santa Cruz 171
Santa Cruz Indians 31
Santa Cruz River 170
Santa Fe 168; climate 8; contemporary Santa Fe 58–69; facts about 8; Hispanic Santa Fe 36–57; lodging 220–224; maps 7, 99; photographing 117; restaurants 207–215
Santa Fe: The Autobiography of a Southwestern Town (La Farge) 50
Santa Fe Art Institute 95
Santa Fe cathedral 56, *56, 57*
Santa Fe Community Theater 70
Santa Fe Farmers' Market 198, *199*
Santa Fe Indians 31
Santa Fe Municipal Airport 229
Santa Fe Opera 40, 90–92, *91, 92*
Santa Fe Plaza 38, *39, 79*, 98, *100*, 101, *101*
Santa Fe River 45
Santa Fe River Park 63
Santa Fe Sage Inn 224
Santa Fe School of Cooking 200 201, *201*
Santa Fe Ski Area *234*, 235
Santa Fe Trail 38, 48, *49*, 49–50, 51, 53, 81, 132
santos carvings 44, 55, 56, 85, 85–86, 131, 165
Santuario de Chimayó *170*, 170–171, *171*, 205
Santuario de Guadalupe 104–106, *105*
Schaafsma, Curtis 28, 29
Scully, Vincent 154
Sena Plaza 103
Seven Cities of Cíbola 36, 37, 93
Sharp, Joseph Henry 39
Sherman, William T. 50
Shidoni *75*
shopping: art 77–78; pottery 80
Short History of Santa Fe, A (Hazen-Hammond) 63

shuttle travel 229
side trips 156–195; Chaco Canyon 193–194;
    Historic Western Loop 185; Los Alamos and
    Jémez Mountains 176–184; map 157;
    Pecos and Las Vegas 174–176; roads to Taos
    and back 159–173
Simmons, Gary 90
Simmons, Marc 45, 47, 103, 151, 198
Simons, John F. 90
Sinagua 25, 28, 140
Sisneros, Manuel Antonio 51
SITE Santa Fe 90
602 Canyon Road 113
skiing 40, 131, 137, 179, 235
smallpox 47
Smith, G.E. Kidder 121, 154
Society of Penitentes 44, 170
Sopyn, Anna 156, *156*, 158, 162
Spaniards and Spanish settlers 33–34,
    36–37, 41–44, 47, 85, 134, 151,
    190–191, 198
Spanish *Entrada* 36, 94, 102, 198
Spanish Market 86, *239*
Spence Hot Springs 158, 182
Stapelman, Eric 210
State Capitol 111
storyteller dolls 84
Strand, Paul 121
Stravinsky, Igor 90, 222
Stuart, David E. 140
Suazo, Anita 82
Suina, Ada 84
Summerhayes, Martha 58

Tafoya, Ray 167
Tafoya family 82, 148
Taladrid, Damaso 57
Talking with the Clay (Trimble) 143
Taos 38, 118–137, 162–165; artists
    124–128; early Taos 122–123; greater
    Taos 135–137; growth and the art market
    128–131; highlights 132, 134–135; lodging
    227; maps 119, 133, 225; restaurants
    212–213, 225; side trips 159–173;
    visiting 131
Taos Art Museum at the Fechin House 132
Taos Institute of Arts 128
Taos Plaza 132
Taos Pueblo 28, 31, *31*, 38, 122, 123, 131,
    137, 143, 151, *154*, 154–155, 162–163
Taos Ski Valley 40, 131, 137, 235
Taos Society of Artists 39, 104, 135
Taylor, John M. 61
Tent Rocks 185
Territorial Inn 223
Tesuque 159
Tesuque Pueblo *141*, 144
Tesuque Pueblo Flea Market 159
Tesuque Village Market 159
Tewa 42, 43, 122, 144, 170
Theory of the Dumbest Sons 59, 61
Thompson, Lewis 18
Tia Sophia's 205, 211
Tibetan Buddhist center *13*
Tiguex 37
timing the trip 228–229
Tlaxcalan Indians 108
Tomasita's 211
tortillas 205, 207
tourism 58
tourist information 238
tours 98–111, 236, 238
Trading Post Cafe 213
train travel 232
Treaty of Guadalupe Hidalgo 38
Trillin, Calvin 59, 61
Trimble, Stephen 143
Trinity Site *178*

Truchas *167,* 167–169
Truchas Peak 167
Tules, la 51–52
Turn Left at the Sleeping Dog (La Farge) 69
Turner, Christy 21, 194
Tyuonyi 29, 180, 182

**U.S. Archaeological Resources Protection
  Act** 80
University of New Mexico 135
Utes 122

Valdez Fruit Stand 162
Valles Caldera National Preserve 182
Vargas, Diego de 38, 43, 43–44, 101, 103
Velarde 162
Vial, Pedro de 38
Vigil, Antonio 187
Vigil, Euralia 168–169
Vigil, Federico 86
Vigil, Robert 93, 95

Vigil, Victor 169
Visual Arts Center 95

walking 98–111, 232
Wallace, Lew 39, 101
Warner, Lane 202
water 40, 62
weaving *166,* 169
Web sites 238
Wetherill, Richard 179
Wheeler Peak 118, 135
Wheelwright, Mary Cabot 90
Wheelwright Museum of the American
  Indian 90
World War II 176, 177–179, *178*

Zamora, Francisco 122
Zia Diner 211
Zia Pueblo 41, 111
Zozobra *66, 67*
Zuni Pueblo 28, 33, 37, 38, 76, 81, *149, 150*

COMPASS AMERICAN GUIDES

Critics, booksellers, and travelers all agree: you're lost without a Compass.

"This splendid series provides exactly the sort of historical and cultural detail about North American destinations that curious-minded travelers need." —*Washington Post*

"This is a series that constantly stuns us . . . no guide with photos this good should have writing this good. But it does." —*New York Daily News*

"Of the many guidebooks on the market, few are as visually stimulating, as thoroughly researched, or as lively written as the Compass American Guide series." —*Chicago Tribune*

"Good to read ahead of time, then take along so you don't miss anything." —*San Diego Magazine*

"Oh, my goodness! What a gorgeous series this is."—*Booklist*

"An abundance of information on culture, and a fine array of historical drawings and photographs." —*Library Journal*

"The most literate and elegant series of guidebooks ever written about North America." —Jan Morris

"Lushly illustrated and intelligently written. Beautiful maps and . . . lots of history." —*National Geographic Traveler*

"Magnificent photography. First rate."—*Money*

"Written by longtime residents of each destination . . . these handsome and literate guides are strong on history and culture, and illustrated with gorgeous photos." —*San Francisco Chronicle*

"The color photographs sparkle, the archival illustrations illuminate windows to the past, and the writing is usually of the utmost caliber." —*Michigan Tribune*

"Class acts, worth reading and shelving for keeps even if you're not a traveler." —*New Orleans Times-Picayune*

"Beautiful photographs and literate writing are the hallmarks of the Compass guides." —*Nashville Tennessean*

"History, geography, and wanderlust converge in these well-conceived books." —*Raleigh News & Observer*

"The authors . . . capture the true character of the locales." —*Tampa Tribune & Times*

"It's a keeper." —*Toledo Blade*

Compass American Guides are available at special discounts for bulk purchases for sales promotions or premiums. Special editions, including personalized covers, excerpts of existing books, and corporate imprints, can be created in large quantities for special needs. For more information, write to Special Markets/Premium Sales, 1745 Broadway, MD 6-2 New York, NY 10019, or e-mail specialmarkets@ randomhouse.com

ACKNOWLEDGMENTS

■ FROM THE AUTHOR

I have worked as a journalist in Texas, New Mexico, Arizona, California, Iowa, Mexico, China, and Russia—a fairly odd geographical patchwork—but of all these places, the people of New Mexico were by far the most receptive, helpful, patient, ingratiating, and just plain friendly. They rewarded my curiosity about their land and their lives with mountains of information and many good stories.

First, many thanks to the staff of the Santa Fe Public Library, which granted me a borrower's card during my temporary residency and dredged up scores of volumes from the basement archives. Librarians even came to my study table from time to time, bearing books or articles I had overlooked. I've never encountered a more user-friendly library anywhere.

Susan Hazen-Hammond, a great friend and writer of two excellent books on Santa Fe, read several chapters, saved me from some errors, and offered valuable suggestions. Help me thank her; buy her books. Lynn Wood, a Tucson schoolteacher, neighbor, and great friend, divided up dozens of research questions and fact-checking with me during the several days we spent together in Santa Fe.

Most of my best insights into Santa Fe and places nearby came from interviews and informal conversation with natives. They include friend and hiking buddy Ann Aceves, Lesli Allison of St. John's College, artist Mary Brown, Truchas weaver Harry Córdova, Ray Dewey of Dewey Galleries Ltd., Judy Dwyer of Palace Avenue Books, William Franke of Hand Artes Gallery in Truchas, architect Michael Freeman, Santa Fe Mayor Debbie Jaramillo, Katherine Kagel of Cafe Pasqual's, Richard Myers of Agape Southwest Pueblo Pottery in Albuquerque, Taos author John Nichols, John O'Brien of Atalaya Restaurant & Bakery, historian Orlando Romero, Pamela Roy of the Santa Fe Farmers' Market, James Rutherford of Copeland Rutherford Fine Arts, Ltd., archaeologist Curtis Schaafsma, fruit vendor and artist Loretta Valdez, orchard magician Euralia Vigil, adobe builder Robert Vigil, and Los Alamos mathematician/writer Larry Winter.

Finally, thanks most of all to Patty Cheek, nurse, musician, wife, and friend, who endured long months of separation while I worked in Santa Fe and even more months of the customary writer's angst and surliness as the book took shape. Only her care, affection, and advice made it possible.

■ FROM THE PUBLISHER

All photographs in this book are by Eduardo Fuss unless noted below. Compass American Guides gratefully acknowledges the following institutions and individuals for the use of their photographs or illustrations on the following pages: **Anschutz Collection, Denver,** p. 124; **Art Institute of Chicago, Alfred Stieglitz Collection,** p. 71; **Buffalo Bill Historical Center, Cody, Wyoming,** p. 122 (Vincent Mercaldo Collection, P.71.143A); **Lawrence W. Cheek,** pp. 84 (top), 121, 129, 156; **Earthship Biotecture,** p. 164; **Georgia O'Keeffe Museum,** pp. 74 (gift of the Burnett Foundation), 87 (Paul Slaughter); **George H. H. Huey,** pp. 24–25; **Lensic Center for the Performing Arts,** p. 106 (Robert Reck); **Library of Congress, Prints and Photographs Division,** p. 149 (LC-USZ62-079646); **Library of Congress, Prints and Photographs Division, Edward S. Curtis Collection,** pp. 23 (LC-USZ62-115803), 150 (top, LC-USZ62-118774 and bottom, LC-USZ62-102040); **Library of Congress, Prints and Photographs Division, FSA/OWI Collection,** p. 141 (LC-USF33-012352-M2); **Los Alamos National Laboratory,** p. 178; **Daniel Mangin,** p. 94; **Mesa Public Library,** p. 180 (Brad Roach); **Palace of the Governors** (MNM/DCA) pp. 9, 31 (neg. 144507), 34 (76958), 37, 40 (3895), 43, 49 (45011), 51, 52 (144638), 54 (35878), 56 (11330), 78 (42317), 96 (144550), 101 (50887), 102 (46776), 110 (133403), 127 (9673); **National Park Service,** p. 30; **New Mexico Museum of Fine Arts,** p. 39; **Santa Fe Convention and Visitors Bureau,** pp. 16–17 (Chris Corrie), 89 (Jack Parsons); **Santa Fe Opera,** pp. 91 (Ken Howard), 92 (Robert Reck); **Taos Chamber of Commerce,** pp. 130 (Rankin Harvey), 237 (Larry Turner); **Taos Historic Museums,** p. 126; **Underwood Photo Archives, San Francisco,** p. 191. The photos on pp. 213, 217, 224, and 226 are courtesy of the restaurant and hotels pictured.

We would also like to thank the following individuals for their contributions to this book: Rachel Elson for copyediting, Ellen Klages for proofreading, Compass senior editor Kristin Moehlmann for shepherding the revision in-house, Mary Jean Cook for her piece on la doña Tules, Arthur Olivas of the Museum of New Mexico photo archives for his assistance supplying the archival illustrations, and Orlando Romero for his expert reading. Also thanks to John O'Brien, and to Donna Pierce from the Palace of the Governors.

■ ABOUT THE AUTHOR

Lawrence W. Cheek now lives near Seattle, Washington, but he spent most of his life in the American Southwest. He has worked as a newspaper reporter, music and architecture critic, and editor for 17 years, and has taught journalism at the University of Arizona. As a freelance writer for the last several years, he has produced eight books, including Compass American Guides' *Arizona*. His journalistic specialties are American architecture, Southwestern archaeology, and food.

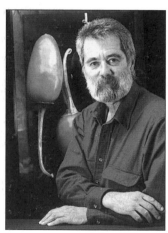

■ ABOUT THE PHOTOGRAPHER

Eduardo Fuss was born in Buenos Aires and has lived in New Mexico since 1980. His photographs have appeared in *Smithsonian*, the *New York Times*, and *Arizona Highways*, among other publications, and have been featured exclusively in numerous books including *Hellish Relish* published by HarperCollinsWest, *Only in Santa Fe* published by Voyageur Press, and the award-winning *Chile Pepper Fever: Mine Is Hotter Than Yours*, also published by Voyageur Press.

HILLSBORO PUBLIC LIBRARIES
Hillsboro, OR
Member of Washington County
COOPERATIVE LIBRARY SERVICES